Praise for *A Soli*

"An 'insider's' story of the UN, ᴛʜᴇ _____ _____ ___ ___ ____ ____
An important contribution to our understanding of conᴛᴇᴍ_
porary international diplomacy."

> **—Paul Sigmund, professor of politics,**
> **emeritus, Princeton University**

"This is an insightful, illuminating, and interesting perspective
on the Iraq imbroglio. ... Ambassador Muñoz, an insider with
the training of a political science professor, offers a nuanced
and balanced assessment, critical of U.S. diplomacy."

> **—Abraham F. Lowenthal, founder and former president,**
> **Pacific Council on International Policy, and professor of**
> **international relations, University of Southern California**

"This lucid analysis and detailed account sheds light on how
future international security threats should be dealt with. A
must read for U.S. policy makers who now need to work on
rebuilding trust on America around the world."

> **—Patricio Navia, Center for Latin American and**
> **Caribbean Studies, New York University**

"In this engaging and extraordinarily candid work, Chilean
scholar/ambassador Heraldo Muñoz ... has supplied the missing perspective—the multilateral one. Unlike many insid-
ers' accounts of how things happened, Muñoz places vivid
anecdotes in a historical and sophisticatedly apprehended
political context."

> **—Tom Farer, dean, Graduate School of**
> **International Studies, University of Denver**

" ... This narrative is compelling history and a must for course
adoption in U.S. foreign policy, contemporary history, and
international organization."

> **—Edward C. Luck, vice president and director**
> **of studies, International Peace Academy,**
> **and professor, Columbia University**

SPEAKER'S CORNER is a provocative new series designed to stimulate, educate, and foster discussion on significant public policy topics. Written by experts in a variety of fields, these brief and engaging books should be read by anyone interested in the trends and issues that shape our society.

A Solitary War

A **Diplomat's** Chronicle
of the **Iraq War** and Its Lessons

Ambassador Heraldo Muñoz
FOREWORD BY Kofi Annan

FULCRUM
GOLDEN, COLORADO

World Spanish rights (excluding Chile) licensed to El Tercer Nombre, 2006
World Chilean Spanish rights licensed to Random House Mondadori, 2006

Library of Congress Cataloging-in-Publication Data
Muñoz, Heraldo.
  A solitary war : a diplomat's chronicle of the Iraq war and its lessons / Heraldo Muñoz.
      p. cm. -- (Speaker's corner)
  ISBN 978-1-55591-676-3 (pbk.)
  1. Iraq War, 2003---Diplomatic history. 2. Iraq War, 2003---Participation, European. 3. United States--Politics and government--2001- 4. Europe--Politics and government--21st century. 5. Iraq--Politics and government--2003- 6. United Nations--Iraq. I. Title.
  DS79.76.M86 2008
  956.7044'32--dc22
                              2007051382

Design by Jack Lenzo

Printed in the United States of America by Malloy Incorporated
0 9 8 7 6 5 4 3 2 1

Fulcrum Publishing
4690 Table Mountain Drive, Suite 100
Golden, Colorado 80403
www.fulcrumbooks.com

For Paloma

Contents

Foreword by Kofi Annan ....*xi*

Introduction.. 1

Chapter One

Early Warnings 7
    A Telling Phone Call from Condi..7
    A War with Multilateral Support..13
    One, Two, Three Iraqs: The Costs
        of the Unilateralist Doctrine.. 16

Chapter Two

War Games in the United Nations:
A Tale of Missed Opportunities 25
    Resolution to Act..27
    A Tug of War...37
    The Blair-Lagos Last-Ditch Effort....................................51
    The Final Diplomatic Bets...62
    High Noon in Iraq: Diplomacy Fails..................................69

Chapter Three

Unilateralism in Retreat:
The Hard Task of Winning the Peace in Iraq 79
    Multilateralism under Fire...79
    The War Deepens: The UN Is a Target.............................92
    A Turn toward Tactical Multilateralism 96

Chapter Four

Why Multilateralism Matters: The United Nations Enables the Transfer of Sovereignty in Iraq and the 2005 Elections 111

A Sense of Loss of Direction and Moral Defeat 113

Negotiating the Establishment of
the Iraqi Interim Government 118

The End of Occupation? 143

The 2005 Elections and the
Nouri al-Maliki Government 150

Chapter Five

Worlds Apart: The Alienation of Allies 159

Chile: The Distant Neighbor 164

Mexico: "So Far from God,
So Close to the United States" 181

The Transatlantic Divide with the "Old Europe" 195

Less-Than-Willing Allies and the
Failed Evidence to Go to War 215

Chapter Six

Conclusions: The U.S. War Backtrack and the Future of Multilateralism 229

The Costs of a War without Friends 229

A Changing Attitude toward the United Nations 235

Why the United States Should
Care about Multilateralism 240

Beyond Iraq: To Lead or to Impose 246

Notes 255

Acknowledgments 265

About the Author 269

Foreword

Heraldo Muñoz, Chile's ambassador to the United Nations, is a known scholar and political leader. I am pleased to have been asked to provide a foreword for this interesting book, which contains his views on a subject that has instigated so much debate around the world.

Muñoz's personal testimony on the events surrounding the Iraq war deserves to be made public. I was, and will always be, a strong advocate for multilateralism, for collective solutions to common security problems. Iraq has offered one more opportunity to validate the benefits of collective action and to understand the problems that may arise by not following that path. As explained in this book, the imperatives of war are always slim, obliging every one of us to look for alternatives that will not be so costly in terms of loss in human lives and destruction of critical infrastructure.

A Solitary War argues that missed opportunities can result in costs, and it makes the case for upholding the legitimacy of the United Nations Security Council. The author provides a detailed narration of the strenuous behind-the-scenes efforts that were made by several countries, at the highest level, to avert war and press the Iraqi government to comply with UN Security Council resolutions.

Muñoz underscores a key point in international policy,

particularly when it pertains to a superpower: no country can ignore the legitimacy the Security Council can confer when it comes to war. He recounts, as a firsthand witness in the Security Council discussions, how the tone in the Security Council changed when the situation demonstrated the need for UN involvement. When the Security Council refused to endorse the U.S. intention to go to war, the UN was described as "irrelevant." However, after the war began, when it was clear that the UN's help and legitimacy was needed, these same actors approached the UN and asked for its cooperation to establish an Iraqi Governing Council. The work of my special representative Sérgio Vieira de Mello was crucial. Vieira de Mello, the experienced, skilled, and evocative representative of UN values, would lose his life in Baghdad during the mission. Later, the Security Council supported delicate negotiations for the transfer of sovereignty to an interim government, chosen largely by my special envoy Lakhdar Brahimi, and asked the UN to organize the 2005 elections and collaborate in the drafting of the new Iraqi constitution. In the end, as Muñoz states, "the UN returned to play a crucial role at the explicit request of the United States."

One of the key lessons of the Iraq war has been the revalidation of the UN seal of approval and recognition of the legitimacy it provides to actions consistent with its charter and agreed upon by member states through its organs, such as the Security Council. I agree with Muñoz's argument that the most efficient way to confront new threats such as proliferation of weapons of mass destruction and terrorism, as well as less conventional threats such as poverty, AIDS, or global warming, is through collective action. True, UN negotiations to reach agreements on common strategies to confront crises can be slow moving and frustrating, but ultimately, such decisions carry greater weight and are sustainable, for they are the expression of the international community's will.

As the author reminds us, "A war of choice is quite different from a war of necessity." Countries must persist in the effort to reinvigorate the UN so that it can serve as the effective international instrument for peace and security, development and human rights that its founders conceived. Heraldo Muñoz's book is a well-informed reflection on this challenge, and an indispensable record on a solitary war and its hard lessons.

—Kofi Annan
Geneva, December 2007

Introduction

On Sunday, January 30, 2005, an upbeat President George W. Bush spoke from the Cross Hall of the White House to congratulate the Iraqi people on their successful election of delegates to a National Assembly.

The election had signified the launch of an unprecedented democratic process in the country. The Iraqis, defying terrorist threats that had created an atmosphere of insecurity, had gone to the polls in massive numbers to exercise their sovereign right to vote.

During his speech, President Bush specifically thanked the United Nations, an organization that he described as having provided "important assistance in the election process." Months later, in September 2005, at a packed UN General Assembly meeting attended by more than 150 world leaders, President Bush thanked the UN once more for having "played a vital role in the success of the January elections" in Iraq, and for supporting the drafting of a new constitution. He then requested that the United Nations "continue to stand by the Iraqi people as they complete the journey to a fully constitutional government."

By contrast, about three years before, in October 2002, Bush had warned the UN that failure to act against the Saddam Hussein regime would lead the organization "to betray its founding and prove irrelevant to the problems of our time." And in the run-up to the invasion, on March 17, 2003, Bush had severely criticized the UN Security Council for not "living up to its responsibilities."

These disparities in the American stance toward the UN were due to the late recognition that the UN was the only legitimate institution able to broker a viable alternative to permanent military occupation so that the United States could begin disengaging, at least politically, from Iraq. The Bush administration's plans for a transition to an interim Iraqi government had been soundly rejected by the Iraqis in 2003. A key player in the process, the Grand Ayatollah Ali al-Husseini al-Sistani, had even refused to meet with *any* American official! So, at the request of the United States, the United Nations stepped in to consult with all concerned parties and develop a solution to hand sovereignty back to an interim government, one that was chosen largely by UN envoy Lakhdar Brahimi. This set in motion an unprecedented democratic transition process, which completed its first key stage in the January 30, 2005 elections, followed by the approval of the new constitution in October 2005.

In November 2005, UN secretary general Kofi Annan made his first visit to Iraq since the invasion. One newspaper reported that the United Nations had become "a crucial advisor in the American-backed political process unfolding in Iraq" and had deployed staff to help organize the December 2005 elections for a full four-year government.[1] That same November, the Security Council voted unanimously to extend the mandate of the U.S.–led forces in Iraq, as it did again repeatedly in 2006 and 2007.

In the absence of political progress and with sectarian violence on the rise in Iraq, during the summer of 2007, the

American representative to the United Nations, Ambassador Zalmay Khalizad, argued for a "larger United Nations role" in Iraq. In an op-ed piece, Khalizad stated that the organization "possesses certain comparative advantages for undertaking complex internal and regional mediation efforts; it can also help internationalize the effort to stabilize the country."[2]

A deepening Iraqi crisis pushed the U.S. government from ignoring the UN to relying on the UN. It was not a full embrace of multilateralism, to be sure. Multilateralism had become both the default U.S. position and a practical requirement of any plan that would begin getting the United States out of the post-invasion quagmire in Iraq. At first, the idea was to put the Iraqis in charge as quickly as possible while maintaining the American-led military presence on the ground.

So, starting in 2004, the United States began working again with the UN in Iraq and slowly repairing its ties with its previously alienated allies. But the long-term benefits of multilateralism were still not fully appreciated, and the U.S. administration felt it was important to show that its hands were not tied and that solitary options were always open. So that there would be no confusion about this, Vice President Dick Cheney asserted at the 2004 Republican National Convention that President Bush had never sought "a permission slip to defend the American people." For his indirect criticism of the UN, Cheney received a thunderous round of applause at New York's Madison Square Garden.

The bottom line was that not long after invading Iraq, the United States executed a dramatic foreign policy reversal by returning to the multilateral table and attempting to woo back those allies who had become distanced. This reversal was not a strategic commitment to multilateralism, but rather an undesired change of course by the Bush administration, one made necessary by the deepening of the war. An American-led invasion with a reduced "coalition of the willing" had seemed to proceed well at first, but had devolved into a veritable nightmare of increasing military casualties, mounting resistance to occupation, bloody suicide bombings, and continued insecurity for coalition forces and Iraqis.

During 2007 and 2008, a growing number of Americans demanded a quick exit strategy from Iraq, with a concrete timetable for the withdrawal of U.S. troops. Numerous press reports revealed the public's increasing unrest with the course of the war. Dissenting voices, well beyond the Democratic Party, included leading Republican senators and conservative commentators. Likewise, the Iraqi government strongly agreed with the idea of designing a strategy for the withdrawal of foreign troops. However, President Bush vowed not to extricate military forces from Iraq "on artificial timetables set by politicians" and suggested that "the allure of retreat" from Iraq could lead to the same disastrous defeat experienced by the United States in the Vietnam War.

...

This book tells the story of missed opportunities and of the costs for the United States of going to war in Iraq without enough significant allies. It discusses the downgrade of multilateralism at a moment when broad alliances and UN Security Council endorsement were needed, and reveals how no single nation, no matter how powerful, can do as it pleases or win a war in a complex environment without real international cooperation and support. Former president George H. W. Bush showed an understanding of multilateralism's value during the Gulf War in 1991, and President George

W. Bush seemed to show a similar understanding during the 2001 war against the Taliban regime in Afghanistan. In the latter war, the United States had major allies because of shared outrage, unequivocal evidence, and a common motive. However, America's decision to go to war in Iraq when there was no evidence of weapons of mass destruction (WMD) was a unilateralist decision, making Iraq an American rather than an international war.

The desertion of the multilateral road in Iraq was costly. The United States lost the favor and support of many friends whom America sorely needed to succeed. This book offers the story of the loyal allies who were initially ignored or rejected when they proposed alternatives to war in order to disarm Iraq and who were later urged to assist the war effort when matters on the ground demanded more partners and greater legitimacy.

The underlying argument of this book is that unilateralism, even when it operates under the cover of a "coalition of the willing," cannot succeed in cases like Iraq, where a strong military force is needed as much as diplomatic alliances are and where the legitimacy of UN endorsement is also a must. The policy reversal to tactical multilateralism may have led to the successful 2005 Iraqi electoral process and the constitution of an elected government in 2006, but that reversal alone may be insufficient to earn the United States sustained support and trust from strong allies in other situations.

In short, the most important lesson of the second Iraq war is that in this world characterized by global media, new threats, and inextricably interwoven political and economic interests, the United States of America needs the support of significant allies and multilateral organizations for the long haul.

Chapter One

Early Warnings

A Telling Phone Call from Condi

When the world learned on the night of Wednesday, March 19, 2003, that the United States had begun bombing Baghdad, it felt, to paraphrase Gabriel García Márquez's novel about an inevitable death, like the "chronicle of a war foretold." United Nations Security Council negotiations had broken down less than a week earlier, and Washington had proceeded to war unilaterally.

Little did I know then that soon after the American rejection of the diplomatic options for a peaceful outcome I would be sitting on the Security Council as ambassador of Chile to the United Nations. As diplomatic envoy, I would be trying with others to pick up the pieces of shattered multilateralism and, later on, negotiating a UN–brokered transfer of formal power from the United States to an interim sovereign Iraqi government after America's military occupation went astray and Washington reversed its course on Iraq.

It became particularly evident that a war with Iraq would prove inevitable once negotiations failed in the UN Security Council on March 15, 2003, with the White House publicly rejecting a Chilean proposal that would have granted more time for the inspections of weapons of mass destruction in Iraq, along with precise and strict goals. But there were signs much earlier that war was coming.

On Friday, February 21, of that same year, when I held the post of minister secretary general of the government of Chile, I received an unexpected call in Chile's presidential palace, La Moneda, from Condoleezza Rice, the U.S. national security advisor. "Condi" was a good friend and a former classmate from the PhD program at the University of Denver's Graduate School of International Studies (GSIS) during the late seventies. Condi was a serious scholar and a bright student of Soviet affairs. Both of us had the same academic advisor at GSIS, Dr. Josef Korbel, Madeleine K. Albright's father, who was a former Czech diplomat and a leading world scholar on Soviet and East European foreign affairs.

Condi's interest in Soviet foreign policy led her to study Russian, and she quickly became Korbel's top student. While I developed a strong intellectual kinship with Korbel— discussing politics and scholarly issues in long chats—I instead chose to specialize in international political economy.

During the summer of 1976, both Condi and I won GSIS scholarships as interns with members of the U.S. Congress. She chose to work with Colorado senator Gary Hart. I went with Denver congressman, and later senator and undersecretary of state for global affairs, Tim Wirth. At that time, Condi was a Democrat.

After graduating, Condi went to teach at Stanford, where she later became provost, while I returned to Chile to participate in the dissident movement against Augusto Pinochet's dictatorship.

After recovering democracy in 1990, I became ambassador of Chile to the Organization of American States in

Washington, DC, and Condi was named director for Soviet affairs of the National Security Council (NSC) under President George H. W. Bush. We met occasionally then to share a cup of coffee and discuss foreign affairs or to chat about the latest news on common friends, former classmates, or our professors from GSIS. Years later, we would stay in touch by phone or e-mail, particularly during the two years I was deputy foreign minister of Chile.

The call I received from Condi on that hot February summer afternoon in the Southern Hemisphere was all business.

From the outset, she made it clear that she was calling both as a friend and as a colleague to convey the White House thinking on Iraq. She was hoping that because of our mutual interest and work, I would seriously evaluate and support the U.S. position. Condi said that Saturday (the next day), President Bush would call Chilean president Ricardo Lagos from his Texas ranch about the Iraq issue. Afterward, he would meet with President José María Aznar of Spain, who would be going to Crawford, Texas.

Condi said that the United States intended to present a new draft resolution to the UN Security Council shortly: "We ask you to consider this draft resolution and not to dismiss it or react negatively outright."

I listened as she went on: "We would like our friends to be with us on this. Of course, when it comes to a vote in the Security Council, it will not suffice to abstain."

In response, I listed the doubts that Chile had about the U.S. position. President Lagos had discussed these with his political cabinet at our regular Sunday working dinners at his residence, during which we prepared the week's agenda. Chile was worried about abandoning the diplomatic route too soon; we believed we should give the UN inspection team more time to unearth the WMD, and we worried that the broad antiterrorist coalition created in the wake of 9/11 could be eroded by a hasty and divided decision to go to war against the Saddam Hussein regime.

I also expressed our concerns about the economic effects of such a war on oil prices, its potential impact on shaky Latin American economies, and the impact an eventual war would have on the Middle East conflict. On this point, Condi tried to ease my apprehension with an interesting piece of information: "Look," she said, "we have an agreement with oil-producing countries that, in the case of war, they will increase production to soften any price increase."

"What about Iraq's neighbors and the impact of war on the Palestinian-Israeli conflict?" I added, groping for arguments against a U.S. invasion.

"I can tell you that the Arab countries are ready for this to be over and done with," she responded.

Our dialogue continued for about half an hour. The last moments of the conversation were most revealing: "Heraldo, I hope you can help us and discuss this with President Lagos. ... We will go with or, if needed, without the UN Security Council."

This phrase echoed in my mind after I hung up the phone. The United States would go alone, if so required.

War in Iraq is inevitable, I thought. *Probably there would be a harsh debate among U.S. allies on the use of force in Iraq.*

I immediately called President Lagos, and he informed me that someone from the Situation Room of the White House had just contacted his staff to communicate that President Bush would phone him on Saturday. Upon hearing why I was calling, he wanted to see me personally.

We met at the presidential summer residence in Viña del

Mar, where I described in detail my conversation with Condoleezza Rice. I referred to the notes that I had quickly jotted down as we talked, and gave him my analysis of the situation.

President Lagos listened attentively. He said he wanted to exchange ideas further with me after he spoke with Bush.

President Lagos's rapport with President Bush was quite good, although it was perhaps not as close as it was with former president Bill Clinton, with whom Lagos had participated in a "Third Way" progressive leaders' group of presidents and prime ministers. That group had included British prime minister Tony Blair, German chancellor Gerhard Schroeder, Italian prime minister Massimo D'Alema, Brazilian president Fernando Henrique Cardoso, South African president Thabo Mbeki, Swedish prime minister Göran Persson, Canadian prime minister Jean Chrétien, and others. However, Bush seemed to appreciate Lagos's influence in Latin America, since the Chilean president had helped him avoid an unpleasant situation with another leader from the region at the 2001 Summit of the Americas in Quebec, Canada. Lagos received occasional calls from Bush and had been invited to the White House. The two men often saw each other at international summits.

Their first phone conversation had occurred on February 3, 2001, after Bush's troubled election as president of the United States. That first time, they compared notes about their respective close presidential elections, from which each had emerged victorious. Lagos took advantage of the moment to refer at length to the importance of the bilateral free trade negotiations initiated during the Clinton administration. Bush responded that free trade would be a priority of his administration and that he expected there would be "good progress" on this front. Lagos inquired about Bush's intended tax cut, but the U.S. president did not elaborate. It seemed that he was sticking to a written script, one from which he would not depart during the conversation with his Chilean counterpart.

Bush then asked, "Is everything else okay in your country?" Lagos replied that he was quite optimistic, as he anticipated that economic growth could reach 5 percent that year. Bush responded candidly, "I wish we could do that!" Lagos then tempered his analysis, reporting that figures on unemployment were well above 8 percent in his country, and Bush said that he similarly expected "a bad first half year" in the United States. The two men explored the possibility of meeting in person soon. "*Quizás* [Perhaps]," said Bush, in a Spanish accent difficult to understand.

But on Saturday, February 22, 2003, the conversation between the two presidents was not about bilateral issues, the world economy, or free trade. It was about war, and only war.

When I returned to see my president that afternoon, he told me that Bush had repeated the exact same words—almost to the letter—that Condi had used with me the day before. Although calm, President Lagos seemed pessimistic about the international situation. With an air of resignation, he said, "The situation looks pretty bad ... I think there will be war."

Some European countries, particularly France, were convinced that the Bush administration was bent on waging war against Iraq independent of the evidence found on the ground or the negotiation of a second resolution.

In January 2003, France chaired the Security Council. President Jacques Chirac sent Maurice Gourdault-Montagne, a trusted presidential diplomatic advisor, to Washington to meet with Condoleezza Rice at the White House and Deputy Secretary of Defense Paul Wolfowitz at the Pentagon. The

French envoy concluded that the Bush administration's message was clear: military action was needed to solve the Iraqi crisis, unless Saddam Hussein was overthrown or left the country. That assessment coincided with what I had heard directly from Condi Rice.

A War with Multilateral Support
The war against Saddam Hussein in 2003 was not the first.

On August 2, 1990, Iraqi troops and tanks invaded Kuwait and seized full control of the country. At the time, many in Washington had a benevolent view of Saddam Hussein's intentions. Since the mid-eighties, the United States had actually intensified ties with the Iraqi regime. A few days before the invasion of Kuwait, Hussein met with American ambassador April Glaspie, at which time she stated that she had "direct instructions from the president to seek better relations with Iraq" and that the United States had "no opinion on Arab-Arab conflicts like your border disagreement with Kuwait." Such declarations no doubt were interpreted by Hussein as a tacit approval for Iraq's invasion, given that the aggression against Kuwait would be "an Arab-Arab conflict."

Yet within hours of the invasion, the U.S. administration reacted multilaterally, requesting, along with Kuwait, an emergency session of the UN Security Council. As President George H. W. Bush had been U.S. ambassador to the United Nations, he knew the practical importance of gaining the Security Council's backing. As a result of that session, resolution 660, condemning the Iraqi invasion, was approved. It demanded that Iraq "withdraw immediately and unconditionally all of its forces to the position in which they were on 1 August 1990."

The invasion of Kuwait continued, however, and four days later, on August 6, the UN Security Council imposed full economic sanctions on Iraq by a vote of 13 to 0, with two abstentions (Cuba and Yemen).

Saddam Hussein tried to rally the support of Islamist mujahideen by adding *Allah Akbar* (God is Great), a phrase important to believers, to the flag of Iraq and broadcasting images of himself praying in Kuwait. In turn, Osama bin Laden offered King Fahd of Saudi Arabia his Al Qaida jihadists to defend his country and the holy cities of Mecca and Medina and to fight Hussein's army, since it was feared that Iraq could next invade the kingdom. The Saudi ruler, however, opted for the United States' protection.

After peace negotiations to achieve Iraq's pullout from Kuwait failed, President George H. W. Bush sought a UN resolution authorizing the use of force against Iraq. On November 29, 1990, resolution 678 authorized the UN member states to "use all necessary means to uphold and implement resolution 660 (1990) and all subsequent relevant resolutions and to restore international peace and security in the area ... unless Iraq on or before 15 January 1991 fully implements [UN Security Council decisions]." When a so-called pause of goodwill and a last-minute Russian compromise proposal still did not produce a peaceful solution, a U.S.–led coalition from thirty-four countries, backed by UN legitimacy, launched an all-out air and missile attack on Iraq on January 16, 1991.

France, led by Socialist president François Mitterrand, aligned with the United States, and French troops entered Iraq, capturing more than 1,000 prisoners. Yet domestic political costs were incurred as a result of France's position: Defense Minister Jean-Pierre Chevènement resigned because he believed that the United States was pushing the war against Iraq beyond the UN Security Council resolutions. The French president disagreed and stood by the George H. W. Bush administration.

Regarding the key issue of proceeding on to Baghdad or not, President Bush Senior believed it was not advisable because it would run counter to the UN–approved use of force, which was restricted to liberating Kuwait. Though, truthfully, the UN role never went beyond authorizing the war (an initiative by Secretary General Javier Pérez de Cuéllar to convince Hussein to withdraw from Kuwait had failed), capturing Baghdad would risk disintegrating that strong multilateral endorsement of the U.S.–led military action. President George H. W. Bush later wrote, "Going in and occupying Iraq, thus unilaterally exceeding the United Nations mandate, would have destroyed the precedent of international response to aggression that we hoped to establish."[1] Though Bush Senior also stated that he would have abandoned the UN route had the Security Council not authorized military action against Hussein, the forty-first American president saw the Gulf War as an opportunity to create a lasting cooperative world order.

In addition, nobody in the administration at the time even considered changing the government in Iraq and installing a democracy there. When asked about the possibility, then secretary of defense Dick Cheney said that a democracy in Iraq would not be appreciated by the Saudis. At the time, Defense Secretary Cheney had other concerns. In the context of the Iraqi invasion of Kuwait, he said: "We are there because the fact of the matter is that part of the world controls the world supply of oil, and whoever controls the supply of oil, especially if it were a man like Saddam Hussein, with a large army and sophisticated weapons, would have a stranglehold on the American economy ... "

What apparently did divide the George H. W. Bush administration was the timing of the president's decision to call a cease-fire and end the ground war. On February 28— barely one hundred hours after the land offensive had begun— Bush announced the cease-fire under the advice of the head of the joint chiefs of staff, General Colin Powell. While Cheney agreed with the decision, Paul Wolfowitz and others in the Pentagon strongly objected to the war's quick end.[2]

Bush acted to preserve the coalition and retain the support of Iraq's neighbors. In addition, images of war being broadcast by the media—in particular, those of the charred bodies of Iraqi soldiers on the so-called highway of death leading from Kuwait to Basra—were beginning to turn the public against further military action. Bush Senior had to be careful about public opinion at a moment when Democrats controlled both houses of Congress—their leaders having been initially skeptical about launching military operations in the Gulf. Anyway, most officials in Washington believed now that a defeated Saddam Hussein would be overthrown by his own people.

The lesson derived from the Gulf War of 1991? The world would follow the United States in using force *for the right reasons* and *if endorsed by multilateral legality*. The UN's cohesion behind the United States had proven a strategic asset.

One, Two, Three Iraqs: The Costs of the Unilateralist Doctrine

The 9/11 terrorist attacks on the Twin Towers and the Pentagon represented a watershed in international relations and U.S. security policy. In the aftermath of 9/11, the United States centralized global antiterrorist strategy and made the "war on terror" the paramount priority of its foreign and security policies.

In the wake of the terrorist attacks, the international community reacted in solidarity with the United States. On September 12, 2001, the UN Security Council met in an emergency session and passed resolution 1368, which asserted that the council regarded those assaults on U.S. soil "as a threat to international peace and security" and, under article 51 of the UN Charter, recognized the "inherent right of individual or collective self-defense." American diplomats were fully satisfied with this resolution.

Shortly thereafter, on September 28, resolution 1373 was approved, reaffirming the need to combat terrorist threats "by all necessary means." For the first time in history, the North Atlantic Treaty Organization's nineteen governments invoked article 5 of the treaty, the collective defense provision that obliges all of its members to use armed force if necessary to protect the territory of any member of the alliance. This had never before taken place, not even in the days of the Cold War.

A few days after 9/11, the U.S. administration's nominee for ambassador to the UN, John Negroponte, gained swift congressional approval; this was interpreted as a signal of support for the UN. The U.S. Congress also approved $582 million toward paying off part of the $2-billion American debt to the organization.

However, anonymous sources in the George W. Bush administration soon warned that this new multilateralism emanated "from the pursuit of highly specific U.S. interests."[3] It seemed to be a new interpretation of the old "American exceptionalism" thesis that, as regards foreign policy, argues that without opting out of multilateral arrangements, the United States should not be restricted by multilateral norms or institutions and could claim some exemptions. Secretary of Defense

Donald Rumsfeld, in a television interview on September 19, stated that the military action in Afghanistan would not depend on the UN's approval. Even the NATO endorsement for the use of force was not seen as vital by the Pentagon.

Still, the multilateral system was backing the United States. A further UN Security Council resolution, on November 14, 2001, condemned the Taliban for "allowing Afghanistan to be used as a base for the export of terrorism by the Al Qaida network and other terrorist groups and for providing safe haven to Osama bin Laden" and also expressed "strong support for the efforts of the Afghan people to establish a new and transitional administration" leading to a democratic government.

In the war against the Taliban, the U.S.–led forces were accompanied by an impressive international coalition composed of Great Britain, Canada, Australia, New Zealand, France, Germany, Denmark, Spain, and Turkey. Small detachments of British, Australian, New Zealander, and Canadian special forces provided intelligence and engaged in skirmishes on the ground. In December 2001, a four-thousand-man International Security Assistance Force (ISAF), authorized by UN Security Council resolution 1386, moved into Kabul and surrounding areas to assist the new government of Afghanistan. After providing 90 percent of the troops, NATO assumed control of ISAF in 2003 under French and German leadership. It was its first mission beyond Europe's frontiers.

After 9/11 and the successful multilateral campaign against the Taliban regime in Afghanistan, some pundits publicly concluded that the George W. Bush administration had reversed its unilateral postures of the first nine months. They were wrong.

When President Bush called Chilean president Ricardo Lagos in January 2003, following that long conversation Condi Rice and I held on Iraq, the gloomy outlook was shared by all. War in Iraq seemed unavoidable, particularly considering the new American foreign policy priorities in a post–9/11 world.

The second Iraq war was launched without UN authorization, and consequently, relations between Washington and the member states of the Security Council that did not agree with the American unilateral course of action became severely strained. One of the costs of the war was a sense of deep mistrust and bitterness that came to exist in the relations between the United States and its allies in Europe, Latin America, and beyond.

The deep differences over the Iraq war completely evaporated the considerable international political capital that the United States had won after the 9/11 attacks, expressed in the concerted military action against the Taliban regime in Afghanistan, though that sympathy had already begun to erode with questions regarding the manner in which the White House had defined and was carrying out the "war on terror." On September 12, 2001, Jean-Marie Colombani, editor of *Le Monde*, wrote a famous editorial entitled "We Are All Americans." That worldwide support for the United States disintegrated with the 2003 Iraq invasion.

In the aftermath of the invasion, allies loyal to the United States were rejected, mocked, and even "punished" in America because of their positions to avoid war or to pursue it solely under strict conditions. One consequence of the United States' decision was that countries became reluctant to contribute troops in any capacity, including even to the UN protection force in Iraq. Many former allies went so far as to withdraw their forces completely. Another is that today, there is a worldwide tide of anti-American sentiment that will be difficult to reverse.

The Iraq war also entailed other costs to America and to shared international objectives. For example, it proved a severe distraction from the war on terrorism and Afghanistan's reconstruction. On October 13, 2003, as chairman of the UN Security Council Sanctions Committee against Al Qaida and the Taliban, I visited Afghanistan to gather information about the resurgent Taliban attacks conducted in alliance with drug lords in charge of opium production and trade. During a meeting with Lieutenant General David Barno, the Coalition Force commander, he complained that the American military priority for Iraq had been pursued to the detriment of his mission in Afghanistan. General Barno told me, "I have 11,000 troops in Afghanistan, in a country geographically larger than Iraq, with Taliban resistance growing, but my colleague in Iraq has under his command 130,000 troops." Priorities had shifted from capturing Taliban leader Mullah Mohammed Omar and Osama bin Laden to removing Saddam Hussein.

Evidence reported in *The Washington Post* suggests that in 2002, as the Taliban regrouped, the Central Intelligence Agency closed bases in the cities of Herat, Mazar-el Sharif, and Kandahar. Also, the agency put off an $80-million plan to train and equip the new Afghan intelligence service, while Task Force 5, a covert command team in charge of hunting bin Laden and his lieutenants in the border area with Pakistan, was reduced by more than two-thirds of its fighting strength. According to *The Post*, the commandos, their high-tech surveillance equipment, and other assets "would instead surge toward Iraq through 2002 and early 2003, as President

Bush prepared for the March (Iraq) invasion."[4] Brent Scow-croft, national security advisor under President George H. W. Bush, had warned before the war that "any campaign against Iraq ... is certain to divert us for some indefinite period from our war on terrorism" and would result "in a serious degradation in international cooperation with us against terrorism."[5] In August 2007, Afghan president Hamid Karzai, on the eve of a meeting with President Bush, candidly admitted that "the security situation in Afghanistan over the past two years has definitively deteriorated."

The Iraq invasion also provoked a loss of American credibility because of the alleged but unproven WMD and Al Qaida–Iraq linkage, as well as the loss of trust stemming from America's changing arguments for going to war. In the future, U.S. allies and friends will very likely not be easily mobilized to war, unless they are provided with hard evidence that a purported threat is indeed an imminent danger.

Another undesired consequence of the war was a clear sense of lowered expectations of burden-sharing by allies for future conflict situations. Allies may not want to commit resources and have to pay domestic political costs for accompanying what may seem to be an American adventure.

One additional result of the war and unilateralism was a weakened but still necessary UN, as became clear when the war in Iraq could no longer be handled by the "coalition of the willing." Despite its slowness to react to some crises, the UN Security Council, through its resolutions, has proven essential to confront the Iraqi conflict, and its endorsement may be demanded as a sine qua non by many more nations being asked to join the use of force against an eventual enemy.

Last, trade ties between the United States and select European countries were negatively affected. But perhaps most important, the United States paid a price in terms of losing authority and respect as the leader of the international community.

No country, and certainly no superpower, needs to win popularity contests, but any nation going to war needs strong and willing allies. Such nations require the legitimacy of *multilateralism*. The United States' solitary action in the Iraq war not only ran counter to previous American war efforts, but also has provoked the most controversial world crisis and most heated domestic American issue since the Vietnam War.

According to the "Bush doctrine" that supported the Iraq war, not only would terrorists be targeted in the United States' efforts, but also the countries that would harbor, protect, or help terrorist movements. The prevailing opinion in the Bush administration was that, whether or not there was evidence of countries such as Iraq owning WMD, it was necessary to act "preventively" against terrorists and tyrants and force a regime change in those nations combining WMD capability and a support for terrorism. In taking this position, the Bush administration abandoned its initial ultrarealist perspective for one of "robust moralism."

The administration was convinced that a preventive war against terrorist movements and nations that support them should be a long-term process. Accordingly, to paraphrase Che Guevara, who advocated "one, two, three Vietnams" to spread anti-imperialist revolutions, there would have to be, if needed, "one, two, or three Iraqs" to bring down rogue governments. Consequently, after the Iraq invasion, Syria, North Korea, and Iran received stern warnings that they were being closely monitored, and that eventually they could be next.

Bush elevated the notion of the importance of preemption to a doctrine so that wars of regime change could be conducted when necessary. The Clinton administration had launched air strikes against Al Qaida camps where Osama bin Laden was believed to be and against a chemical plant in Sudan in the wake of the terrorist bombings of the U.S. embassies in Tanzania and Kenya. However, no new doctrine on the use of force had been advanced.

This unilateralist doctrine of preventive war contradicted Harry Truman's 1945 warning: "We all have to recognize [that] no matter how great our strength ... we must deny ourselves the license to do always as we please." In the post–9/11 world, neoconservatives thought differently and were ready to test their new doctrine in Iraq.

Theoretically, no state in the world would relinquish the last-resort right to strike preemptively in the face of a clear and imminent armed attack. But U.S. Secretary of State Daniel Webster's cautious interpretation, offered in April 1841, is still valid: for self-defense to be invoked, there must be "a necessity of self-defense, instant, overwhelming, leaving no other choice of means, and no moment of deliberation."[6]

Some argue that in the age where WMD are potentially in the hands of terrorists, the use of force as a last resort in the face of a clear and present danger seems reasonable. But a war of opportunity is quite different from a war of necessity. Yet, under existing international law, legitimacy for the use of force still resides in the hands of the UN Security Council.

America's decision to disregard the UN in the pursuit of war against Saddam Hussein only to re-embrace it in the chaotic wake of war demonstrates a key point of this book: that there are benefits to the United States of multilateralism, and costs resulting from unilateralism. Even an American administration criticized by many for its penchant for unilateral action came to pragmatically recognize that the

UN was important in dealing with Iraq's predicaments. A war waged with strong allies and international backing is always easier to win than a war fought alone.

As seen in the Iraq case, a "coalition of the willing" can be large in numbers but limited in quality, and those countries that did support the United States' position "did so on the basis of an elite calculation of national interest—in almost all cases against the wishes of large majorities of their own population." Thus very few countries were willing to put "boots on the ground" during the active phase of combat, and many withdrew their forces as the war dragged on.[7]

Nothing can replace the legitimacy and the weight of solid international alliances behind a UN Security Council mandate. This is what presidents Franklin Delano Roosevelt and Harry Truman had in mind when they pushed for the establishment of the United Nations in 1945. It was the Americans who principally designed the world organization, drafted its charter, and lobbied other nations to join in. The UN gained attributes that even nowadays a superpower lacks: moral authority to focus global attention, the ability to summon the international community to respond, and the influence to generate a consensus on difficult issues and legitimacy behind its actions. The United States is undisputedly the world superpower, but it cannot succeed without broad and stable coalitions and solid decisions negotiated in the organization that Washington was instrumental in creating. This is one fundamental lesson derived from the Iraq crisis.

Chapter Two

War Games in the United Nations: A Tale of Missed Opportunities

President Bush took the Iraq issue to the UN in September 2002. Many had advised Bush to avoid the Security Council, since no useful agreement could emanate from such a diverse body. In addition, France or Russia could exercise veto power.

Neoconservative advocates William Kristol and Robert Kagan wrote in an editorial of their magazine, *The Weekly Standard*, "The inspections process on which we are to embark is a trap. ... It was designed to satisfy those in Europe who oppose U.S. military action against Iraq; and it was negotiated by those within the Bush administration who have never made any secret of their opposition to military action in Iraq." Yet they trusted that the president would "ensure that his administration's vision remains unclouded by the smoke emanating from the UN, and that, at the right moment, he will thank the UN and our 'allies' for their efforts and order his military to get about the urgent business of removing Saddam Hussein's regime in Iraq."[1]

Despite misgivings about the inspections process, President Bush agreed to attend the September 2002 UN General Assembly. There, at 10:30 A.M., he delivered a key speech focused on Iraq in which he depicted Saddam

Hussein's regime as "a grave and gathering danger," adding that "to suggest otherwise is to hope against the evidence." For President Bush, the Iraqi regime represented "a threat to the authority of the United Nations, and a threat to peace." After reminding the packed audience at the main hall that the UN Security Council had been created so that its "deliberations would be more than talk"—unlike the League of Nations—Bush asked, "Are Security Council resolutions to be honored and enforced, or cast aside without consequence? Will the United Nations serve the purpose of its founding, or will it be irrelevant?"

Yet the message delivered at the General Assembly Hall by Secretary General Kofi Annan on that same morning, September 12, 2002, seemed to reflect the majority of the views in the room: "I stand before you as a multilateralist," Annan said, adding, "Every government that is committed to the rule of law at home must be committed also to the rule of law abroad. And all States have a clear interest, as well as clear responsibility, to uphold international law and maintain international order." Annan called on Iraq to comply with its obligations, but he warned against unilateral action. "There is no substitute for the unique legitimacy provided by the United Nations," said the secretary general. Annan's speech had been released, unusually, the prior evening, thus appearing in the press that same morning and annoying White House aides who felt the American president had been upstaged. But nobody could ignore the ominous tone and contents of the Bush speech.

In November 2002, after almost two months of deliberations, the UN Security Council toughened measures on Iraq as the Bush administration wanted. Bush's words from his September speech were still fresh: "We will work with the UN Security Council for the necessary resolutions. But, the purposes of the United States should not be doubted. The Security Council resolutions will be enforced—the just demands of peace and security will be met—or action will be unavoidable."

Resolution to Act

After the September General Assembly, the Hussein government formally permitted the return of the UN weapons inspectors to Iraq "without conditions." Baghdad realized that it was better to accept inspections under the existing legal framework of past resolutions dating back to 1991, not those under a new resolution that would be much more demanding, one that Iraq feared could be used as a justification for military action.[2] The inspections didn't begin until the unanimous vote supporting resolution 1441, the so-called last chance, on November 8, 2002. The Americans, who were not exactly happy at the Iraqi acceptance of inspectors in September, were now satisfied, as Iraq had a tough challenge in front of it, and Washington began to shift its discourse from that of "regime change" to "disarmament."

Through the years, Baghdad had not fully cooperated with the UN inspections process, at times expelling and then readmitting inspectors. Now, in 2002, the Saddam Hussein regime grudgingly accepted resolution 1441 within the brief one-week period provided for a response. In his letter to Kofi Annan, Iraqi foreign minister Naji Sabri Ahmed expressed that his government would "deal with resolution 1441" and was prepared to receive the inspectors within the assigned timetable. In a second letter, sent a few days later, the Iraqi government complained that the resolution was "inconsistent with international law, the Charter of the United Nations, the relevant resolutions of the Security Council, and the relevant constitutive instruments of organizations of the UN system concerning the inspections and monitoring regime in Iraq." Nevertheless, Iraq had no choice but to accept the new inspections regime. Annan had pressured the Iraqis for an unconditional acceptance of inspections, and since he had managed to get it, hard-liners in the Bush administration were actually annoyed at him because a good excuse to trigger military action had been removed.

The climate surrounding the resolution's approval had been extremely tense: the United States had mobilized thousands of troops in the Persian Gulf region, and, moreover, on October 10, 2002, a joint resolution of the U.S. House of Representatives and Senate had passed, authorizing the use of military force against Iraq. Bush had declared that the bipartisan action was "clear and strong" and would "show to friend and enemy alike the resolve of the United States."

Although there is ample evidence that Iraq had been a target of the Bush administration since 9/11, there were several reasons to give Saddam Hussein a last chance. First, the Blair government of Britain needed to go the UN Security Council route for domestic political calculations; second, the UN option smoothed internal Washington differences on Iraq; and third, polls showed that voters in the November midterm congressional elections favored UN backing when it came to American policy on Iraq.

Inspections by the UN team on the grounds of Iraq began on November 27 and proceeded swiftly, according to the stipulations of resolution 1441. Another push toward war occurred when, on December 19, 2002, a self-declaration required from Iraq on all aspects of its WMD and delivery programs did not meet the expectations of the inspectors and the Security Council. The United States then advanced the view that Iraq was "in material breach of its obligations." It seems that at that point, the Bush administration re-affirmed its conclusion that war was the only way to deal with Saddam Hussein. The questions remaining would be when to use force and how far to accommodate U.S. allies.

Since no clear judgment had been reached that Iraq indeed possessed WMD, the Security Council agreed that the inspection process should accelerate and bring forth solid evidence on any wrongdoing by Baghdad. The work of the Hans Blix team of the UN Monitoring, Verification and Inspection Commission for Iraq (UNMOVIC) and that of Mohamed ElBaradei, the director general of the International Atomic Energy Agency (IAEA), was increasingly becoming the focus of international debate on Iraq.

The year 2003 was inaugurated with a Security Council meeting on January 9, where chief inspectors Blix and ElBaradei agreed that the Hussein regime was providing adequate access and that a "smoking gun" of culpability had yet to be discovered—although the above-mentioned self-declaration by Iraq was still viewed as insufficient. Washington and London had been asserting publicly that proscribed weapons, materials, and activities did exist in Iraq and were ready for use. In contrast, UNMOVIC stated that there were no finds at inspected sites, but that it could not be ruled out that "such items and activities could not exist elsewhere." The inspectors had to perform a delicate balancing act to maintain credibility and gain time to carry out their work as patience ran out in Washington.

At the January 9 Security Council session, Hans Blix argued that since the Iraq inspection process had begun in 1991, not in 2002 as referred to by resolution 1441, the inspections process would not end on January 27. In accordance with relevant Security Council resolution 1284 of 1999, the next quarterly inspections report would be released on March 1, 2003. Such an interpretation was strongly challenged by the United States, which viewed it as an unnecessary delay.

In informal council talks held on January 16, American ambassador John Negroponte stated, "Moving directly into the timetable called for by resolution 1284 would send the wrong message to Iraq: a message of business as usual." He added that Security Council resolution 1441 gave Hussein a "final opportunity to comply" and required Iraq to "cooperate immediately, unconditionally and actively" and that, by contrast, resolution 1284 had been drafted "under a different context to establish a path to suspending and ultimately lifting sanctions." The U.S. envoy concluded that it was "difficult if not impossible to visualize the application of the timetable contained in 1284." Other countries, however, opined that resolutions 1284 and 1441 were complementary, that no "deadlines" existed for the inspections, and that, in the end, the important point would be Iraq's compliance with the disarmament requirements.

As the Iraqi debate heated up, the foreign ministers of most of the fifteen member countries of the council descended on New York to be present at its January 27 session. Blix noted there was progress in terms of inspections access but suggested that a "similar decision was required on substance." The key conclusion of the UN inspectors was that it could be neither confirmed nor denied that WMD existed in Iraq.

As is customary in this type of meeting, once the reports on the respective subjects were presented publicly by UN officials, the session was adjourned, to be followed by closed consultations limited solely to the fifteen member countries of the council.

In the closed session of the Security Council, the ministers and representatives of member countries posed many questions to inspectors Blix and ElBaradei. Russia, Germany, China, and France underscored that Iraq was cooperating with the inspections process, but that it needed to do so more actively, by answering all queries and facilitating interviews with scientists and specialists. On the other hand, Spain, the United Kingdom, and the United States stressed the lack of cooperation by Iraq and that inspections could not continue indefinitely. Secretary of State Colin Powell emphasized that inspections were not the ultimate goal of resolution 1441, "disarmament" was. He added that there was "no evidence to indicate that Saddam is voluntarily disarming his nation of its biological and chemical weapons, nuclear capabilities, and ballistic missiles."

The next day, President Bush delivered his State of the Union address to Congress, where he suggested that Hussein was seeking to manufacture nuclear weapons. He cited what would later become two highly contentious assertions: (1) that "The British government has learned that Saddam Hussein recently sought significant quantities of uranium from Africa" and (2) that "Evidence from intelligence sources, secret communications, and statements by people now in custody reveal that Saddam Hussein aids and protects terrorists, including members of Al Qaida."

During the same speech, Bush announced that the United States would ask the Security Council to convene on February 5 to receive from Secretary Powell information and intelligence "about Iraq's illegal weapons programs, its attempts to hide those weapons from inspectors, and its links to terrorist groups." Bush ended with an ominous warning: "We will consult, but let there be no misunderstanding: If Saddam Hussein does not fully disarm ... we will lead a coalition to disarm him." It sounded like what Condi Rice had told me a few days earlier: "We will go with or, if needed, without the UN."

By that time, rumors had intensified about a second Security Council resolution, one that some council members did not want, but one that President Lagos and I knew would come soon, as we had learned from our respective démarches by President Bush and Condi Rice on January 14 and 15. Chile's position was that war should be avoided, that sufficient, not indefinite, time should be given to UNMOVIC for intrusive inspections, and that any eventual use of military force in Iraq would require a new resolution that the Santiago government would analyze with an open mind.

Tony Blair was behind the drive for the second resolution, just as he had contributed to Bush's decision to follow the UN Security Council path in November 2002 and support resolution 1441 to disarm Iraq. Yet opposition to Blair was growing not only in the streets of London, but also, more dangerously, within his own Labour ranks.

Why would Blair stand behind the United States posture so steadfastly? Philip Gould, a leading political and communications strategist as well as key advisor to Blair, once told me in a conversation we had in London in 2002 that one of the great successes of Tony Blair and the New Labour movement had been to outflank the conservatives "on the right" by committing fully to the transatlantic alliance. The Labour Party had always been hesitant about the alliance with America in moments of crisis, while the Tories profited from their unconditional alignment with Washington, a posture strongly shared by British public opinion. In short, Blair had pulled the rug out from under the Conservative Party by siding firmly with Bush.

In late January 2003, Bush invited Blair to Camp David to discuss the launching of a new resolution. The British prime minister had been to the mountain retreat outside Washington in February 2001, when he had been invited there to meet Bush and talk about European defense, and, more importantly, in September 2002, when the president had agreed to take the Iraq question to the UN, in part to help Blair maintain the leadership of his Labour Party.

On Friday, January 31, a bitterly cold Washington winter day with light snow and strong winds grounded the helicopters that were to take the two leaders to the Camp David cabins. They were forced to remain for the weekend in the residential area of the White House, holding a summit that began over lunch and continued through dinner. Bush agreed to Blair's request for a second resolution, which was actually confirmation of a decision already adopted by all the top players in the Bush administration.

But since Colin Powell would address the UN Security Council within a few days to attempt to reveal a "smoking gun" on Iraq's WMD, the communications experts at the White House recommended lowering the emphasis on the need for a second resolution. This bothered Blair. At the joint press conference the next day, Bush avoided an explicit reference to the expected resolution, but in response to a question he said, "Should the United Nations decide to pass a second resolution, it would be welcomed if it is yet another signal that we are intent upon disarming Saddam Hussein."

Back in November 2002, the United States and the United Kingdom had reasoned that with resolution 1441 in place, they did not need an additional resolution to act against Hussein. But since that time, political conditions had changed in Britain. Key Labour figures such as Robin Cook, leader of the House of Commons, and Secretary of International Development Clare Short had publicly expressed the view that a proper interpretation of international law required a new, explicit council resolution authorizing the eventual use of force in Iraq.

In late January 2003, attention was concentrated on Powell's alleged evidence about WMD in Iraq, which would be presented before the Security Council on February 5. On January 31, a council meeting about the format of the February 5 session supported the U.S. proposal that the meeting be public and open to the press and that only members of the council could intervene in the discussion, although the possibility of speaking was given to the Iraqi delegation.

The Security Council chamber was absolutely packed by 10:15 A.M. of the day in question. Powell proceeded to make his hour-and-a-half-long presentation, supported by two giant screens situated near the corners of the chamber. The backdrop was a huge, bright, and magnificent painting on the east wall symbolizing the promise of peace, freedom, and progress completed in 1952 by Norwegian artist Per Krohg. Central Intelligence Agency Director George Tenet was also present as a member of the U.S. delegation, seated right behind Powell. All fifteen countries were represented by their foreign ministers, with Germany presiding through its Vice Chancellor and Foreign Minister Joschka Fischer. Kofi Annan was seated to his right at the horseshoe-shaped table, next to the foreign ministers of France, China, and Chile.

Powell began by quoting Blix and ElBaradei that Iraq had not yet demonstrated a "genuine acceptance of the disarmament that was demanded of it" and that on the nuclear issue, no new information "relevant to certain questions outstanding since 1998" had been provided. Then he proceeded to play a tape of what was supposed to be a secret conversation between two senior officers of Iraq's Republican Guard on the day before the UN resumed Iraqi inspections (November 26, 2002), illustrating how items had been removed and hidden, but not destroyed.

Colin Powell asserted that Hussein was not only concealing weapons, but "also trying to hide people," meaning those scientists who would need to be interviewed by the UN inspectors. Moreover, Powell said that there were mobile biological weapons factories "on wheels and on rails ... designed to evade detection by inspectors."

Another tape was played, this one suggesting the removal of "nerve agents." This led Powell to strongly affirm that "Saddam Hussein has chemical weapons" and, furthermore, that there was "no indication that Saddam Hussein has ever abandoned his nuclear weapons program" and that there was "proof that he [Hussein] remains determined to acquire nuclear weapons." Powell's PowerPoint presentation repeatedly emphasized his desired message through slides showing thick yellow and white letters against a blue background: "Iraq fails to disarm: denial and deception. Nuclear weapons. Terrorism. Chemical weapons." Powell did not repeat, however, the allegation by President Bush that Iraq had sought to buy uranium from an African country.

Powell affirmed that his statement that day was "backed up by sources, solid sources. These are not assertions. What we are giving you are the facts and conclusions based on solid intelligence."

These words would later come back to haunt him.

Approximately one year later, in April 2004, Powell admitted to reporters during a transatlantic flight that his allegation about Iraq's mobile biological weapons labs appeared not to have been "that solid," suggesting that he had been misled by the CIA.[3]

Powell's speech to the Security Council would be questioned later by David Kay, the chief American weapons inspector, who said that months of searching in Iraq under U.S. and coalition control suggested that further searches for WMD would not turn up any unconventional weapon.

The foreign ministers asked that the information provided by Powell be made available to the UN inspectors. They expressed their appreciation for the American commitment to a multilateral approach to Iraq. Most of the ministers also expressed that morning a desire for a peaceful outcome to the crisis, and while some emphasized the need for immediate results, others explicitly supported the longer timetables for inspections set by resolution 1284.

The Security Council met again on the morning and afternoon of February 14, 2003. Many television networks transmitted live the public portions of the Security Council session that journalists would come to dub the "St. Valentine's Day massacre." The meeting was taking place a week after inspectors Blix and ElBaradei had been in Baghdad as inspections on the ground continued. Positive developments on the Iraqi front were reported, for Iraq had allowed U-2 flights to pass over the country, something that Saddam Hussein had adamantly opposed for months. But the U.S. government was growing impatient with the Security Council and the inspection process, and the authorization of U-2 flights did not impress Washington at all.

In the morning meeting, Blix was cautious: "There is

some hope," he said, adding that he had reasons to be more optimistic than in his last report, even though the change or progress was not drastic. Both he and ElBaradei argued that if Iraq continued to cooperate, then the inspections process should simply proceed. Blix said that no one should jump to the conclusion that WMD exist in Iraq, although he warned, "That possibility is also not excluded."

The Blix report was at odds with the intelligence evidence provided by Downing Street and the White House, through Colin Powell, one week before. Consequently, the British and the Americans were furious at the inspectors' reports. The differing opinions among members of the Security Council were becoming more and more evident.

A Tug of War

France was of the idea that the inspections regime could be strengthened with, among other elements, more inspections, increased aerial surveillance, inspections of road traffic, and a better flow of intelligence from national agencies to the inspectors. Paris suggested all of this with the purpose of avoiding a war. China stated that the inspections should continue and become more efficient, yet worried that any intensification of inspections could lead to a political solution. The Russian foreign minister agreed that the inspections should continue, and he raised the idea that, in line with resolution 1284, a list of "key remaining disarmament tasks" should be developed to provide objective criteria against which to evaluate Iraq's degree of cooperation.

On the other side of the debate, the United States and the United Kingdom were losing their patience not only with Iraq, but also with their partners on the Security Council. At the February 14 meeting, Colin Powell dismissed the idea of more inspectors and inspections and felt that "this is as far as we will go [in the inspections process] and there is no justification to continue." Powell added forcefully, "Compliance is compliance; time will pass and we will continue to say that we do not see the level of compliance we wanted." British foreign secretary Jack Straw expressed his skepticism that interviews with Iraqi scientists would yield better information about WMD, and he reminded his colleagues that in 1991, Iraq had been given ninety days to disarm and it had not complied. Hence, he concluded, there should be "a credible threat of force" and taking action in Iraq would send a powerful signal to other potential WMD proliferators.

Chile and Mexico, nonpermanent members of the Security Council, saw polarization grow in the council. The position that they would adopt was becoming increasingly vital.

The Security Council adopts binding resolutions and can impose sanctions, send peacekeeping missions around the world, and authorize the use of military force. If a resolution for the use of force in Iraq came to a vote, the decision would have to be backed by a quorum of at least nine of the fifteen members of the council, assuming that none of the five permanent members—the United States, Great Britain, France, China, and the Russian Federation—used their veto power. Hence, the inclination and eventual vote of the ten nonpermanent members—elected in the General Assembly by a two-thirds majority, from different regions, to serve on a rotating basis for two-year periods—was becoming critical.

Presidents Vicente Fox of Mexico and Ricardo Lagos of Chile had agreed to coordinate positions on the Iraq question. If they opposed an invasion of Iraq, it would be very difficult for other nonpermanent members such as Pakistan or Angola to endorse war. There had to be clear evidence and strong reasons, the presidents agreed, to approve a resolution endorsing going to war.

Meanwhile, Colin Powell invited his colleagues from the council's ten elected-member countries to an informal dialogue. The first surprise for the foreign ministers as they entered the Waldorf Astoria Towers was in the meeting room where the conversation would take place: British secretary Jack Straw was present and sitting at the head of the table.

The informal session started with the American secretary of state welcoming his guests. He then went directly into his briefing. Washington, he said, was already "making preparations for humanitarian assistance" in the Gulf region to attend to the needs of the civilian population in the event of military action. The United States, he asserted, would exercise its leadership, and that action would be against the Saddam Hussein regime—not the Iraqi people. Powell added that Washington had no interest in prolonging military action beyond what was needed and would favor, upon victory, a process of reconstruction that would ensure economic development, peace, and stability for Iraq and its neighbors. Could there be any clearer message that war was *ad portas*?

The most interesting point of the conversation hosted by Powell was German foreign minister Joschka Fischer's suggestion of identifying "objective elements" as a yardstick to measure Hussein's cooperation. Why not make an effort to set up concrete criteria that would allow an effective evaluation of the degree of progress of the inspection process and the work plan that Hans Blix would have to present on March 27? asked Fischer. Powell's reaction was noncommittal, although he did not dismiss the idea. From that point on, several countries began mentioning the term *benchmarks* to refer to the objective yardsticks for measuring cooperation by the Saddam Hussein regime.

Several ministers reiterated concepts such as a need to maintain the "unity of the Security Council" while making sure that the requirements outlined in resolution 1441 would be complied with. Powell insisted that Iraq should remain pressured to fully comply with the resolutions, and he stated that he was keeping his "fingers crossed" for an eventual regime change in Iraq promoted from inside or for a decision on Hussein's part to go into exile.

At the time, it had become known that the Saudis were trying to persuade Hussein to go into exile. It was reported that Foreign Minister Prince Saud al-Faisal had met with Bush on Thursday, January 30, to discuss the initiative, after the Saudi minister had consulted with Chirac and Blair. Rumors abounded about a hypothetical UN Security Council resolution to offer Hussein amnesty for war crimes charges in exchange for exile and compliance with resolution 1441. Prior to this, Egyptian foreign minister Ahmed Maher had denied any involvement in the exile plan, although Philippine foreign secretary Blas Opple confirmed that there was an Arab initiative to have Hussein voluntarily step down and leave the country.[4] Apparently, the exile proposal had originated in Saudi Arabia and Turkey, and Saudi intelligence had gone as far as contacting Hussein's son Qusai about the plan.

In fact, a secret memo from the Spanish government leaked in the fall of 2007 transcribing a conversation held in Crawford, Texas, on February 22, 2003, between President Bush, Spanish president José María Aznar, and their top aides, had Bush affirming that the Egyptian authorities were "talking to Saddam."[5]

"It seems that he [Hussein] is willing to go into exile if he is allowed to take along US $1 billion and all the information available on WMD," said Bush in the conversation transcripts. "[Muammar El] Qadaffi has told [Prime Minister Silvio] Berlusconi that Saddam Hussein wants to leave," Bush added.

The exile option was pursued up until the day of the eventual invasion into Iraq. In early March, the president of the United Arab Emirates called publicly for Hussein's exile, and on March 19, the king of Bahrain, Sheikh Hamed al-Khalifa, offered Hussein asylum on the Gulf island. On the weekend of March 16 and 17, both Bush and Vice President Cheney even proposed the "flight or fight" choice to Hussein.

Around the time of the February 14 New York City meeting, many countries outside the Security Council were clamoring to get their views heard about this crisis that was dominating world affairs. Thus, an open debate of the UN Security Council was held in February 2003, where sixty-one delegators lined up to speak their minds, uninterrupted by council members. Among the many declarations, the European Union (EU) voiced the view through its Greek president that "war is not inevitable" and that "force should be used only as a last resort." The EU urged that parallel efforts be made to "invigorate the peace process in the Middle East and to resolve the Israeli-Palestinian conflict."

The time for a final resolution was at hand, and on February 24, during a closed meeting in the tight and uncomfortable consultations room located on one side of the Security Council hall, the United Kingdom introduced the text Condoleezza Rice had announced back on January 14, cosponsored by the United States and Spain. The key introductory paragraph stated, "Iraq has submitted a declaration pursuant to its resolution 1441 (2002) containing false statements and omissions and has failed to comply with, and cooperate fully in the implementation of that resolution." The sole substantive operative paragraph, mentioning the chapter of the UN charter that allows for the use of armed force, read, "Decides that Iraq has failed to take the final opportunity afforded it in resolution 1441 (2002)."

The U.S. ambassador intervened to underline that this draft resolution was justified because the objective of resolution 1441 was "disarmament" and not inspections, and Iraq had not actively or genuinely cooperated with UNMOVIC and the IAEA. Iraq "should demonstrate that it does not have WMD," added the American representative, who closed with a lament that Iraq had not taken advantage of its last opportunity.

France reacted to the draft resolution by proposing "reinforced inspections" and distributed a memo, cosigned by Germany and Russia, with ideas on how to strengthen the inspections process according to a clear work program to be submitted by inspectors on March 1, instead of simply "before March 27." The French representative stated that the military option "should be the last resort." Russia expressed that no proof had been presented of the existence of WMD in Iraq and, moreover, questioned several of the arguments used by the United States and its cosponsors in defense of the draft resolution. Several members of the Security Council thought that Russia's position was harsher than that of France, although the American media would later portray the Chirac government as the main obstacle to the U.S. push toward war.

A few days later, on March 5, Foreign Ministers Dominique de Villepin of France, Ivan Ivanov of Russia, and Joschka Fischer of Germany met in Paris and released a joint statement in which they affirmed that inspections in Iraq were "producing increasingly encouraging results."

They called on Iraqi authorities "to cooperate more actively with the inspectors to fully disarm their country" and asked that "inspections be accelerated" according to their memo submitted to the Security Council specifying the remaining issues and calling for limited and detailed timelines. The conclusion of the trilateral declaration read: "In these circumstances, we will not let a proposed resolution pass that would authorize the use of force. Russia and France, as permanent members of the Security Council, will assume all their responsibilities on this point."

It was clear that a veto action was looming over the draft resolution introduced by the United States, the United Kingdom, and Spain. The prospects for the approval of another resolution paving the way for war looked grim.

Friends and allies of the United States made sincere attempts to bridge the growing gap among positions. Canada distributed a non-paper—as an informal note is called in diplomatic lingo—in which it recognized that both sides had a point, and proposed "a deadline for cooperation" of March 28 as a possibility, preceded by a "timetable and disarmament requirements." The central idea was a prioritization, with deadlines, of the key substantive tasks to be accomplished by Iraq. It was a further-evolved version of the benchmarks idea that had been discussed in general terms in the French memo of February 24.

On March 3, the Canadian representative met at the Mexican mission with the ten nonpermanent members of the Security Council (the so-called E-10, or the elected ten members, as opposed to the "P-5," or the five permanent members, of the council). Canadian ambassador Paul Heinbecker clarified his government's document and informed that group that his prime minister, Jean Chrétien, had visited Mexico, where he had held positive talks with President Vicente Fox. He also said that Chrétien had exchanged views with British prime minister Blair, President Chirac, and President Lagos. Comments were made at the meeting about the rumors that the United States would put the draft resolution to a vote on March 7. Most agreed that there was only a small possibility of pushing an alternative solution.

The E-10 group welcomed the Canadian document and generally backed the notion of benchmarks within limited time frames. The Canadian compromise of initiating tests on a "pass or fail" system, however, was not accepted, even though, at the time, the Canadian ambassador was apparently "encouraged to persevere by many, including members of the so-called coalition of the willing."[6]

On Monday, February 27, new closed consultations of the Security Council focused on the inspections report presented over the weekend. Not much had changed, and the countries' positions had not shifted either. A press communiqué by the inspectors informed the members that Iraq had, on that very day, accepted "the request for the destruction of the missiles and other items listed by UNMOVIC." This referred to the Al Samoud 2 missiles that had to be destroyed because they exceeded the range limit of 150 kilometers established by the Security Council. Previously, the Hussein regime had been very reticent to destroy these missiles.

The ten elected members of the council began to feel the pressure of polarization, and there was a split. Spain had already joined the U.S. and U.K. coalition, and soon Bulgaria followed suit. The opposite bloc, led by France and Russia, including China, was joined by Germany and Syria. That left six countries caught in the middle: Cameroon, Pakistan, Guinea, Angola, Mexico, and Chile.

Consequently, in early March, Mexico and Chile began intensive rounds of talks with various groups of countries in a search of a viable alternative to war.

The ambassador of Chile, Juan Gabriel Valdés, and his colleague from Mexico, Adolfo Aguilar Zinser, met jointly with Hans Blix at his UN office on the thirty-first floor to explore peaceful alternatives to the crisis. They told Blix that the Canadian proposal reflected, to some degree, the concerns of their respective countries because it had "benchmarks with time frames," but that a consensus could not be generated with such an imminent deadline (March 28) or with an automatic decision to go to war after a certain date. On the other hand, the latest French "memo," they argued, was "atemporal" and did not completely take into account the full gravity of the situation at hand.

Blix revealed to them that in his report to the council on March 7 he would refer to elements of the work plan that he was due to present on March 27, but that even though the March 27 work plan was ready, the United States, United Kingdom, and Spain had, unfortunately, blocked its immediate delivery to the council. The plan, he said, included concrete tasks to be accomplished by Iraq within specified time limits. Blix suggested that he had the support of Secretary General Kofi Annan and had also communicated his concern about the "nebulous" nature of the coalition draft resolution.

On March 4, during the monthly lunch of the secretary general with the members of the Security Council, in a dining room overlooking the East River, Kofi Annan stated that in his view and according to the latest information provided by the inspectors, Iraq was working much better with UNMOVIC and IAEA. Then he proceeded to make an appeal to the representatives who were present:

I urge all of you to find a point of convergence. I am not naive, but it is evident that we need real dialogue. I am ready to work with each and every one of you to find a solution that allows the peaceful disarmament of Iraq.

The luncheon discussion shifted to the draft resolution and its legal implications. According to UN secretary general legal advisor Ralph Zacklin, in the case of war without authorization of the Security Council, the Geneva Conventions would apply between an occupying and occupied country. In addition, it was believed that another resolution would be required to deal with the pending and ongoing issues between the UN and Iraq.

On March 6, the night before another Security Council meeting, President Bush gave a prime-time fifty-minute news conference during which he committed "not to leave the American people at the mercy of the Iraqi dictator and his weapons" and asserted that it was "a fact" that Hussein had failed to disarm. For some observers, the occasion of Bush's rare press conference—the first in a year and a half—was believed to reflect Washington's determination "to preempt a report on Friday [March 7] by one of the chief arms inspectors, Hans Blix, who was expected to say that Mr. Hussein [was] finally destroying some of his weapons and that the inspectors need more time to complete their job."[7]

On Friday, March 7, the Security Council meeting began at 10:35 A.M. It was the third time within a month that the council had convened at a ministerial level to discuss the Iraq crisis. Most of the foreign ministers were in attendance, including Colin Powell, Jack Straw, and Dominique de Villepin. The council chamber's 232 seats reserved for the public and the 118 reserved for the press and other UN members were packed.

Meanwhile, far from New York, 250,000 U.S. troops massed around Iraq.

At the session, Blix and Mohamed ElBaradei proceeded to brief the council on the inspections process. Blix reported that the destruction, under UNMOVIC supervision, of Al Samoud 2 missiles constituted "a substantial measure of disarmament ... the first since the middle of the 1990s." Indeed, he added, "we are not watching the breaking of toothpicks. Lethal weapons are being destroyed." However, he also complained that destruction work was not proceeding further. Evaluating other aspects of the inspections process, Blix affirmed, "After a period of somewhat reluctant cooperation, there has been an acceleration of initiatives from the Iraqi side since the end of January."

ElBaradei then discounted several accusations regarding a renewed nuclear-weapons production program by Iraq. His team judged the import of aluminum tubes, previously alleged to have been for the manufacture of centrifuges, to have been for the production of rockets. ElBaradei said the supposed uranium acquisition attempt from Africa, which Bush had cited in his 2003 State of the Union address, was based on documents "not authentic," a finding he based "on the concurrence of outside experts." ElBaradei added that there was "no indication that Iraq [had] attempted to import uranium since 1990." He concluded that "after three months of intrusive inspections, we have to date found no evidence or plausible indication of the revival of a nuclear-weapon program in Iraq."

Secretary Powell intensely questioned Iraq's true cooperation with the inspections process, stating that progress "with respect to substance" was coming "in a grudging manner ... I still consider that what I heard this morning to be a catalogue of noncooperation." Powell insisted that "the inspectors should not have to look under every rock, go to every crossroads, and peer into every cave for evidence or proof. We must not allow Iraq to shift the burden of proof onto the inspectors."

Powell did not concur with ElBaradei's stance on the aluminum tubes, and he even criticized the IAEA for having been close to "determining that Iraq did not have a nuclear program" back in 1991. He ended by stating that "limited progress" comes from the "unified will of the council—and from the willingness to use force" and called on the Security Council to bring the coalition draft resolution to a vote "in the very near future."

The growing transatlantic divide—at least as far as France and Germany were concerned—became ever more evident at this session. German minister Joschka Fischer recognized that Iraq's cooperation did not yet fully meet UN demands but added that "in recent days, cooperation has, nevertheless, notably improved. ... It shows that peaceful disarmament is possible and that there is an alternative to war."

For his part, the French secretary did not mince words. He began by asserting that "significant evidence of real disarmament" was being observed in Iraq and then asked, "Why should we wish to proceed by force at any cost when we can succeed peacefully? War is always an acknowledgement of failure. Let us not resign ourselves to the irreparable."

De Villepin proposed three initiatives based on the French-German-Russian memo: (1) that the inspectors establish a hierarchy of disarmament tasks and, on that basis, present a work program in line with resolution 1284; (2) that the inspectors submit progress reports every three weeks; and (3) that a schedule be established for assessing the implementation of the work program.

The French minister then added that his country could not "accept an ultimatum as long as the inspectors are reporting progress in terms of cooperation. That would mean war." Then he unloaded a diplomatic bomb: "As a permanent member of the Security Council, France will not allow a resolution to be adopted that authorizes the automatic use of force." In short, if the U.S.–U.K. resolution were brought to a vote, Paris would veto it.

Russian minister Ivanov emphasized his observation of "a real disarmament process in Iraq for the first time in many years" and expressed that his country was "firmly in favor of continuing and strengthening inspection activities and of making them more focused in nature." Chinese foreign minister Tang Jiaxuan pointed out that on New York's First Avenue, right outside the UN building, he had heard "justified cries of 'peace not war' from the peoples of many countries" and that the ministers had "no reason to remain indifferent to those strong demands and outcries." He concluded that there was "no reason to shut the door to peace" and that China was "not in favor of a new resolution, particularly one authorizing use of force."

The key move of the meeting came in the form of an intervention by U.K. foreign secretary Jack Straw. Addressing his colleagues around the table of the council, he declared that it defied experience "to believe that continuing inspections with no firm date, as suggested in the French, German, and Russian memorandum, will achieve complete disarmament. ... The memorandum is not even a formula for containment." Disputing that the February 24 resolution presented by the coalition proposed an automatic use of force, he announced that an amendment was being introduced to "specify a further period beyond the adoption of a resolution for Iraq to take the final opportunity to disarm and to bring itself into compliance."

The U.K.–sponsored amendment specified conditions that Hussein would have to meet quickly to avoid war, including admitting, on Iraqi television, to his possession of WMD; allowing twenty scientists to be interviewed outside the country (with their families safely outside the country as well); and surrendering all his stocks of and production facilities for biological and chemical weapons. All of this was to be accomplished in ten days. Iraq would be considered to have "failed to take the final opportunity" if, by March 17, 2003, the council had concluded that Hussein had not complied with the demands.

The sixth introductory paragraph of this new draft resolution noted that Iraq so far had "failed to comply with and cooperate fully in the implementation" of resolution 1441. In the UN corridors after the public meeting adjourned, the comment was that the new amendment entailed "war by preamble."

Still, the introduction of this proposed resolution meant that the British were opening space for a negotiation. In a private meeting held on February 21 at the Mexican mission between the E-10 ambassadors and British envoy Sir Jeremy Greenstock, the latter had suggested that it had been London that had convinced Washington about the introduction of this second resolution. "The U.S.," he stated, "did not want a second resolution." The United Kingdom had persuaded Washington otherwise, however, because that "would allow for more time for debate" and the Iraq question would remain under Security Council control. Greenstock also had warned that the United States' hurry to action was primarily due to the Bush administration being convinced that "it now has the support of public opinion for war, but that there is no certainty that it will have it in the future."

The ten-day deadline posed by the United Kingdom in the new draft resolution accelerated efforts on the part of Chile and the other undecided nonpermanent members to find a middle ground. It also mobilized the British to gain a viable deal.

The Blair-Lagos Last-Ditch Effort

Given their good personal rapport, Prime Minister Tony Blair and Chilean president Ricardo Lagos maintained regular phone contact on the Iraq issue. In fact, prior to submitting the second resolution to the council, Blair had called Lagos, on Tuesday, February 18, to tell him about the planned draft resolution and what had transpired in a NATO meeting days before. Blair told the Chilean president that "time was running out," although the United Kingdom had agreed to continued inspections and that "the burden of proof" lay upon Hussein's shoulders. Lagos replied that Iraq had to comply with resolution 1441, that time was needed to carry out the inspections, and especially that the "Security Council had to act united." The Blair-Lagos connection was so strong that on March 6, Tony Blair almost traveled to Chile to convince Lagos to support the February 24 resolution— the very one that Blair, in turn, had persuaded Bush to submit to the Security Council.[8]

Lagos told Blair in one of the conversations they held during those days, "Tony, the shortest route between London and Santiago, in case you don't know, is Moscow." Lagos wanted Blair to bring Putin in on the eventual agreement for the second resolution, particularly since the position Russia had taken seemed more reluctant than that of France.

Besides, the climate was not propitious for Blair—or even foreign secretary Jack Straw—to visit Chile to discuss Iraq.

Blair's foreign policy advisor, Sir David Manning, secretly flew to Santiago for a Sunday appointment with President Lagos. His presence was known only by a reduced circle of officials, one that included the commander-in-chief of the Chilean Army, who was in charge of providing the location for the meeting. It was a good exchange, and though Manning failed to obtain an endorsement of the British posture, dialogue and the search for a consensus with Chile continued.

A genuine personal and political affinity between Lagos and Blair had developed years before. In fact, when Lagos was a candidate for the presidency of Chile, he received a formal invitation by the British prime minister. As Lagos's foreign policy advisor, I arranged the details for the visit to London. The invitation, coming in the midst of election time, was an important and courageous political signal of sympathy to Lagos, a modern social democrat like Blair. The schedule for the planned visit included a personal meeting with Blair, a visit to the think tank Demos close to the New Labour movement, interviews with other key British authorities, and lectures at leading academic institutions in London.

I was to accompany Lagos on that October 1998 trip, which also included a stopover in Madrid to attend a meeting of intellectuals and political leaders, but the visit never materialized, because an opposition member of the Chilean Parliament requested an investigation of a construction project undertaken while Lagos was minister of Public Works. Lagos decided to cancel the trip to give the matter his full personal attention. I told him that it was a mistake to turn down an invitation from the British prime minister. Lagos replied that I should request "a postponement" of the visit.

"I just cannot leave Chile now, with this accusation coming," Lagos concluded. "Although it is totally baseless, it would not look good if I left for Madrid and London."

A few days later, on October 16, 1998, former Chilean dictator General Augusto Pinochet was arrested in London by Scotland Yard. The British government was responding to an extradition warrant by Spanish judge Baltasar Garzón, who was conducting an investigation into the deaths and disappearances of political prisoners of various nationalities under the Pinochet dictatorship.

Lagos and I were stunned to learn the news of Pinochet's detention in London. Lagos commented wryly, "If we had gone to London and Madrid, nobody, not even our closest friends and fellow party members, would have believed that we did not have anything to do with Pinochet's arrest. Everyone would have thought that we [were] behind a cleverly designed and executed plan to jail Pinochet in London. ... It would have been impossible to demonstrate that our presence in Spain and the United Kingdom and the interviews with the highest authorities in London were totally unrelated to Pinochet's troubles."

The first formal meeting between President Lagos and Prime Minister Blair finally materialized much later, on September 8, 2000, in the context of the UN General Assembly of the millennium. On that occasion, the two men expressed their mutual satisfaction for having overcome the "Pinochet affair." The former Chilean dictator had remained under house arrest in England for a year and a half. Pinochet was finally freed and sent back to Chile on March 2, 2000, nine days before Lagos was inaugurated as president of Chile. There, Pinochet would face trial for human rights violations.

When they met in New York in September 2000, Lagos

and Blair focused their talk on bilateral issues and on the ongoing "Third Way" debate among democratic socialists. Several other encounters followed between Blair and Lagos, perhaps the most memorable being the Chilean president's official visit to London on September 11, 2001. That day, the discussion—which I attended in my condition of deputy foreign minister—was marked by exchanges between the two leaders about the terrorist attacks against the Twin Towers and the Pentagon.

In March 2003, however, the talk between Blair and Lagos was about the impending war in Iraq.

President Lagos thought that the amended resolution was not viable. Among other reasons, he cited the short, ten-day deadline and the requirement for Hussein to go on television and yield to all the stated conditions. Lagos felt it was not politically realistic and would prove humiliating. But Lagos did believe that the Blair-modified resolution at least opened a way to move forward. Hence he instructed his Chilean ambassador in New York to explore an alternative to the U.K.–amended resolution in close coordination with Mexico and the other countries of the so-called U-6, the six undecided members of the council. The U-6 countries based their strength on withholding their vote intentions on a second resolution until the Americans and British actually called for a ballot on a concrete date and time; thus Washington and London could not count in advance the necessary nine votes required to approve a resolution.

On Saturday, March 8, the representatives of Chile, Mexico, Guinea, Cameroon, Angola, and Pakistan—the U-6—met for breakfast at the Beekman Hotel, an old but distinguished terra-cotta-colored building one block from the UN, to discuss the elements of an alternative text to be put forth by the Chilean mission. The proposed text would support the idea of requiring concrete benchmarks to be accomplished by Iraq, but it would do so in more flexible terms than those offered by the amended draft resolution. The next day, the ambassador of Guinea informed the British representative and the French envoy that the U-6 would prepare a text that would seek a compromise with the amended text. In the following days, the Chilean draft would suffer changes from the suggestions of the other U-6 members.

On Monday, March 10, at 7:45 P.M., President Lagos phoned Hans Blix at his UN office. "I haven't found WMD in Iraq. I need more time to verify if there are or if there are not [any]," Blix told Lagos. For almost an hour, the Chilean president inquired about the viability of concrete benchmarks and time frames that he wanted included in the U-6 draft resolution. He wanted these answers before submitting the resolution to the Security Council.

Lagos explained to Blix that the Chilean proposal extended the ten-day deadline and that the required Hussein television address would be substituted with a letter to the secretary general and the president of the Security Council indicating that Iraq would allow UNMOVIC and IAEA to destroy, without delay, all remaining prohibited weapons, proscribed items, and related documentation. The letter would also specify a complete willingness on Iraq's part to immediately address and resolve all outstanding questions.

Blix wrote later that the Chilean document "was clearly a more 'realistic' paper than the British, except that the time allowed went beyond what the U.S. would tolerate."[9] In addition, the document did not authorize the automatic use of force if Iraq did not comply; the council would have to assess afterward whether Iraq had attained the benchmarks or not and then decide on any further action.

The Chilean president spoke to Blix twice about the draft. One of the questions he posed to the arms inspector was how much time he would need to complete his tasks. Blix initially responded, "Forty days." When Lagos said it was too long, Blix replied, "Thirty days." The Chilean president settled on three weeks, given the pressing circumstances.

As the U-6 drafted its alternate text, Deputy Secretary of Defense Paul Wolfowitz, in a speech delivered on March 11 to the Veterans of Foreign Wars, called for the urgent invasion of Iraq. "Should we wait until the people inside Iraq who are willing to help us give up all hope? Or, should we wait until Saddam Hussein finishes preparing weapons of mass terror, weapons that will further endanger our troops?" he asked.

In the meantime, Blair frantically sought support for his own draft. The British even offered to drop some of the ultimatums in the document if they got "traction" on it.

To make matters worse, Blair had received a trans-atlantic missile in the back when, on March 12, Defense Secretary Rumsfeld publicly stated that if the British could not solve their political problems regarding Iraq, the United States would go without them. Furious phone calls were exchanged between Geoff Hoon, the British defense minister, and Rumsfeld, which resulted in the Pentagon issuing a "clarification" that was not much of an apology. Rumsfeld explained that "obtaining a second UN Security Council resolution is important to the United Kingdom, and we are working to achieve it." After a couple of further phone conversations between Blair and Bush, the U.S. president explained that Rumsfeld was actually "only trying to help," thus soothing Blair's anger.[10]

On Thursday evening, March 13, the U-6 received a

revised text of the Chilean-led draft resolution at the office of the Security Council president, Guinean ambassador Mamady Traoré. It contained contributions from some of the members of the group and ideas derived during the Lagos-Blair conversation. The Chilean-led proposal was, in fact, not that far off from the amended U.K.–led draft resolution, but by then, time was of the essence.

For Chile, it was essential to preserve multilateralism and to avoid a breakup of the collective-decision process in the Security Council. A country traditionally known to be a promoter of international law and a defender of the UN Charter, Chile had to do the utmost to impede the unilateral use of force.

The following morning, an amazing situation took place. As the deputy permanent representatives of the U-6 met around 11:30 A.M. at the Chilean mission on East Forty-Seventh Street to discuss the final text, they were called by their respective chiefs of mission to leave the meeting immediately. This situation arose because U.S. ambassador John Negroponte had phoned the Mexican representative to warn him that if the proposal that he knew was being discussed at the Chilean mission was submitted to the council, the United States would see it as an "unfriendly act" that sought to isolate the United States. In turn, Colin Powell phoned Chilean foreign minister Soledad Alvear and the other foreign ministers of the U-6 with the same message.

The delegates disbanded, and the Chilean initiative seemed dead. Mexico and the other members of the U-6 decided to hit on the brakes regarding the common effort. The Angolan ambassador Ismail Gaspar Martins told me that he received immediate instructions from his capital to stay away from the initiative, even more so since it seemed—

according to Gaspar Martins—as if Chile had taken the proposal "off the negotiating table." *The New York Times* reported that the envoys from Mexico and Angola had distanced themselves from involvement in the draft by saying that it was "a Chilean proposal." A UN official said that evening that "the unified front of the six had fallen apart."[11] Nonetheless, President Lagos decided to make the initiative public that same Friday.

The document offered five compliance tasks with a deadline of three weeks, but no automatic trigger for war. The United States rejected the Chilean draft only twenty-one minutes after its release. According to White House spokesman Ari Fleischer, the Chilean-led proposal was "a nonstarter." The proposal was then withdrawn from any formal consideration.

Council members gathered that Friday afternoon in closed consultations, hoping that a Sunday summit at the Azores on March 16 by the leaders of the United States, United Kingdom, and Spain would perhaps provide for a peaceful compromise.

Yet phone conversations had not ended. On Saturday the fifteenth, Tony Blair spoke to Lagos and told him that the Chilean proposal was indeed "very close" to the British one, but that since time was running out, it was bound to be seen by the United States as "encouraging more delay." Blair then complained, as he had before, about the toughness of the French position, specifically their threat to veto the amended second resolution. Lagos's close personal rapport with Blair allowed him to make a joke as the two were on the telephone. As a Royal Guard band played loudly in the background, Lagos quipped, "Did you begin with the martial music already?" Blair then explained that no martial music—only "the usual band"—was playing as of yet.

In Lagos's last talk with Blair in those prewar days he complained about the White House's negative reaction to the Chilean proposal and asked him to convey to Bush and other leaders during the Azores summit that Chile's proposal had been in good faith and had not been proposed to serve as a delaying tactic. Blair responded, with little conviction, that perhaps the two could talk again and that he would explore alternatives "right to the end."[12] In the secret Spanish memo of the Bush-Aznar conversations on Iraq leaked in 2007, President Bush had told Aznar, "This is like the good cop, bad cop routine. I don't mind being the bad cop and that Blair be the good one."

Several of the players in the Security Council had actually shown their final cards a few days earlier—on Tuesday, March 11. That day, Lagos had received a phone call from Tony Blair while the Chilean president was in the isolated northern desert town of Diego de Almagro inaugurating the national school year and celebrating his administration's third anniversary. The minister of education was present at the ceremony, as well as regional and local authorities. Everyone wondered what a British diplomat was doing there, but only Lagos knew. The diplomat was there to carry the secure phone with the codes for the Lagos-Blair conversation.

During their conversation, the two heads of government exchanged comments on the alternative draft that both were pushing and Blair informed Lagos that Bush would be calling the Chilean president the next day.

Bush phoned Lagos on his return to Santiago. He assured Lagos that he had a solid eight votes out of the nine needed to pass a Security Council resolution—provided no permanent member vetoed the resolution—and, therefore, he needed Chile's vote. Lagos doubted Bush had eight strong votes, but at the time, he did not challenge the White House numbers, something he later lamented. In a cabinet meeting afterward, President Lagos stated that his country's coordination with Mexico was essential. Assuming there was no veto from a permanent member on the resolution and there was no other choice left, Chile could not vote in favor of the Iraq invasion if Mexico abstained, and Chile could not abstain if Bush truly had nine votes, including that of Mexico.

The Lagos-Bush conversation on March 11 was cold yet respectful. Lagos tried to persuade the American president not to bring the resolution to a vote if a consensus could still be reached, but Bush shot back: "It's time to bring up the vote, Ricardo. We've had this debate too long." When Lagos argued that progress in terms of the inspections was being made based on the Blix and ElBaradei reports, Bush responded that such progress was "illusionary," since it had occurred only because the United States had about 200,000 troops surrounding Iraq. Bush then commented that he just could not keep his men sitting around there. The Chilean president outlined his compromise proposal, to which Bush responded: "There's no more space, Ricardo. Next Monday, time is up." When Bush asked him how he would vote, Lagos replied, "Chile is not available to vote yes because I feel [there is] still time for negotiations."

Throughout the conversation, Bush had referred to the Chilean president as "Ricardo." But as the conversation drew to a close and Lagos refused to support the resolution as it stood, Bush shifted to a cool and aloof "Mr. President." That very morning at the National Security Council daily meeting, plans were being discussed on how to revamp the Iraqi foreign ministry as well as the military and intelligence services in a postwar period.[13] It was clear the American mindset was not on negotiations.

This had been confirmed to me separately in a conversation I had with a high-ranking U.S. foreign policy career official. He confided to me that, in his many years in government, he had never seen the White House team so fired up and holding such definite positions as in the Iraq case. He said there was no room for negotiation when it came to the resolution.

Later on that same Tuesday, Tony Blair phoned Lagos again, at 9:00 P.M. Chilean time (2:00 A.M. London time). He wanted to know how it had gone with Bush. Lagos was giving him the details of the conversation when the prime minister asked him, "Let's say we go with the alternative draft. How many votes do you have out of the six who are undecided? Do you have the six?" Lagos replied, "I have three for sure: Chile, Mexico, and Pakistan. I do not know about the Africans, but [earlier] this evening, Bush told me he had all the African votes for the amended second resolution. If that is the case, I imagine you could bring them onto our alternate draft."

In the weeks leading up to these conversations, Bush had phoned Lagos repeatedly. On Saturday, February 22, Bush had lobbied for the long-announced second resolution that would be introduced by Britain a few days later. Two weeks before that, on Wednesday, February 5, Bush had called the Chilean president to emphasize Hussein's alleged cheating in terms of the UN inspections. And on March 8, Bush had telephoned to discuss the amended second resolution; he considered the call to be a goodwill gesture for those nations that had requested more time. Bush had also sent his presidential envoy for the Americas, Otto Reich, to Santiago to meet with Lagos on February 28 to discuss Iraq. On all these occasions, Lagos had insisted on the need to stick to multilateral negotiations, to demand Iraq's collaboration through intrusive and time-limited inspections, and to consider the use of force as the last resort, under the authorization of the Security Council. Evidently, Bush was not optimistic about support for his resolution, based on his conversations with the Chilean president or with Mexican President Vicente Fox, for that matter, and he conveyed his skepticism to Tony Blair.

The Final Diplomatic Bets

The phone calls and consultations on Iraq during the months of February and March 2003 included various other leading political figures as well.

French president Chirac worked the phones. He called President Lagos three times between late February and mid-March.

On March 8, Foreign Minister Dominique de Villepin traveled to those African countries on the Security Council to pressure them for abstention regarding the U.S.–U.K.–Spanish–amended resolution.

On Monday, February 10, Chirac telephoned Angolan president José Eduardo dos Santos to argue against the U.S. posture. The next day, Bush picked up the phone and called the Angolan leader to counter the French offensive. A few days earlier, on February 5, it had been Vice President Dick Cheney who had talked to President dos Santos, but the action Chirac had taken had forced the Americans to raise the ante to the presidential level. Almost a month later, on Thursday, March 13, Bush contacted dos Santos, as well as the presidents of Guinea and Cameroon, in the hope of winning their votes for the amended second resolution. Around that same time, South African president Thabo Mbeki called all three African countries to argue for a united African front against military intervention in Iraq.

The Africans were also lobbied by the British through phone calls from Tony Blair and a visit from British deputy foreign minister Baroness Valerie Amos. She traveled to Cameroon, Guinea, and Angola on the week prior to the United Kingdom's presentation of the second resolution.

Chirac also spoke to Bush on several occasions in February and March to argue that war was not inevitable and to look for compromise. At the beginning, Bush, Rice, Powell, and others in the administration felt that France could be won over. But after the second resolution was presented on February 24, it became clear that the White House could not count on Chirac. Moreover, on Friday, February 21, Jean-David Levitte, the French ambassador to the United States, went to the West Wing of the White House for an interview with Stephen Hadley, deputy national security advisor to Condoleezza Rice. The French representative urged the White House, on behalf of President Chirac, to drop the second resolution because of the damage it could cause to transatlantic ties. He did not succeed in his plea. Almost simultaneously, President Aznar of Spain was also advising Bush not to go ahead with the second resolution, but for different reasons: he said that the coalition did not have the necessary votes.

During private talks between de Villepin and Alvear, which were held at the UN on the occasion of the March 7 Security Council session, the French minister continued to assert that the United States did not have the necessary nine votes. "I can assure you," he said, "the Africans will not be on board. ... The case of Cameroon is clear and Guinea also because they experienced ten years of war." Moreover, de Villepin added that there would be not one veto, but very likely three: France, Russia, and maybe China.

Later on that same day, Minister Alvear exchanged notes with Mexican foreign minister Luis Ernesto Derbez. The Chilean minister passed him a similar message: the United States did not have the nine votes, and he should continue to abstain, although de Villepin made it clear that he was open to an alternative draft that did not present an ultimatum.

President Lagos and President Chirac had frequent phone conversations during those final days before the war. Lagos asserted to the French president that benchmarks with concrete deadlines were indispensable in the Iraqi situation. In Chile's view, benchmarks without time limitations, as the French had suggested, were not feasible.

A rather tense conversation between Chirac and the Chilean president ensued on February 27, after the presentation of the second resolution by the United Kingdom. Lagos was bothered over France's inquiry as to whether Chile would abstain, while Paris remained reluctant to clarify if it would veto the resolution. He told Chirac, "Mr. President, for me to abstain on the resolution is equivalent to voting against the United States, but if you abstain it means you are voting for Bush. Obviously, the political cost is much greater for me than for you. I would like to know for sure if you will use your veto or not."

Chirac was alarmed by President Lagos's observation. Thus, the next day, French ambassador Jean-Marc de la Sablière requested an urgent meeting with Chilean colleague Juan Gabriel Valdés in New York to clear up the veto issue.

On Saturday morning, March 1, 2003, the two men met at the Chilean mission. They were accompanied by their respective deputy permanent representatives, although there were no note-takers present, as requested by the French. That Saturday, de la Sablière went straight to the point. The French envoy said that President Chirac had personally instructed him to meet with the Chileans as a consequence of the Lagos-Chirac conversation that had transpired less than forty-eight hours earlier. The message he was bringing to the table was that Chirac was determined to veto any second resolution. A French official told me years later that Chirac had considered Lagos's demand to know about France's eventual use of the veto a reasonable point that required a formal signal.

Thus, President Chirac ordered Foreign Minister de Villepin to use the word *veto* that very weekend; the word was one that France had carefully avoided in the Security Council or elsewhere. And sure enough, over the weekend world newspapers reported that during a press conference in Algeria, de Villepin had announced that France would veto any second resolution.

On March 9, President Fox of Mexico had a similar dialogue with Chirac. Fox explained his country's position and demanded to know whether France or some other permanent members might use the veto. If France vetoed, then the Chilean-Mexican search for a compromise would not make much sense. The responsibility for the failure of the U.S.–led resolution would not fall upon those abstaining, but upon France's shoulders.

Chile's and Mexico's relations with France during these days became distant—and even more so as a result of the March 15 television program *Newsnight*, when Foreign Minister de Villepin, in referring to the U-6 effort to reach consensus on a new proposal, declared that the undecided six "would not be allowed to dictate policy." For his part, Blair said in early March, "Why should Chileans or Africans take the risk of voting for war at the United Nations if France is going to ensure that their vote is never counted? This is irresponsible."[14]

Meanwhile, the Americans intensely lobbied the Russians and the Chinese. In late February, Undersecretary of State for Arms Control and International Security John Bolton visited Moscow, where he tried to convince President Vladimir Putin to distance himself from the French stand of opposition to a war in Iraq. But Russian foreign minister Ivan Ivanov traveled to China, where both governments expressed their opposition to any new resolution that would endorse war with Iraq. Colin Powell, who had been in Beijing around the same time to press the Chinese for support, did not achieve any positive results.

During a phone conversation with Putin on March 12, President Bush insisted on Russian support, without success. The day before, the U.S. ambassador to Moscow, Alexander Vershbow, warned Russia that its ties with Washington could suffer if the Kremlin vetoed the amended second resolution in the Security Council. The American ambassador said that there was a great difference between a Russian veto and an abstention. Tony Blair also phoned Putin several times, including when Britain presented the second resolution, on February 24. Both men failed to change Russia's position.

To complicate matters even further, on March 1, the new Turkish government had failed had to win parliamentary support for American troops to use Turkish bases and deploy troops through its territory to enter Iraq from the north. This only caused additional impatience on Washington's part.

A key player in the Iraqi crisis was Pakistan. Bush called

Pakistani president Pervez Musharraf a number of times in both February and March. A pivotal conversation took place on Wednesday, March 12, when Bush appealed for Pakistani support for the amended second resolution. The Pakistanis were cautious, however; together with the U-6, they sought an alternative to the British proposal.

Two days later, on March 14, President Bush authorized an extended waiver of all sanctions imposed on Pakistan after the 1999 coup d'état by Musharraf. The waiver paved the way for Congress to approve an aid package of $1 billion for debt relief and $104 million for economic and military aid. (Congress had first waived the sanctions in October 2001, after Pakistan leaned in favor of Washington in the war against the Taliban in Afghanistan.)

Although Bush, Blair, and Chirac lobbied the remaining members of the Security Council worldwide, other players, including some rather secondary to the crisis, intervened.

Seeking a peaceful solution to the crisis, the Vatican sent Cardinal Roger Etchegaray to Iraq on February 11 as a special envoy of Pope John Paul II. His mission was to prepare a visit to Rome by Deputy Prime Minister Tarek Aziz. On March 5, the pope sent Cardinal Pio Laghi as his personal envoy to meet with Bush and advocate a peaceful road when it came to Iraq. The cardinal had served as the Vatican ambassador to Washington, and so he knew the Bush family well.

This time, however, Bush could not reach a consensus with the Holy See, and when the president was received by Pope John Paul II in June 2004, he was admonished for initiating the Iraq war. The pope reminded Bush of the Vatican's "unequivocal position" against the use of force in Iraq and urged him to normalize the situation "as quickly as possible with the active participation of the international community."

Meanwhile, Prime Minister José Durao Barroso of Portugal lobbied Angola's president, while Spanish president José María Aznar attempted to get the votes of Chile and Mexico.

As a proxy for Bush, Aznar flew to Mexico on Friday, February 21, to persuade President Vicente Fox to support the U.S. resolution. Aznar had been invited to spend the weekend at Bush's ranch in Crawford, Texas, but stopped over first in Mexico City. He felt that he could sway Fox, since both belonged to right-of-center parties. Fox was actually irritated by his visit, since he felt he did not need an intermediary to communicate with Bush. Thus, to show his displeasure with the Spanish visitor, he received a formally dressed Aznar in a sport shirt and blazer.

The Mexican press reacted angrily to Aznar's visit. *La Jornada*'s headline prior to the arrival of the Spanish leader was "Aznar, el Capataz de Bush ante Fox" (Aznar, Bush's Butler, faces Fox), accompanied by a caricature of Aznar as a Franco look-alike. In *El Universal*, a columnist referred to "the inopportune visit of the proconsul." Political leaders, and even the Spanish community in Mexico, denounced the alleged purpose of the trip, and a demonstration outside the Spanish embassy in Mexico City protested the Aznar visit. Most media and observers concluded that the brief joint communiqué Fox and Aznar issued after they met at the Los Pinos presidential residence clearly implied that Mexico was not changing its position on Iraq.

That same morning, on a trip to Yucatán, Fox had reaffirmed his country's posture: "No to war, no to unilateralism, yes to the strengthening of the UN Security Council, yes to multilateralism, and that, among us, we decide the roads to follow." The furor that the visit was creating was such that the U.S. State Department, through its spokesman Richard Boucher, clarified that President Aznar was going to Mexico on behalf of Spain and not the United States. On the eve of the Spanish president's arrival in Mexico, Boucher stated, "Let Aznar decide what he wants to tell President Fox. [Journalists] can ask him what issues he will raise and why." Long after, former Mexican ambassador to the UN Adolfo Aguilar Zinser reflected that Aznar had "wanted to take Fox's head on a platter to Bush's ranch," but it did not happen.[15]

Aznar never visited Chile during this time, but he did phone President Lagos on several occasions. Once Lagos commented that if all legal conditions were met and Chile decided that there was no other way but to vote in favor of authorizing the use of force by means of a Security Council resolution, he would communicate it "directly to Bush and certainly not through Aznar."

High Noon in Iraq: Diplomacy Fails

The barrage of consultations and phone calls was unable to bridge the gap that existed between the U.S. bloc and those led by France. Thus, negotiations began to give way to exhortations.

On March 11, at the request of the nonaligned group of countries, an open debate took place on Iraq. Forty-seven ambassadors took the floor, and the debate dragged on for two days. Most representatives supported a peaceful disarmament of Iraq through enhanced inspections as the solution to the Iraqi crisis.

Since France, Russia, China, and others, publicly and in closed consultations on March 12, had rejected the ten-day ultimatum and the automatic use of force called for in the amended draft resolution presented by the United Kingdom, a gloom hung over the closed Security Council consultations on Thursday, March 13. It was announced that UNMOVIC personnel were being pulled out of Iraq and sent to the Kuwaiti border and that other UN personnel were being relocated, in anticipation of war. A British non-paper that offered to suppress some paragraphs of the amended resolution was rejected by several delegations—Chile included—because it still left intact the eventual use of force.

The differences of opinion among the Security Council members continued unabated, and the frenetic diplomatic activity of the last few days gave way to a growing sense of resignation that war was about to start, despite a world divided about its merits. Not even Bush's announcement in the Rose Garden of the White House on Friday, March 14, about an agreement reached on a "road map" for peace between Israel and the Palestinians improved the pessimistic international mood.

That same Friday afternoon, the president of the Security Council announced that a weekend meeting of the Security Council was cancelled. He saw no point in scheduling further meetings at that moment, as earlier that same day Washington had summarily rejected the Chilean compromise proposal.

Ironically, Saddam Hussein also dismissed the Chilean alternative. On March 16, Hussein stated, "In Chile, they know nothing about the situation in Iraq, or they are at the service of the diabolical purposes of the government of the United States. Two days ago, I heard on the radio that I think it was Chile that proposed to give Iraq a few more weeks to destroy its weapons of mass destruction. It made me wonder why our press did not attack such a bad proposition, because it is truly bad."

International attention now focused on the Portuguese Azores mini-summit of Sunday, March 16, with Bush, Blair, and Aznar attending. The prime minister of Portugal, Durao Barroso, was present as the host and as a coalition supporter.

The same day as the mini-summit, President Chirac fired his last diplomatic volley, suggesting thirty days be given for UN weapons inspections in Iraq. While Chirac had phoned Blair on Saturday to discuss this idea and reassure him that "we are not fighting against you," his last-minute move was not seen as conducive to compromise. If the White House had already rejected the Chilean proposal that gave Hussein three additional weeks, a longer time frame was bound to fail—and this is exactly what happened. Chirac's suggestion was seen as a desperate "delay and divide" tactic. At this point, Washington viewed any new initiative undertaken by Security Council members as an unfriendly action intended to slow down the inevitable use of force.

Some still harbored hopes that the Azores summit would become a last try for peace. The U.K. ambassador to the UN, in fact, had suggested as much. But the absence of countries such as France, Russia, or Germany at the summit proved a bad omen.

In addition, Condi Rice had declared, "It is time to bring the UN Security Council process to a conclusion." B-2 stealth bombers were already heading to the Gulf region and dozens of U.S. warships were moving into the Red Sea. In the meantime, millions of Europeans stopped work for fifteen minutes in a symbolic strike to protest the imminent war, and massive antiwar protests raged worldwide.

At the end of the Azores meeting, Bush announced that the next day, Monday, March 17, would be "a moment of truth for the world. ... The Iraqi regime will disarm itself, or the Iraqi regime will be disarmed by force." Bush then added, "We'll push as quickly as possible for an Iraqi interim authority, if military force is required." The message from the Azores mini-summit was clear: diplomatic compromises would no longer be pursued, and Hussein's time was up.

In the meantime, President Chirac announced on French television from the Elysée Palace in Paris, "Whatever the circumstances, France will vote no. ... We will vote no," he said, "because we consider that there is no reason to wage a war to reach the goal we have set ourselves, that is, the disarmament of Iraq." The British foreign secretary refused to believe that Chirac had actually slammed the door on any compromise until he read it the next morning in *Le Monde*. The Americans, however, were not that surprised.

Later on, the French attempted to explain Chirac's words, saying that "whatever the circumstances" referred to a rejection of a resolution that included "automaticity" for the use of force if Iraq did not comply. The Americans and British thought that without "automaticity," there would be a never-ending string of Security Council resolutions. But by this point, it was too late for explanations or interpretations.

On Monday, March 17, the Security Council met in a closed session at 10:00 A.M. with Secretary General Kofi Annan and UNMOVIC chief Hans Blix. The mood was somber rather than acrimonious. United Kingdom envoy Sir Jeremy Greenstock informed council members that the cosponsors of the amended resolution no longer planned to bring it to a vote, and he advised the UN to suspend inspections and withdraw all personnel from Iraq. United States ambassador Negroponte lamented that voting on the draft resolution would no longer serve any purpose given the threat of a veto.

A few days earlier, White House press secretary Ari Fleischer had challenged Security Council members to a vote. "The moment will come this week," he said, "for members of the UN Security Council to raise their hands and take a stand." But that Monday, Colin Powell arrived at dawn at his office at the State Department and began to phone his colleagues in the Security Council to explain that Washington and its allies had decided to withdraw the resolution. Instead, he asked for cooperation when it came to the reconstruction of Iraq after the war.

At the council, French representative Jean-Marc de la Sablière responded that his country was interested in continuing with the inspection work program, and he reiterated that if the "veto threat" alluded to France, his country could not endorse the use of force. Several UN envoys expressed their disillusionment and frustration at not achieving a compromise solution.

A surreal moment occurred when Hans Blix announced that the disarmament work plan, with benchmarks and timetables, was ready and could be distributed in the afternoon. As this would occur just as the allies were about to invade Iraq, however, Secretary General Annan, who recognized the grim situation, announced that he was withdrawing all UN humanitarian personnel, including the Oil for Food program personnel. This would lead, then, to the disarmament plan's suspension.

The council decided to hold an additional meeting on Wednesday the nineteenth. Some delegates expressed their desire that it be attended by foreign ministers from member states, while several coalition representatives said their foreign ministers would not participate. Russian minister Ivanov managed to convince his colleagues from France and

Germany to be present, however.

During the following hours, Secretary Powell called several colleagues to request that they not attend the upcoming council session and that they not present any new resolution. That same Monday, Bush called Spanish president Aznar to request that he call President Lagos to dissuade him from any last-minute initiative at the Security Council. However, Lagos had no intention of pursuing another alternate course. The American military juggernaut could not be stopped by anybody, not even Washington's staunchest allies. In the transcript of the conversations between Bush and Aznar on February 23, 2003, President Bush had said that the "time [had] arrived to get rid of Saddam," and he had warned, "My patience is exhausted. I do not intend to wait beyond mid-March. ... We will be in Baghdad by the end of March." Bush was being true to his word.

Chile, Mexico, and other nations in the Security Council had attempted to present real alternatives to the U.S.–British proposal that might have made the rush to war unnecessary. Some believe that more time for the UN inspectors would have made no difference, since no WMD would have been found and that would not have convinced the Americans to unravel the war drive. But at least if diplomatic efforts had been exhausted and Hussein still refused to comply with strict benchmarks, Security Council support for the use of force would have been greater, even under the threat of a veto, thus having the effect of lending needed legitimacy to America's use of force.

On Monday evening, March 17, 2003, President Bush spoke on television from the White House to announce that the end had come for the Hussein regime. He said that for the last four and a half months, the United States and its allies had "worked within the Security Council ... yet some permanent members of the Security Council have publicly announced that they will veto any resolution that compels the disarmament of Iraq." The UN Security Council, continued Bush, "has not lived up to its responsibilities, so we will rise to ours." Then, he concluded, as if addressing the Iraqis, "Saddam Hussein and his sons must leave Iraq within 48 hours ... The tyrant will soon be gone. The day of your [Iraqi citizens'] liberation is near."

Blair convinced the British Parliament to cast a vote on going to war on Tuesday, March 18. Blair won, 396 to 217. While he was missing one-third of the Labour Party votes, a number of Tory votes were cast in the war's favor. In the Iraqi conflict, Blair lacked the full support of his own government. Clare Short, the British secretary for international development, said that going to war without the specific authority of the UN Security Council would be "reckless for the world, reckless for the undermining of the UN, reckless with our government, reckless with our future." And Robin Cook resigned his post as Labour leader of the House of Commons in protest of the war. But Blair weathered the rebellion and won a vital vote.

On Wednesday, March 19, the Security Council convened at 10:45 A.M. with the presence of few ministers, including de Villepin, Fischer, and Ivanov. Hans Blix was present on behalf of UNMOVIC, but only a representative for IAEA chief ElBaradei was present. Blix expressed "sadness that three and a half months of work carried out in Iraq have not brought the assurances needed about the absence of WMD or other proscribed items in Iraq, that more time is not available for our inspections, and that armed action now seems imminent."

The foreign ministers spoke more about the future than about the moment at hand. Fischer stated that it was important to counter the myth that the Security Council had failed. The council, he said, "has made available the instruments to disarm Iraq peacefully. The Security Council is not responsible for what is happening outside the United Nations."

For the French foreign minister, the choice was "between two visions of the world." He affirmed that in contrast to "those who choose to use force and think that they can resolve the world's complexity through swift preventive action, we [the French government], in contrast, choose resolute action and a long-term approach. For in today's world, to ensure our security, we must take into account the manifold crises and their many dimensions, including the cultural and religious ones." De Villepin concluded that the council had "fully shouldered its obligations."

United States representative Negroponte referred to the Blix report by declaring that "the situation on the ground will change and so will the nature of the remaining disarmament tasks." He then observed that "considering a work program at this time is quite simply out of touch with the reality that we confront. ... Under the current circumstances we have no choice but to set this work aside for the time being."

Further discussions in the Wednesday session focused on the need to provide any needed humanitarian relief, and the possibility of drafting a resolution that could ensure the continuity of the Oil for Food program. That same day, the secretary general sent a letter to the president of the council requesting authorization to provide emergency humanitarian assistance to Iraq on an interim basis.

Barely a few hours had passed since the Security Council meeting when, at 9:35 P.M. eastern standard time, the first American bombs fell on Baghdad. Washington acted only an hour and a half after the expiration of the forty-eight-hour ultimatum dictated by Bush. At 10:15 P.M., the president spoke from the White House to announce the formal initiation of hostilities against Iraq.

The next day, the ground assault began. It was covered by journalists "embedded" in U.S. military units. American warplanes dropped about 2 million leaflets on southern Iraq calling on Iraqi troops to surrender to "avoid destruction."

The United States released a list of countries that it identified as the "coalition of the willing," although only the United Kingdom and Australia were sending troops to engage in combat. Most of the others were minor countries providing symbolic aid.

In the early morning of March 20, the Pentagon launched its "Shock and Awe" bombardment of Iraq. F-117 pilots dropped three-thousand-pound bombs, followed by several dozen Tomahawk Sea-Launch Cruise Missiles and abundant precision-guided bombs, on strategic targets in Baghdad and other cities in a single twenty-four-hour period. Diplomacy had fallen silent, although it would be resuscitated later on.

Chapter Three

Unilateralism in Retreat:
The Hard Task of Winning the Peace in Iraq

As the war in Iraq proceeded swiftly on the ground in favor of the occupying forces, multilateralism, the UN, and particularly the Security Council became the target of harsh criticism from the U.S.–led coalition. Hours before the invasion, Vice President Cheney had fired the first rounds: "The United Nations has proven incapable of dealing with the threat that Saddam Hussein represents, incapable of enforcing its own resolutions, incapable of meeting the challenge we face in the twenty-first century of rogue states armed with deadly weapons." Ironically, from a different direction, those who had opposed the war were disillusioned with the UN's incapacity to have prevented a war they viewed as illegal and dangerous.

Multilateralism under Fire
Richard Perle—then chairman of the Defense Policy Board, an advisory panel to the Pentagon—wrote an op-ed piece as the Iraq invasion began. It was a blistering attack against the United Nations. In the article, entitled "Thank God for the Death of the UN," Perle noted, "Saddam Hussein's reign of terror is about to end. He will go quickly, but not alone: in a parting irony, he will take the UN down with him." Coalitions

of the willing were, according to Perle, not a threat to a new world order but, "by default, the best hope for that order, and the true alternative to the anarchy of the abject failure of the UN."[1] Media such as *The Weekly Standard*, the *New York Post*, Fox News, and others owned or partly owned by Rupert Murdoch, gave ample coverage to such negative perspectives on the UN and multilateral institutions.

Neoconservative thinkers began speculating about alternatives to the UN. David Gelernter, in *The Weekly Standard*, wrote that "America's problem is not with the idea of a world organization: its problem is with the UN. The UN is no good. ... Now it is time to start thinking post–UN, not merely because the Security Council has made such a mess of Iraq, but because we have remarkable opportunities." His proposal: a new organization of the "big three"—the United States, Great Britain, and Russia—where democracies or aspiring democracies could apply to be junior members.[2]

Yet these pipe dreams of enduring unilateralism and doing without the UN were unrealistic. Predicting what would happen later, former leading congressman Lee H. Hamilton stated, "I don't agree with those who say the United Nations becomes irrelevant. It won't happen because the United States and other countries need the skills the United Nations has, not least the food-delivery, humanitarian, and civil-administration expertise that will likely prove essential in a postwar Iraq."

But in early April 2003, as coalition troops advanced toward Baghdad and seized the international airport on April 3, the UN's role in Iraq seemed marginal at best.

On April 5, when asked about a definition of the UN's role in Iraq, Condi Rice declined to comment, saying, "We are not in a position, with the liberation of Iraq still going on, to know what is going to be needed." Then she cautioned that the U.S.–led coalition "will have the lead role ... having given life and blood to liberate Iraq."

But some U.S. allies looked forward to a larger UN role in Iraq. The UN was being considered as a "Plan B" if things went wrong.

On April 8, Bush and Prime Minister Blair met at Hillsborough Castle in Northern Ireland. Present at that meeting, in a comfortable room with a large fireplace, were U.S. National Security Advisor Condoleezza Rice; Secretary of State Colin Powell; White House spokesman Ari Fleischer; Alastair Campbell, communications advisor to Tony Blair; and Jack Straw, British foreign secretary. The previous day, Kofi Annan had named Raffendin Ahmed as a special advisor for Iraq and had stressed the need for a meaningful UN role in the new Iraqi scenario, an appeal few believed would be well received.

Hence it caused some surprise when the joint communiqué issued by Bush and Blair after the Hillsborough Castle summit stated that the UN "has a vital role to play in the reconstruction of Iraq" and welcomed "the appointment by the United Nations Security Council of a Special Advisor for Iraq to work with the people of Iraq and coalition representatives." But when asked at the press conference on April 8 what the UN "vital role" would be exactly, President Bush referred to a function constrained to humanitarian matters: "A vital role for the UN would be as an agent to help people live freely. That's a vital role, and that means food, that means medicine, that means aid, that means a place where people can give their contributions. That means suggesting people for an Interim Iraqi Authority. That means being, you know, a party to the progress being made in Iraq."

For the UN Secretariat and many members of the Security Council, the worst political scenario was beginning to take shape: a highly rhetorical UN involvement in Iraq. In real terms, this meant a truly minor and subordinate role. An image would emerge of a strong UN responsibility while the reality was the UN would have only a marginal presence. This meant the UN could possibly share in the costs of any potential failure while having little power to influence the course of events.

According to a newspaper report, the perception in Great Britain was that the Bush administration wanted "the UN restricted to acting as little more than an aid agency and [saw] the collapse in its authority as a beneficial side effect of the Iraq war. That view runs contrary to Mr. Blair's. ... He wants the stamp of the UN authority on the postwar settlement. ... The UN will be involved in some way, but nobody is suggesting that they be involved in the administration of the country."[3]

In the meantime, on April 9, the Iraq regime collapsed as U.S. forces gained control of Baghdad approaching from west of the city, moving east, and seizing the presidential palace, government ministries, and Baath party offices. Then they pushed northward, finding minimal resistance. In the following days, U.S. forces and Kurdish fighters would take control of the northern cities of Kirkuk and Mosul. On April 14, American troops took over Tikrit, the last main Iraqi city to fall to coalition forces.

Due to the large number of American forces on the ground, there was no longer a need for the UN to help seek out WMD, weapons that, by late April 2003, American troops also had not found. The assistance of Hans Blix and UNMOVIC was not desired any longer. Marc Grossman, undersecretary of state for political affairs, announced that changes would be introduced in the inspections system. To begin, "the security situation is not ready for civilians to be involved," he declared at that time.

On May 1, 2003, Bush declared victory in the Iraq war. In a speech aboard the USS *Abraham Lincoln*, Bush, wearing a flight jacket after having completed a dramatic landing in an S-3B fighter jet, announced that combat operations in Iraq had ceased. It was a well-crafted production. The president spoke with a large White House–made banner placed behind him that read Mission Accomplished. Many believed that the aircraft carrier was near the theater of operations, but actually it was at sea off the coast of San Diego, California.

In May 2003, L. Paul Bremer III arrived in Baghdad to see to the administration of Iraq. He was to replace retired general Jay Garner, who had directed the Office of Reconstruction and Humanitarian Assistance. Bremer's approach would be to put into practice some of the Pentagon's ideas about Iraq. The Defense Department had drafted the document "Principles for Iraq—Policy Guidelines," which, among other goals, sought to create an Iraqi government made up mostly of Iraqi exiles, excluding any remnants of the Saddam Hussein regime. This project was coordinated by Deputy Secretary of Defense Paul Wolfowitz, who had traveled months earlier to Michigan to recruit high-level professionals among the Iraqi American expatriate community. Some of them were later trained at the Pentagon, under Wolfowitz's watchful eye, to simulate a government in action. After the invasion, exiles were transported into Iraq from various countries.

Bremer designated a governing council composed mainly of Iraqi exiles. In reality, the council had little decision-making power, since the administration would remain in the hands of the occupation authority. One of Bremer's first measures was to disband Saddam Hussein's army, a decision some questioned. By June, Bremer was promising to dismantle the country's state-run economy by privatizing companies and writing new laws to encourage foreign investment.

The hiring of senior Coalition Provisional Authority (CPA) staff was directed from Washington by Donald Rumsfeld and his Pentagon assistants. Instead of Iraqi or foreign administration experts or diplomats, amateur private sector ideologues who wanted to change Iraq were recruited. For example, Michael Fleischer, the brother of then White House spokesman Ari Fleischer, went to teach Iraqis the concept of competitive bidding for government contracts, as the intent was that Iraq would be an example of free-market capitalism.

Elizabeth Cheney, Vice President Cheney's daughter, who had been appointed deputy assistant secretary of state for the Near East in March 2002, spearheaded economic and political reform in Iraq and the region through the project known as the U.S.–Middle East Partnership. Critical of "state control economies," she supported Bremer's ideas of legal reforms and privatization, insisting that the purpose was not "imposing the U.S. model" but assisting the countries of the region to make "the difficult decisions that are required to undertake the necessary reforms." Yet such ambitious objectives would prove hard to implement on the ground.

The United States' main interest in the United Nations at this stage was that it would swiftly lift the economic sanctions that had had a stranglehold on Iraq for almost thirteen years. While some American officials implied that the UN sanctions might simply be bypassed, Colin Powell urged caution and focused on a draft resolution—discussed in advance with Kofi Annan—that was presented to the Security

Council by the United States and the United Kingdom on May 9. The purpose was to gain, among other things, the approval of an Iraqi Interim Authority, lift UN sanctions, phase out the Oil for Food program, request the secretary general to appoint a special coordinator for Iraq, and seek acceptance for coalition presence in Iraq for a minimum period of twelve months. Within the Security Council, some representatives raised the issue of the Geneva Conventions regulations regarding armed conflicts and proposed that the resolution should make reference to the United States' responsibilities as an "occupying power" under such conventions. "Okay!" U.S. ambassador Negroponte responded to what many believed would be another polemical proposal. "At the time, there was a sense of hubris on the part of the Americans," one ambassador present in those conversations told me.

Some of the U.S. media were not tolerant of this ongoing multilateral discussion. An editorial in the *New York Daily News* put it bluntly: "The UN must wake up to the fact that Saddam Hussein is no longer in charge, despite the worst intentions of his friends on the Security Council. ... If the UN wants to prove that it has not—as many believe—become irrelevant, it had better get on board with the plan. ... It is extremely gracious of the allies to offer the UN a place in postwar Iraq. If the diplomats blow the chance, Bush and the coalition should go ahead and do the job without them."[4] Interestingly, on April 5, the *Los Angeles Times* had published the results of a poll on the Iraq war that posed the question "Who should lead the reconstruction effort in Iraq?" Twenty-nine percent responded with the United States, but 50 percent answered with the United Nations. The rest preferred another country (7 percent), a United States–United Kingdom joint effort (7 percent), or Iraq (3 percent).[5]

By mid-May, the United States was pushing for a quick decision on the draft resolution. President Chirac made it clear this time that his government would not veto but that France wanted an increased UN role. Two days later, the foreign ministers of France, Russia, and Germany gathered in Paris and communicated that they would support the Security Council resolution for lifting sanctions on Iraq, despite reservations about the limited UN involvement in Iraq's future. Minister de Villepin summed up their collective feelings that they no longer wanted to pick a fight: "Even if this text does not go as far as we would like, we have decided to vote for this resolution." It was all the multilateralism that seemed possible at that point.

The following day, on May 22, the Security Council adopted resolution 1483 with fourteen votes in favor and none against. Syria was absent, although the deputy representative would later state that he could have voted in favor if more time had been allowed for him to receive instructions from his capital.

Resolution 1483 resolved that "the United Nations should play a vital role in humanitarian relief, the reconstruction of Iraq, and the restoration and establishment of national and local institutions for representative governance." Sanctions were immediately lifted, and the Oil for Food program was given a six-month phase-out period. The resolution stated that Iraqi resources would be transferred to a development fund for Iraq. However, the establishment of the fund's International Advisory and Monitoring Board was considerably delayed, and, even when it was set up, it only submitted one report to the Security Council. Instead, emphasis was placed on the investigations into the Oil for Food program employing Iraqi money.

The resolution also requested the secretary general "to appoint a special representative for Iraq whose independent responsibilities" would involve coordinating the activities of the UN and various international agencies engaged in humanitarian assistance and reconstruction activities in Iraq. Additionally, he was to work in coordination with the authority (the occupying powers) to undertake tasks ranging from promoting economic reconstruction and human rights protection to encouraging efforts to rebuild the capacity of the Iraqi civilian police force and promote legal and judicial reform. The resolution asked the special representative to support the formation of an Iraqi interim administration.

De Villepin offered a moderately optimistic view afterward; he judged that the resolution meant that "the United Nations is back in the game." But a cartoon in *Le Monde* showed its skepticism about the concession wrested from the United States in the Security Council resolution.

Two days later, on May 24, Secretary General Kofi Annan named then UN human rights commissioner in Geneva, Sérgio Vieira de Mello, as the special representative for Iraq. The Americans had requested Vieira de Mello due to his outstanding role as UN administrator in East Timor while the country was in the process of stabilization. Eventually, the former Portuguese colony gained independence. The UN was now trying to recuperate lost ground. The only problem the UN had to face was avoiding the appearance of being a subcontractor of the occupying powers. But if it tried to play a bigger role, it could become an easy scapegoat if things went wrong.

And things in Iraq began to go wrong. First, the occupying forces could not deal with the initial instances of looting, slow restoration of basic services, insecurity, unemployment, and the sense of generalized chaos as fighting dragged on beyond the declared end of combat operations. This led to the replacement of Jay Garner by Ambassador Bremer as administrator of Iraq.

Moreover, by June it became clear that a guerrilla movement was developing. As U.S. soldiers died in increasing attacks against occupation forces, it was evident that Iraqi resistance went beyond Hussein loyalists or possible foreign fighters.

The armed resistance was made up of members of the old regime, estimated by U.S. sources to number between five thousand and nine thousand hard-core loyalists; Sunni Islamists, including Islamist Kurdish Ansar al-Islam; resistant tribes, which were motivated by heavy-handed coalition raids in places such as Fallujah, Mosul, Ba' Quha, and al-Majar al-Kabir; criminal groups that, with the fall of the Baathist regime, had improved their organization and were strengthened by disenfranchised ex-military; foreign volunteer Islamist militants; and Shiite sectors, particularly the group led by Moqtada al-Sadr.

During the first months after the invasion, U.S. and coalition commanders dismissed the Iraqi attacks as isolated acts of violence. But by mid-July, U.S. Central Command commander General John Abizaid had to admit in a Defense Department briefing that U.S. forces were facing what increasingly bore the hallmark of a well-organized, classic "guerrilla-type campaign."

The political process leading to the establishment of an interim Iraqi authority was not easy either, as ethnic, cultural, religious, and political differences among a number of leaders and aspirants—some of them just returned to the country after years of exile—made consensus difficult to achieve. This convinced the United States that any substantive administration had to remain in U.S. hands.

Nevertheless, by July 13, 2003, Iraq's twenty-five-member Governing Council was constituted and met for the first time as the principal body of the interim administration called for in Security Council resolution 1483. The Governing Council would exercise limited powers, with the final word going to the Coalition Provisional Authority.

By mid-July 2003, I was invited, as ambassador of Chile in the UN Security Council, for consultations at the U.S. State Department in Washington. On Thursday, July 17, I took advantage of my visit to meet with Condi Rice at the White House. At the time, there were rumors that, given the growing complexity of the situation on the ground, the United States would return to the UN Security Council in pursuit of a new resolution to stir up support for occupation forces and encourage other countries to contribute troops.

As always, my meeting with Condi was cordial and fluid. I had already been in her West Wing office before; it was bright and spacious, by White House standards, and particularly so on that sunny summer day. I updated her on what I had done since our last talk and then focused on my tasks at the Security Council as chairman of the Al Qaida and Taliban Sanctions Committee and on the council's broader agenda.

On the matter of Iraq, I asked Condi if the United States intended to present a draft resolution to motivate other countries to contribute troops under a new and different mandate. She responded that the issue was "under study" but that if there was a positive decision, a text would not be presented immediately, "but probably within a few months." She inquired about how I envisioned support in the council for such a resolution. I told her that I had noticed resistance by the UN Secretariat to deeper involvement in Iraq, but that seemed to be changing. Regarding members of the council,

I said that it all depended on the specific contents of the eventual draft. I mentioned that under present circumstances and the current council mandates, there was no predisposition for countries to send military forces. A new mandate with a stronger UN role and a positive political signal from the Islamic world, I said, could convince some nations otherwise. Still, I warned, it would be a difficult challenge.

On a related issue, I conveyed to Condi the misgivings of some states about the recently constituted Governing Council and its relationship with the CPA. I noted that the upcoming trip of some of its members to New York had raised a debate about whether the Iraqis should be allowed to attend and speak at the Security Council meeting where Sérgio Vieira de Mello would report. I went on to say that the rules under article 39 allowed the council to hear individuals who could provide relevant information in a personal capacity. My meeting with Condi had been good, though it was interrupted twice by phone calls from President Bush.

The upcoming July 22 council meeting with Vieira de Mello and the members of the Governing Council continued to generate debate. Some countries felt that allowing the leaders of the Governing Council to speak could implicitly constitute some sort of diplomatic recognition. In the end, the July 22 open session of the council, which was attended by a large crowd of observers and press, heard the report by Vieira de Mello as well as commentary from Adnan Pachachi, head of the Governing Council delegation. Pachachi spoke under article 39 of the council. The foreign minister of Spain, Ana Palacio, presided over the meeting, which was also attended by Kofi Annan.

Vieira de Mello made a forceful speech emphasizing that Iraqis had to begin making decisions about their future or, at the minimum, should be duly consulted first. He said that he perceived a desire for a larger UN role in the stabilization and reconstruction process. He defended the Governing Council as a major step toward the institutional normalization of the country, and he reported that the council would soon name ministers and representatives to international organizations and countries of the region. Vieira de Mello also stressed the importance of human rights and international cooperation with Iraq's development.

Pachachi candidly revealed that the security and living conditions of the Iraqi population had not improved as swiftly as expected, although the citizens now had "a degree of freedom." He noted that it had become necessary to "reduce the time of military occupation" and to move forward in the drafting of a new constitution and key pieces of legislation about political parties, electoral law, and so on. Pachachi also referred to the need to reform the judicial branch, the armed forces, and the police.

August 2004 was a key month in the war and in the international mood concerning the future of Iraq. As the members of the Security Council considered—some more reluctantly than others—that the Governing Council in Iraq deserved a chance, the Security Council approved resolution 1500 on August 14. There were fourteen votes in favor and one abstention (Syria).

This resolution welcomed the establishment of a widely representative Governing Council of Iraq "as an important step toward the formation by the people of Iraq of an internationally recognized representative government that will exercise the sovereignty of Iraq." It also established a UN assistance mission for Iraq for an initial period of one year.

The War Deepens: The UN Is a Target

But dark clouds hovered on the horizon. On August 7, the Jordanian embassy in Baghdad was hit by a terrorist bomb that killed eleven people and injured more than fifty. Following the attack, the embassy was stormed by people who smashed portraits of Jordanian king Abdullah II.

A few days later, on Tuesday, August 19, at about 4:30 in the afternoon, the United Nations headquarters in Baghdad was turned to rubble as a truck carrying explosives came crashing through the weak defenses surrounding the Canal Hotel, the organization's headquarters. United Nations envoy Sérgio Vieira de Mello, who was trapped under piles of rubble, lived for a few hours, but as communications with him faded, so did hopes for his survival. He died, along with twenty-one other UN staff members. More than one hundred people were injured.

The event caused a shock wave across the world, and an emergency session of the Security Council was called. Most of the fifteen representatives were out of town on vacation and had to quickly return to New York. Media from all over the world centered their full attention on the bombing. It was a sad and emotionally exhausting time for all of us on the council.

I recalled that only a few weeks earlier, Vieira de Mello he had come to brief the council about the political situation in Iraq. At the time, he passionately defended the Governing Council as a major step forward in the Iraqi political transition. As fellow South Americans, Vieira de Mello and I had had private conversations—in Portuguese, as it brought an air of camaraderie to our talks—about the challenges of Iraq. In one of those discussions, on Thursday, July 24, Vieira de Mello recognized that it would be difficult to work with the Iraqi Governing Council due to the diversity of viewpoints and life experiences (its members included religious leaders, politicians, businessmen, and several exiles who had lived outside Iraq for decades). I pushed him for a transition timetable, and he responded that it was "too early to tackle that issue" since the Iraqi council had to set up its work plan and then adopt decisions regarding an eventual referendum on a constitution, followed by elections. Vieira de Mello argued strongly against any federalist structure for Iraq because it could lead to the division of the country into a Kurdish north, a Sunni center, and a Shiite south.

I asked Vieira de Mello about the security situation on the ground. Ironically, the UN envoy, who was a native of Brazil, explained to me, "You know Rio de Janeiro. Well, the security conditions in Baghdad are not any more dangerous than what you find in Rio." He said it was "largely a police problem, and it will be controlled when the new police force is duly trained." Sadly, he was wrong.

Vieira de Mello had convinced U.S. administrator Bremer to focus on the configuration of the Governing Council, even though it was known that Bremer initially resisted the creation of the Governing Council altogether. Vieira de Mello was on better terms with, and better able to gain the trust of, important power players in Iraq. Bremer was known to be an overpowering and unyielding personality. Actually, Vieira de Mello had charmed Bremer and had become instrumental in assembling the Governing Council. Later on, though, when the Governing Council was functioning, we heard in the Security Council corridors that Bremer had begun to push Vieira de Mello away. Bremer wanted to limit the UN representative's influence.

Vieira de Mello had told me that his plans were to return

to his permanent position in Geneva toward the end of September. I had joked that Kofi Annan would be reluctant to let him go, seeing that he was doing such a good job in Iraq. Vieira de Mello replied that the UN chief had promised him a short mission in Baghdad. Though the Americans had requested that he remain in Baghdad for six months, Vieira de Mello wanted only two months, and he and Kofi Annan had settled for four.

So when the Security Council met on Tuesday, August 19, its members were in a state of shock. The first reports that came in from Iraq were relayed by Assistant Secretary Danilo Türk. A press statement strongly condemning the terrorist attack was drafted and issued. A few hours later, the news of Vieira de Mello's death blackened the mood even further. Some speculated that the bombing could have been retaliation for the Security Council's approval of the resolution welcoming the Governing Council and authorizing the UN mission for Iraq. Others commented that the bombing of a "soft target" showed an inability on the coalition's part to maintain minimal conditions of security.

The following day, the council met again, in closed session, with the secretary general, who had arrived from Scandinavia. Annan avowed, "Yesterday was one of the darkest days in the history of the United Nations." He paid homage to Sérgio Vieira de Mello and confirmed the rescue of sixteen bodies, saying that some people were still missing and many more were gravely injured. Security measures were being reevaluated for all UN personnel in Iraq. Annan reflected that the UN had always been considered part of the solution to conflicts and never the target and that it was necessary to forge onward so that extremism would not succeed.

Many wondered what would become of others that did

not enjoy the UN's legitimacy now that the organization itself had become a war target. Beyond the sorrow, there was a shared perception that the Iraq war had become entrenched and harder to control. Everyone was a target now.

Mary Robinson, former president of Ireland and Vieira de Mello's predecessor as UN high commissioner for human rights in Geneva, warned, "It is not healthy for the UN to be playing a secondary role to an occupation power, as it is perceived." At the same time, the British foreign secretary declared that his government was "open-minded" about giving the UN a broader role in Iraq.

I addressed precisely this issue with U.S. ambassador Negroponte on August 20, after an emotionally charged day of closed and open sessions of the Security Council with Kofi Annan. At a social gathering that evening, the American representative told me that the next day, Colin Powell would visit Annan to present his condolences and take advantage of the moment to inform him of the elements of a possible new resolution on Iraq. Negroponte said that at a scheduled open session of the Security Council the next morning, he would request a closed session in the afternoon to discuss those elements. I recalled that Condi Rice had told me in mid-July at the White House that a new resolution might be presented a few months down the road. Obviously, the bombing of the UN headquarters in Baghdad had hastened those plans.

The proposed resolution stressed calling on more countries to send troops to Iraq or contribute funds. This caused a feeling of disappointment among council members, as it appeared as if the Security Council was being asked to put its stamp of approval on the presence of coalition military forces on the ground. Aware of this perception, Secretary Powell declared, "Perhaps additional language and a new resolution might encourage others [to participate in the military force in Iraq]. Other issues with respect to the role that the UN has to play, all of this can be discussed in the course of our negotiations on a resolution."

The situation on the ground worsened as the days passed, with new bombings and growing armed conflict. On August 29, top Shiite cleric Ayatollah Mohammed Baqr al-Hakim was among ninety-five people killed in a car bomb explosion in the holy city of Najaf. Al-Hakim was the leader of SCIRI, the Supreme Council for the Islamic Revolution in Iraq. In September, Dr. Akila al-Hashimi, a female member of the Iraqi Governing Council, was shot dead by attackers wielding machine guns and a bomb.

A Turn toward Tactical Multilateralism

On September 4, editorials in four different newspapers coincided in their views that it was time for the UN to play a bigger role in Iraq. The *New York Post*, not exactly a critic of the Bush presidency, wrote, "There may be no harm in the Bush administration's decision this week to offer the United Nations a greater role in Iraqi affairs—so long as America continues to run the show. President Bush's detractors ... are trying to paint the decision as a defeat for Bush & Co.—an acknowledgement by them that things are out of control in Iraq ... in seeking a forced admission that America cannot, after all, go it alone."[6] *The New York Times* indicated that "with terrorism on the rise in Iraq and American forces stretched to the limit, the Bush administration has stepped back from its stubborn resistance to greater United Nations involvement. ... The administration's sudden embrace of a broader UN role should not be limited to security issues. ... Fuller UN involvement would not only reduce the costs in American lives and dollars—it would also improve the chances for success."[7]

The Wall Street Journal reflected that "As a matter of strategy, President Bush's decision to seek another UN resolution for rebuilding Iraq may well make sense," but it warned that this should proceed under the assumption "that the price of the UN's blessing isn't too high." Believing that the war in Iraq was "winnable," the editorial concluded by expressing its desire that "this new UN strategy is about strengthening America's commitment to victory in Iraq, not the first step toward walking away."[8] Last, *The Washington Post* pointed out that "President Bush's decision to return to the United Nations for a new mandate and greater assistance in Iraq is an important step toward overcoming the growing difficulties of an occupation authority the administration unwisely sought to dominate ... the draft resolution being circulated by the administration yesterday appeared to offer a reasonable basis for agreement. ... A new UN mandate might make the challenge more manageable, and success more likely—and yet this country must still prepare for a difficult, expensive, and prolonged effort."[9]

Actually, many commentators had been advocating a larger role for the multilateral institution in Iraq after the bombing of the UN headquarters. Senator Robert C. Byrd put it thusly in his no-nonsense style: "The bombing at the UN headquarters has clearly exposed our vacant policy in Iraq. ... While the secretary of state has opened a dialogue with the United Nations, it must be a true exchange and not a U.S. monologue." Moderate Democratic senator Joseph Biden focused on the costs of the war, claiming they were "staggering" and arguing that America should "turn to the UN for help for a UN–sanctioned military operation that is under U.S. command."

Colin Powell had counseled President Bush to return to the UN for a new resolution. The Pentagon civilian leadership resisted such an idea. In a conversation held around that time between Pakistani finance minister Shaukat Aziz, who later became prime minister, and Deputy Defense Secretary Paul Wolfowitz (the two were friends), the Pentagon authority referred in harsh terms to Colin Powell's insistence on the UN road. A Pakistani high official present in the meeting told me that Wolfowitz spoke in "abusive terms about Powell, using the 'F' word." But Bush and Condi Rice finally agreed with Powell's approach. A *Washington Post* article affirmed that "for months Rumsfeld and his civilian aides had successfully resisted wishes of the State Department and the British government for UN help, arguing that U.S. troops and foreign troops assembled outside UN authority could get the job done. But this time was different, because the situation in Iraq made Rumsfeld's view look increasingly doubtful to the White House."[10]

Negotiations on the new resolution continued at an intense pace. Many council members felt that more emphasis had to be placed on the political process. Hence, a paragraph dealing with a "timetable and a program for the drafting of a new constitution" had to be more concrete so that a "horizon of sovereignty could be perceived by the Iraqis." Chile suggested amendments, including that a timetable for a new constitution be presented to the Security Council "within sixty days."

Yet discussion of the resolution at the ambassadorial level was interrupted as the General Assembly sessions approached. It seemed that no one in the council wanted to block the draft resolution, even though the changes that were ultimately accepted for the proposal were very minimal in nature. While we might well have the fifteen votes in support of the proposal, putting those changes into practice would not have any substantial effect on the ground.

New York was becoming hectic as presidents, prime ministers, and foreign ministers and their respective delegations arrived in town to attend the inaugural week of the UN General Assembly. On September 25, 2003, Secretary Powell invited the foreign ministers of the ten elected council members to a meeting at the Waldorf Astoria Towers.

After television cameras and photographers left and the meeting started, Colin Powell focused on the Iraq situation. He began manifesting his surprise over the total collapse of Iraqi institutions after the fall of Hussein. The military units had disappeared, he said, with strong consequences: in 1991, during the Gulf War, Americans had captured eighty thousand Iraqi prisoners; in 2003, only seventy-seven hundred. I wondered if this time the Iraqi tactic had been to lay low, keep their arms, and reemerge later with guerrilla attacks. The political price of the total collapse, continued Powell, was that a "quick turnover of the administration to nonrepresentative Iraqis is not possible." He made an apologetic interpretation of U.S. interventions, saying they "were always liberating and non-colonizing"; it was a message apparently aimed at the Europeans in the room. The serious atmosphere was broken when the Syrian foreign minister interjected: "The U.S. is not a colonizer power, but it could rapidly learn." Everyone laughed at the comment, including Powell.

The secretary of state then referred to the draft resolution, requesting support for it and asking opinions about the option of constituting a provisional government before elections. Powell stressed the importance of drafting and approving a constitution before an electoral process. Most foreign ministers stated that they had a constructive attitude toward the resolution and wanted to leave past differences behind.

Talks continued feverishly during the days of the General Assembly. A meeting between the E-10 foreign ministers and Kofi Annan touched upon the same themes that had been addressed at the Waldorf Astoria gathering with Colin Powell. The secretary general highlighted the need for a good Security Council resolution on Iraq, one with real impact on the ground. He suggested that the sequence of events during the political transition was more important than the mere acceleration of the process. A rumor started among foreign ministers that Colin Powell was working on a new draft resolution that would incorporate some of the concerns of the French, but now Powell was worried about Kofi Annan's reticence to return UN staff to Iraq.

During a luncheon of the Security Council members with the secretary general on Thursday, October 2, Annan dropped a veritable political bomb. In a soft but firm voice, he delivered a stern message: the Secretariat could "not be expected to play a larger role in Iraq under the present security circumstances on the ground." He went on to say that the conduction of the political process should either lie in the hands of the UN or the coalition authority; two parallel administrations would be "confusing and a recipe for disaster." However, the UN should not be given the responsibility for the political process now, although this could perhaps be possible at a later stage, when security conditions had improved. (At this time, the UN staff was operating from Kuwait and Jordan, and the UN Assistance Mission for Iraq, UNAMI, was being administered by Deputy Special Representative Ambassador Ross Mountain of New Zealand.)

That same morning, Negroponte had formally presented the draft resolution to the Security Council. Several representatives expressed their opinion that the draft introduced was insufficient and still would be difficult to implement on the ground.

Annan's luncheon comments served to reduce the attempt by some council members to garner a greater role in Iraq for the UN. The secretary general insisted that the problem with the resolution that was on the table was not merely one of drafting, but was truly substantive in nature: If the UN were to face grave security risks and put its credibility on the line, it would have to exercise a commensurate leading political role. Why play a marginal role and, in so doing, endanger the security of UN staff? In addition, many thought that if things on the ground continued to worsen, the UN could share part of the blame for them.

The secretary general suggested a way out of this dilemma by touching upon a theme he had mentioned in recent days: if the sequence of events were changed and a provisional government was established quickly, it would improve the security environment. The U.S. ambassador disagreed: "There is no evidence that installing an interim government right away would improve the security conditions in the country."

Council members left the luncheon with a sense of unease as we watched our bargaining chips slipping away vis-à-vis the coalition sponsors. Annan apparently would accept the leading role for the UN, but not a larger role. That would be difficult to achieve. But still, Washington wanted a resolution, particularly before a financial donors' conference for Iraq in Madrid, and further consultations would be needed before the vote.

Ambassador Negroponte warned that his government was not going to be able to accommodate further modifications to the resolution: "This is just about as far as we can go," he said. A few days earlier, an article in *The New York Times* quoted anonymous Bush administration officials as saying that the United States might drop its initiative to get a vote on the Iraq resolution in view of the stiff resistance to the text.[11] It seemed like a bluff.

On Monday, October 13, the United States circulated yet another draft of the resolution. The UN role would depend on adequate security conditions. The draft introduced the Chilean suggestion of a concrete date for submitting the proposed transition timetable to the Security Council; this would be no later than December 15, which amounted to the sixty days proposed in the Chilean amendments delivered to the Americans. The draft also touched on the issue of "transparency in the management of financial resources" and established for that purpose an international advisory and management board.

I was pleased. I felt that the critical aspect of this resolution was the concrete timetable of transition to be presented to the council at the earliest possible date, since such an agreement would transfer sovereignty to the Iraqis and bring an end to occupation. Chile also wanted a leading role for the UN in the political process, but given the secretary general's security requirements and the U.S. reticence to yield on the conduction of this transition, the resolution's reference to the "strengthened UN role as circumstances permit" was realistic and allowed for the improvements Chile desired.

The U.S. delegation wanted a vote on the resolution by Wednesday, October 15. But France, Russia, and Germany presented a joint proposal with additional changes. They indicated that during the past weekend, their respective presidents and chancellor had held a phone conversation during which they had decided on a common posture on the resolution.

The Chinese ambassador then announced that his country was joining the other three.

Near midnight on Tuesday the fourteenth, the American representative offered yet another version of the resolution, which partially incorporated the changes sought by France and others, excluding a modification that transferred immediate sovereignty to a transition government.

Negotiations continued all day on Wednesday the fifteenth between the United States on the one hand and France, Russia, and Germany on the other. For the latter group, the final text of any resolution still had to be approved by their heads of government. A consensus was finally reached, and on October 16, all fifteen Security Council members voted in favor of what became known as resolution 1511.

However France, Russia, and Germany then read a communiqué that explained their votes. They declared that the resolution should have gone further in terms of the UN role in leading the political process and on the issue of transference of sovereignty to the Iraqi people. Given the resolution's weaknesses, the communiqué stated, the three countries therefore would not contribute troops to Iraq, nor would they make additional financial contributions.

Pakistan and China also expressed misgivings about the resolution, and the Pakistani ambassador, Munir Akram, announced that his government could not participate in the "multinational force" it created because "it should have had a different mandate from the occupation forces" and "should have been requested by an Iraqi government."

The United States and its cosponsors had gotten the council to authorize "a multinational force under unified command to take all necessary measures to contribute to the maintenance of security and stability in Iraq." However, since no significant number of countries later committed troops to that "multinational force," another opportunity to broaden the coalition had been missed.

As desired, resolution 1511 was ready in time for the October 24 Madrid donors' conference on Iraq. The countries that assembled in Spain pledged $33 billion in donations, loans, and other types of aid.

Meanwhile, the security situation in Iraq continued to deteriorate. On Sunday, October 26, at 6:00 A.M., the Al-Rashid Hotel, considered safe within the protected "Green Zone" of Baghdad, was hit by rocket fire. One of the rockets blasted out rooms below the twelfth floor, where Paul Wolfowitz was staying during a visit to Iraq. Several people died, and scores were injured.

The next day, October 27, coordinated suicide bombing attacks against the International Committee of the Red Cross headquarters in Baghdad and four police stations killed forty-three people and wounded more than two hundred. In early November, two U.S. helicopters were shot down and coalition forces were attacked in various cities, with a loss of more than sixty soldiers and scores wounded.

The resolution had called for a timetable and a program to be presented to the Security Council no later than December 15, 2003, "for the drafting of a new constitution for Iraq and for the holding of democratic elections under that constitution." Surprisingly, the timetable issue came up earlier than expected. On Saturday, November 15, an "Agreement on Political Process" that laid down the timetable was signed by the Iraqi Governing Council and Paul Bremer on behalf of the coalition authority. It declared that a fundamental law would be agreed upon between the CPA and the Governing Council by February 28, 2004. Once this fundamental law was approved, a national committee of select Iraqis would organize "caucuses" in the eighteen governorates in Iraq, and the caucuses would choose a transitional national assembly by May 31, 2004. In turn, this assembly would elect an executive and appoint ministers who would make up the transitional government, to be formed by June 30, 2004.

The transitional authority constituted on June 30, 2004, would assume sovereign powers, and the CPA would dissolve. Later on, in 2005, a constitution would be drawn up and put to a referendum. Finally, elections would be held for an Iraqi government by December 31, 2005, on the basis of the new constitution.

On November 24, Jalal Talabani, interim president of the Governing Council, sent a letter to the president of the Security Council explaining the agreed-upon program and timetable. At the end of the letter, it was suggested that the Security Council "adopt a new resolution, taking into consideration the new circumstances." Many council members felt that, in addition to this letter, a formal presentation of the timetable and program was in order.

A few days earlier, at the monthly luncheon of council members with the secretary general, Kofi Annan had anticipated the contents of the Governing Council letter on the transition timetable. In addition, Annan had disclosed that the UN was resuming its activities in Iraq from Nicosia, Cyprus, while awaiting an improvement of security conditions on the ground. More importantly, at the luncheon he made public the establishment of an advisory group of countries to Iraq, to be known as the Group of Friends of Iraq.

Welcome news came on Sunday, December 14, when Saddam Hussein was captured by U.S. troops in an underground bunker in a rural farmhouse fifteen kilometers from his ancestral hometown of Tikrit. The capture provided a shot of pure adrenalin for the coalition spirit. A jubilant Paul Bremer exclaimed, "We got him!" before a roomful of journalists, and Condi Rice awakened President Bush at dawn to give him confirmation of Hussein's capture.

A few days earlier, the Iraqi council had created a special tribunal to judge war crimes and human rights crimes committed under the Hussein regime. One alternative provided was that the dictator, who had been responsible for torturing and murdering thousands of his people and burying them in unmarked graves, would be given a fair and open trial under the auspices of the UN, with all the guarantees of due process that he had never given his countless victims. Still, upon his capture, the preferred option seemed to point toward a hearing before the Iraqi Special Tribunal, which by May 2004 had appointed an administrator, together with seven investigative judges and five prosecutors. Some of the Iraqi judges had already received training in The Hague, and the same was contemplated for investigative judges and prosecutors.

The timetable for the transition was finally presented by Iraqi foreign minister Hoshyar Zebari to the Security Council at a morning session on Tuesday, December 16. There, the foreign minister, as well as all the ambassadors on the council and the secretary general, applauded that weekend's capture of Saddam Hussein. It was an appropriately symbolic day: the Baathist regime had ended with the arrest of Hussein, and a timetable leading to a sovereign government was being submitted to the UN Security Council.

Most delegations welcomed the transition timetable but underscored that the security situation in Iraq was still very critical and would not improve by the mere detention of

Saddam Hussein. The secretary general expressed the same concern when he said, "In taking the difficult decisions that lie ahead, I need to weigh the degree of risk that the United Nations is being asked to accept against the substance of the role we are being asked to fulfill." The return to multilateralism was not proving simple.

Unfortunately, the timetable and program put before the council by the Iraqi foreign minister soon began to unravel. Shiite leader Grand Ayatollah Ali al-Husseini al-Sistani challenged the caucus-like selection of the National Transitional Assembly, preferring direct elections for the assembly to duly reflect the Shiite national presence. So, in his capacity as temporary president of the Iraqi council, Sayid Abdul Aziz al-Hakim wrote to the secretary general on December 30 to request "an opinion from a specialized United Nations team about the possibility of conducting elections for the Provisional National Assembly." The letter continued, "We request your kind cooperation and prompt initiative to support us and the Iraqi people to achieve quick results to permit us to uphold our undertaking of the timetable presented."

To attempt to solve what amounted to an impasse and to clarify the UN's role in the transition process (as the timetable accord drafted by the Iraqi council and the CPA did not refer at all to the UN presence in the process), a meeting was arranged in New York between the UN Secretariat, the Governing Council, and the CPA (Bremer). Prior to that meeting, however, on January 8, Kofi Annan wrote back to the president of the Iraqi council, "There may not be time to organize free, fair, and credible elections for a provisional government within the framework of the 15 November agreement between the Governing Council and the CPA." He added that he was conscious "of the importance of ensuring that the deadline for the transfer of effective sovereignty" be maintained.

Ayatollah al-Sistani was not satisfied or convinced by Annan's letter that direct elections were impossible, given the June 30 deadline. Imam Jalaladeen al-Sangheir, a close associate of al-Sistani, countered that the ayatollah would only listen to a UN delegation that would be willing to assess the situation directly in Iraq. "What if a delegation from the UN says it's impossible to have elections; what will happen then?" Imam al-Sangheir said. "In that case, Ayatollah al-Sistani will change his opinion."

At the time, I was president of the Security Council, and I had received a letter from the Iraqi mission requesting that Planning Minister Mahdi Hafedh, who would accompany the Governing Council delegation that was coming to New York for the January meeting, be received by the Security Council. After a conversation with the U.S. ambassador, who knew nothing about the minister's request to be heard by the Security Council, we agreed that the full delegation, headed at the time by President Adnan Pachachi, should meet the council in a private session, without the press, public, or even other UN delegations.

When I conveyed to Ambassador Negroponte the opinion of some representatives on the Security Council that perhaps Bremer should also be invited to attend the meeting, Negroponte jumped. "By no means!" he screamed over the phone. "Cool it," I responded, "and don't raise your voice. As president of the council, I am transmitting to you what other colleagues are thinking." The American ambassador changed the tone of voice and explained: "What happens is that if Bremer appears in the council, some will turn the session into an indictment of the U.S. occupation."

The ambassador and I agreed that neither Paul Bremer nor Sir Jeremy Greenstock, the British representative in Iraq, would be present at the session, in this way avoiding a discussion focused on the coalition's occupation. The Security Council accepted these terms. And since I knew the Americans were also worried about divisions within the Governing Council if more than one delegate spoke, I stated that I would invite the whole delegation but would offer the floor only to President Pachachi.

In the meantime, the security environment in Iraq continued to deteriorate. On February 1, 2004, more than one hundred people died, and many more were wounded, in a double suicide attack on the offices of the two main Kurdish parties. Then March 2 proved to be the bloodiest day in Iraq since the official end of the war: 271 Shiite Muslims were cut down as they celebrated the holy day of Ashura, which commemorated the death of Imam Hussein in 680. These attacks in Baghdad and Kerbala were well-coordinated aggressions, employing suicide bombers, mortar fire, preset bombs, and automatic rifle fire.

An extensive report in *Newsweek* in late 2003 described the situation in Iraq as one of chaos, disorganization, waste, and fraud in the reconstruction efforts. Citing Republican senator John McCain, the magazine compared the situation in Iraq to Vietnam.[12]

To make things worse, in December 2003, a U.S. Army War College study criticized the Bush administration for "an unnecessary preventive war of choice against a deterred Iraq that has created a new front in the Middle East for Islamic terrorism and diverted attention and resources away from securing the American homeland against further assault by an undeterrable al-Qaida. The war against Iraq was not integral to the global war on terror, but rather a detour from it."[13]

The meeting of the Iraqi council delegation and the CPA with Kofi Annan, and the Security Council private session over which I presided on Monday, January 19, both yielded the same diagnosis: there would not be enough time between January and May to hold credible direct elections to designate the transitional authority.

The Bush administration requested Lakhdar Brahimi, the UN troubleshooter who had just stepped down as UN envoy to Afghanistan, to lead the electoral mission and try to broker a deal with Ayatollah al-Sistani. But Brahimi was reticent to take on the post.

By January 24, al-Sistani asked his thousands of followers to suspend all street demonstrations demanding direct elections and await the UN's final decision on whether to send an electoral team or not. The ayatollah refused to meet with any American mediator, including Administrator Bremer. Only the UN seemed to be able to offer al-Sistani the opportunity for a solution. An observer described the shift in U.S. policymaking that he saw: "The Bush administration believed that it had within its control the political trajectory of Iraq. Since those early days, the administration has watched Iraq come undone and now it is going back to the UN and saying, 'Please help us.'"[14]

Multilateralism seemed to be the only practical option open to the White House.

Chapter Four

Why Multilateralism Matters:
The United Nations Enables the Transfer
of Sovereignty in Iraq and the 2005 Elections

As bloodshed in Iraq escalated and support for the U.S.–led coalition declined worldwide, the voices in favor of returning to multilateralism increased. Also, those advocating the desire to regain the backing of Russia, China, and Western European allies in the Security Council multiplied and spread.

Jean-Marie Colombani, the editor of *Le Monde* who had written the editorial entitled "We are All Americans" after 9/11, reflected on the change in mood in postwar Iraq when he noted in March 2004 that deep divisions had developed within the Atlantic community. But in view of the "United States' difficulties in the field," Colombani went on, Washington was now "more lenient with those of its allies—France and Germany—that it had drifted from: and the allies are calling to get involved once more now that the banner of the UN, and therefore of international legality, is raised again."[1]

One year after the invasion of Iraq, a *New York Times* editorial made a grim evaluation of the situation on the ground and called to make "the best of a very disturbing situation" by, among other things, "winning the cooperation of countries like France and Russia." According to the analysis, "the Bush administration [had to] be far more serious about turning responsibility in Iraq to the United Nations and NATO."[2]

Along similar lines, an editorial in *The Economist* in June 2004 admitted that "The transatlantic alliance will probably never be again as strong as it was when the Red Army was poised to storm through the Fulda gap and NATO was poised to repel it." Then the editorial concluded:

> Iraq did after all show that France and Germany cannot prevent America from going to war if it wants to. But their opposition has made the post-war job in Iraq very much harder. And that is where to start mending relations. For all their prewar differences, both sides have an interest now in making sure that Iraq enjoys peace and prosperity rather than degenerates into another terror-breeding failed state.[3]

On May 25, 2004, Bush eased tensions with France and paved the way to the agreement on the Iraqi sovereignty resolution by telephoning President Chirac about voting in favor of the resolution and talking about his coming trip to France to attend D-day commemorations on June 6. Unlike on other occasions, the reaction from the Elysée to this news was positive. In its view, Washington was now moving in the right direction in terms of the Security Council resolution.

Significant discrepancies would still linger on between the United States and its Western European allies, but the wounds of the Iraq war were slowly beginning to heal as the White House realized that it needed the multilateral organizations and allies it had rejected at the time of the Iraq invasion. The help of European allies was not only needed in the Iraq conflict, on several other key international security matters, the active engagement of countries that opposed the war in Iraq would be indispensable. North Korea and Iran became, increasingly, two emblematic cases where multilateralism and collaboration by formerly distanced allies would prove to be essential.

A Sense of Loss of Direction and Moral Defeat

The Abu Ghraib scandal exploded in early May 2004. The gruesome pictures of American soldiers torturing and ridiculing prisoners in the very same jail where Saddam Hussein tortured his victims became a symbol of a war gone wrong. A debate ensued on whether Secretary of Defense Rumsfeld should be removed from office, since Bush complained that he had been "blindsided" by his secretary on the prison abuses. But later, the president reiterated his confidence in Rumsfeld.

As more and more photographs of this kind of abuse appeared in the media, the public's outrage mushroomed. Moreover, there was a sense of chaos, or at least a loss of direction, which was heightened by the horrible beheading in Iraq of a hostage from Pennsylvania. French foreign minister Michel Barnier said in a *Le Monde* interview, "What strikes is the spiral of horror, of blood, of inhumanity, that we're seeing on all fronts, from Fallujah to Gaza, and in those terrible pictures of the murder of that poor American hostage. It all gives the impression of a total loss of direction."[4]

Abu Ghraib struck a blow to the argument of the Iraq war being a war for liberation and human rights. Many recalled President Bush's address to the UN General Assembly in September 2003 when, referring to Hussein, he said, "The true monuments of his rule and his character—the torture chambers, the rape rooms, and the prison cells for innocent children—are closed."

Worse yet, the International Committee of the Red Cross had given the U.S. military a preliminary report on Abu Ghraib as early as November 2003. The report had uncovered prisoner abuses not just in that jail, but also in other U.S.–run Iraqi prisons.

With all this unfolding, former national security advisor Anthony Lake determined that the Abu Ghraib scandal "further undermined whatever credibility or legitimacy the U.S. presence in Iraq may once have had. ... In Iraq today, America no longer offers a solution. It has become part of the problem."[5]

Samuel P. Huntington, the conservative thinker and former American government official, made public his own critical view: "Bush took us to a war against the Iraqi people, a war that the United States will never win. The only solution is to begin to immediately reduce our military presence and transfer power to the Iraqis." Huntington added, "Washington does not have the moral upper hand in the Iraqi conflict, and the revelations of torture in Abu Ghraib put in an even more difficult position those governments friendly to the United States, such as Jordan, Egypt, and Saudi Arabia."[6]

An impression of lack of plans for winning the peace and rejecting multilateralism seemed to be growing among key commentators and foreign policy experts. Republican senator Richard Lugar, chairman of the Senate Foreign Relations Committee, declared that the Bush administration had failed to "offer solid plans for Iraq's future" and commented that preventing terrorism worldwide required "repairing and building alliances." It seemed the only possible sensible outcome could derive from sticking to the UN handling of the transition and the naming of the caretaker government.

Even Paul Wolfowitz, a leading advocate of the Iraq

intervention, recognized his administration's errors before the Senate Foreign Relations Committee: "We had a plan that anticipated, I think, that we could proceed with an occupation regime for much longer than it turned out the Iraqis would have patience for. We had a plan that assumed we'd have basically more stable security conditions then we've encountered."

On the other side of the ocean, British foreign secretary Straw also conceded in a BBC interview that the Iraq situation was much worse than predicted: "It's palpable that the difficulties which we faced have been more extensive than it was reasonable to assume nine months ago."

The new mood of bewilderment and disappointment was reflected in a blistering *New York Times* editorial entitled "America Adrift in Iraq": "At times the only unifying theme for Washington's policies seems to be desperation. ... In the diplomatic arena, White House aides are now beseeching the same United Nations they once belittled to rescue the transition, hoping that its special emissary, Lakhdar Brahimi, can somehow produce a plan for an interim government after June 30. ... If President Bush is now prepared to yield real authority to the UN over transition arrangements, for example, it may create a sense of legitimacy that Washington itself is no longer in any position to bestow."[7]

A parallel process began to unfold. On the one hand, Brahimi returned to Iraq on the morning of May 6 to continue the process of consultations to select the members of the transitional government that would be inaugurated on June 30. On the other, informal negotiations began in New York among Security Council members for a draft resolution on multiple aspects of the new key phase in the life of Iraq.

Brahimi stayed in New York for several days in late

April and early May, calibrating the views and wishes of the major players in Washington, DC, the UN Secretariat, and the Security Council. After his return to Baghdad, he renewed an intense agenda aimed at putting together a roster of names that would constitute the Iraqi transitional authority of June 30.

Different names were rumored for the posts of president and prime minister. There was speculation that Lakhdar Brahimi's idea of naming a caretaker government of technocrats was running into trouble as Iraqi leaders, fearing they would be left out, were pressing for a transitional authority with greater political weight. But, in fact, Brahimi never excluded the possibility of including some politicians in the caretaker government and said so to council ambassadors in private conversations. His main concern was that those responsible for integrating the new government be capable and honorable people who would administer the transition and, ideally, hold no further electoral ambition for the following stage. Still, some leaders and power groups were worried about being marginalized by Brahimi.

The state of affairs in Iraq was symbolized by Ahmad Chalabi. Once a favored Pentagon candidate for president of Iraq, he had become one of the harshest critics of U.S. occupation. Chalabi became particularly critical of Brahimi and a strong advocate of including Governing Council politicians in the caretaker government. In addition, since Bremer had accepted Brahimi's recommendation for relaxing the ban on former Baath party members from jobs in the new government, Chalabi had likened this decision to "allowing Nazis into the German government immediately after World War II."

Moreover, U.S. intelligence services believed that Chalabi might have passed on classified information to Iran regarding American security operations and internal political plans in Iraq. *The New York Times* also revealed, on June 2, 2004, that Chalabi had disclosed to an Iranian official that the United States had broken the secret communications code of Iran's intelligence service, thereby "betraying one of Washington's most valuable sources of information about Iran." Citing security concerns, the same newspaper divulged that the Bush administration had asked it not to publish details of the case, but that it had withdrawn this request on June 2, after information about the code-breaking began to appear in news reports.[8]

Despite such serious charges, Chalabi's allies in Washington blamed the CIA for mounting a smear campaign against him. Some of them—including Newt Gingrich and Richard Perle—went to see Condoleezza Rice at the White House to defend Chalabi. Condi Rice expressed appreciation for the views they conveyed but made no concessions to their perspectives on the former Pentagon favorite.

On Sunday, May 23, 2004, the UN Security Council learned that on Monday night, President Bush would deliver a speech to the nation on Iraq's timetable and the transfer-of-sovereignty resolution that we had been discussing informally at the UN. *The Christian Science Monitor* suggested that President Bush was beginning "a series of speeches on Monday to reassure the American people that his administration has a plan of transferring power in Iraq on June 30."[9] An administration official in Washington was quoted in *The New York Times* as saying that the resolution presentation and Mr. Bush's speech would outline a plan of action to dispel "this idea that we don't know what we are doing" on Iraq.[10]

The president had to move quickly, as domestic criticisms had mounted and uncertainty over Iraq's future remained.

Only one week before, in a congressional hearing, Chairman of the Joint Chiefs of Staff General Richard Myers had said ominously, "There is no way to militarily lose in Iraq. There is also no way to militarily win in Iraq."

The UN, once sidelined by Washington, was now brokering the political transition that would chart Iraq's future and impact the internal debate in the United States. As a *Wall Street Journal* report put it: "Now it seems clear that Mr. Bush will have to exit Iraq's political mess with the UN, the organization whose influence he once tried to limit in Iraq—and that later pulled out of the country over safety concerns. ... [Iraq's political future will be] charted by a special UN envoy, Lakhdar Brahimi, who has been sent to stitch together a caretaker government to take over on June 30."[11]

Negotiating the Establishment of the Iraqi Interim Government

At the council's monthly luncheon with the secretary general, on Wednesday, May 19, a good part of the conversation revolved around Iraq. Kofi Annan stated his demands for the resolution. It should start with the restoration of sovereignty; clearly define the powers of the interim government (he suggested that perhaps it could impose "self-denying" limitations on its authority, given its caretaker nature); precisely delineate UN tasks within boundaries and as circumstances permit (i.e., political process, elections, assistance in drafting a definitive constitution); ensure the security of the UN staff; and detail the relationships between the interim government, the UN, and the former coalition authorities.

Most ambassadors who interjected at the luncheon agreed with the words of the secretary general. I asked Ambassador Negroponte, who was sitting next to me, what his opinion was, since he soon would be the U.S. ambassador to Iraq. "Look," he said, "we want to assist the interim government to gain ownership of the political process as soon as possible. This is my official mission statement and determination." He added in plain terms, "To put it frankly, we don't want this new government to fall on its ass." He also lamented that in Iraq, there was no obvious President Karzai (as in Afghanistan) in sight.

The draft resolution was presented on Monday, May 24, at a closed-door meeting of the council. Its contents were disappointing, as the informal discussions in New York had offered more-constructive suggestions than the actual text submitted. Washington was running the decision-making process.

Several representatives, myself included, objected to the fact that one paragraph about the multinational force (MNF) was directly linked to the authorization of the MNF under the occupation. Along the same lines, some delegates, including those from France, Chile, Germany, and Brazil, felt that the mandate for the MNF to be "reviewed 12 months from the date of this resolution or at the request of the transitional government" was too extensive, and that, furthermore, it was the new government that should decide on the duration of the MNF. Others found the text to be lacking elements, such as a reference to the sovereign interim government's control of Iraqi armed forces and police.

That night, President Bush spoke to the nation from the U.S. Army War College. Unlike at other times, this speech was carried live only by the cable television networks.

With his speech, the president did not add much to the timetable that he had supported previously. He laid out the Iraq agenda brokered by the UN, ranging from the transfer of sovereignty to an Iraqi government by June 30 to the preparation, with the assistance of the UN, for free national elections, to be held no later than January 2005. The president also promised to tear down the notorious Abu Ghraib prison and build a new complex.

Again President Bush spoke of America's "full support for Brahimi's efforts" and informed the public that the UN special envoy intended "to put forward the names of interim government officials this week." He referred to the ongoing elections work by UN Chief Carina Perelli and announced that the United States and the United Kingdom had just "presented a new resolution in the Security Council to help move Iraq toward self-government." Bush added that he had instructed Secretary Powell "to work with fellow members of the council to endorse the timetable the Iraqis have adopted, to express international support of Iraq's interim government, to reaffirm the world's security commitment to the Iraqi people, and to encourage other UN members to join in the effort."

The changing U.S. attitude toward multilateral negotiations was noted in a *New York Times* editorial that stressed that the president had opted for "a new United Nations resolution being developed in consultation with American allies, not imposed in defiance of them, and a timetable for moving Iraq toward elected self-government." It added that Bush had spoken "after nearly 14 months of policy failures, none of them acknowledged by the president, which have left Iraq increasingly violent and drained Washington's credibility with the Iraqi people and the international community."[12] In other words, the United States had suffered grave costs from its unilateralist stance and had reversed course toward multilateralism.

A *Financial Times* editorial shared a similar perception: "At last the U.S. and Britain have put on the UN Security Council table their long-awaited draft resolution on the transfer of power in Iraq to a 'sovereign government' on June 30." Then it added, "Mr. Bush's unwillingness to make a clear break with his disastrous mishandling of Iraq is part of the problem. He has shifted position, particularly toward the UN on which he is relying to broker the composition of the interim government. But he does not say so publicly in a way that could change the overall climate."[13] Obviously, it was not easy for the White House to recognize a shift from unilateralism toward multilateralism.

The climate of pessimism over Iraq did not improve noticeably with the presidential address. A somber tone continued to dominate multiple editorials, news analyses, and diplomatic talks. Some of these avenues pointed to reasons behind the shift from unilateralism to multilateral engagement. A *Financial Times* op-ed referring to the Bush speech noted, "After rejecting a role for the UN for more than a year, the Bush administration now wants it to assume responsibility for the transition process." Recalling Dick Cheney's claim that the UN "had failed for more than a decade, unable and unwilling to enforce its own resolutions," the article asked if now "the UN has become America's exit strategy." It closed with a warning: "Setting the UN up for failure is a tactic that has become all too common. ... The UN, having shouldered more than its share of intractable burdens in recent years, needs to be very careful how it approaches this latest challenge." This caution was shared by many at the UN: was the United States' reversal of policy toward multilateralism a genuine effort on America's part to work with the UN, or was it an attempt to spread the blame in case of failure?

After his Monday-night speech, Bush phoned French president Chirac to pave the way for constructive negotiations on the resolution just submitted to the Security Council. The

American president reported that he had "a great conversation with Chirac," adding that Chirac wanted "to make sure that the transfer of sovereignty to the interim government is a real transfer and that's what we want." From their own side, a top-ranking French diplomat clarified it this way: "We want real change" and genuine sovereignty. "We are in a constructive mood, but we are not in the mood to give a blank check."

Other countries sounded even more cautious in their approval of the draft resolution. German chancellor Schroeder stated that the process endorsed in the resolution should ensure that the new Iraqi government "be able to make decisions over security issues, or it won't be truly sovereign."

And London appeared to have a different understanding of the draft resolution than Washington. Tony Blair offered an interesting interpretation of the resolution: that the Iraqi sovereign government would have an effective veto not only over its own military participation in some operations, but also over American or MNF military actions in places such as Fallujah. "If there is a political decision," said Blair, "as to whether you go into a place like Fallujah in a particular way, that has got to be done with the consent of the Iraqi government. That's what the transfer of sovereignty means."

Washington's interpretation was that there would be consultations. "Obviously," asserted Colin Powell, "we would take into account whatever they [the Iraqis] might say at a political or military level. And to make sure that happens, we will be creating coordinating bodies, political coordinating bodies and military-to-military coordinating bodies so there is transparency." Powell also added something that few would dispute: the U.S. forces would remain under American command and would do whatever was necessary to protect themselves.

This was one of many points raised at a May 26 breakfast

meeting at the Chilean mission over which I presided. Present were the ten elected members of the Security Council, and the common feeling was that if the new government were to be truly sovereign, it should have to lend its consent to any major military operation conducted by the MNF. To this end, an operational paragraph in the draft resolution that referred to "a close coordination" between the MNF and the interim government seemed insufficient. Another related issue agreed upon at the meeting was that the long-term presence of the MNF should be limited and that the "twelve months from the date of this resolution" merely referred to a "review" by the Security Council that the transitional government of Iraq could also request. Moreover, some of the ambassadors felt that it should be up to the new government to decide how long MNF personnel should stay in Iraq.

In an interview with Spanish newspaper *El País*, Condoleezza Rice dismissed the idea of any U.S. intentions to stay in Iraq for an indefinite period: "[The] Iraqis alone are not yet capable of guaranteeing security and someone will have to help them. Multinational forces guarantee security in various parts of the world to sovereign governments that are not capable of doing it. ... The United States will remain [in Iraq] only with the consent of the government."[14]

As negotiations on the draft resolution proceeded in New York City and the capitals of the other council member countries, Brahimi struggled in Iraq to build the political architecture of the new government.

On Tuesday, May 25, the members of the Security Council gathered at the secretary general's meeting room on the thirty-eighth floor of the UN for a briefing on Brahimi's work. Kofi Annan warned that the council should not expect results until Brahimi's return to New York.

Indeed, Brahimi was facing a difficult exercise in equilibrium. The Shiite leaders demanded that they hold the majority in the government; the Kurds wanted to safeguard their autonomy as the second largest minority in the country; the Sunnis sought reassurance about their presence; the Turkomen demanded due space as the third largest minority; and the Christians wanted adequate representation. Also, the UN envoy had to do even more of a balancing act when it came to members returning from abroad, the exiles, and the "internals."

Kofi Annan discussed the progress in the electoral work being led by Carina Perelli, particularly the configuration of the Independent Electoral Commission, composed of seven Iraqis—more than one thousand candidates had applied for the seven posts—and one foreign representative, to be chosen by the UN. After some observations and questions from council representatives, the secretary general reaffirmed the date of May 31 for the formation of the government and recommended that the council allow the "government in waiting" sufficient time to participate in the discussions of the resolution so as to contribute their ideas on the various aspects of it. He concluded with an ominous warning: "There is no Plan B; Lakhdar [Brahimi] is the last best hope."

Brahimi's complicated mission became even more troublesome when the name of Hussain Shahristani, a Shiite nuclear scientist close to Ayatollah al-Sistani who had spent more than a decade in the Abu Ghraib prison after refusing to work in Hussein's nuclear weapons program, surfaced in the Western press as the chosen prime minister of the new government. Brahimi had just appeared on al-Iraqia, the U.S.-controlled television station, to reassure viewers that he was in careful consultations with all sectors as to who would compose the government. He had underscored that he had not yet reached any final conclusions nor made any final choices. (His appearance was part of a series of interviews given to demonstrate transparency and highlight the leading and independent role the UN was playing in the process.)

The next day, the UN Secretariat in New York declared, "No names have yet been decided and all of this is speculation which is not helpful to the process. No slate has been put forward." But a high State Department official also noted, "Shahristani is the candidate to beat."

Diverse Iraqi players reacted unenthusiastically to Shahristani's name. Shiite politicians in the Governing Council went as far as suggesting to Brahimi that they could openly oppose the interim government proposal if Shahristani were named prime minister. When the candidate heard of this, he withdrew his name from consideration. Brahimi, a calm man under most circumstances, was irritated at the leaking of Shahristani's name as the leading candidate for the prime minister's post.

In short, Shahristani had failed the "political market test," as Brahimi personally told me.

During his third visit to Iraq, in May 2004, Brahimi met and consulted with more than six hundred people in Baghdad and Erbil. He talked often to Governing Council members and the CPA, but most importantly, he met with the heads of the leading tribes of Iraq; the Caldo Assyrian community; university authorities and professors; professional associations, including those for engineers, economists, lawyers, and physicians; labor unions; groups of editors and journalists from the main Iraqi media; business leaders; religious leaders and clerics; prominent civic and religious leaders from Fallujah; representatives of the Arab

Socialist Movement and various other parties; the Iraqi Women's Network; Kurdish leaders and the Iraqi Kurdistan National Assembly; Turkomen tribal leaders; and representatives of the Arab Nationalist Movement and the local diplomatic corps. Brahimi also attended countless other gatherings and working dinners.

Brahimi threatened to quit his mission during the Battle of Fallujah, when a U.S. Marine division attacked the city following the brutal murder of four American contractors in that Sunni community. Bremer and other Americans authorities had to plead with Kofi Annan to convince his envoy to stay on. Brahimi was glad to hear President Bush's declaration that not all Iraqis fighting the occupation were terrorists, since Brahimi was also talking to people in the "insurgency movement." He even tried to recruit some who were on the margins of the movement for the interim government, but those whom he contacted said they could not be part of the government "at this time." The UN envoy maintained almost daily contact with Annan, and with Colin Powell as well.

In Iraq, Brahimi constituted a working group in which the criteria for candidates were established and representative people were chosen. The CPA, represented by Bremer and Ambassador Robert Blackwill of the NSC; a Governing Council troika of past, current, and future Iraqi presidents Massoud Barzani (a Kurd), Ezzedine Selim (an Arab Shiite), and Sheik Ghazi al-Yawar (an Arab Sunni); and the UN, as represented by Brahimi, made up the working group. The group's negotiations were interrupted when, after meeting one day in the town of Erbil, Selim, then president of the Governing Council, was assassinated in Baghdad. Soon thereafter, Hamid Majid Moussa, chairman of the council's committee on the transfer of sovereignty, was invited to replace Selim.

Surprisingly, on Friday, May 28, the Iraqi Governing Council publicly announced the choice of Iyad Allawi, a secular Shiite Muslim and former Baathist who had lived in exile in Britain for more than twenty-five years, as prime minister of the interim government. The UN's initial reaction to this choice was cautious: "The secretary general respects the decision" was the diplomatically worded statement from New York. Colin Powell, in turn, let it be known that he expected to hear from Ambassador Brahimi on this new name. But soon thereafter, a White House official confirmed the American backing of Allawi.

Allawi, a doctor by training born in the southern town of Hilla, was indeed on Brahimi's short list, but he was, in effect, a compromise choice. Brahimi himself put the issue in simple terms: "At the end of the day, you will have to have a compromise between all these views of people in power and people who are not in power. I hope that Iraqis will find him [Dr. Allawi] acceptable. ... I hope that the Iraqis will pass judgment on the whole government."[15]

Brahimi appreciated the background and political assets that Allawi brought with him. Allawi remained close to the pan-Arabist parties, and he was known to be tough, an advocate of competent security services and a strong government. Once a dedicated Baathist during his student years, Allawi had broken with the Iraqi regime and quit the party in 1975. And, like Brahimi, he had been highly critical of the de-Baathification campaign and of the dissolution of the Iraqi army by the U.S. occupation authorities. Allawi's weaknesses, however, were that he belonged to the Governing Council; his Iraqi National Accord Party had been funded for years by the CIA; and his party did not enjoy particularly smooth relations with the Shiite clergy, although Ayatollah al-Sistani did not oppose his designation.

Allawi's appointment was an apparent victory for the Governing Council, considering the surprisingly short-lived emergence of Hussain Shahristani's name for the post. Could Shahristani's name have been leaked on purpose by the Americans in order to burn him and, instead, favor Allawi? It seemed that way, but that was not the whole story.

Once Brahimi and the rest of the working group agreed on Allawi for the prime minister's post, two meetings were arranged to communicate the decision to the Governing Council. During the first one, at 4:00 P.M., the CPA and the troika would advance Allawi's name to test the waters. At the second one, planned for 5:00 P.M., Brahimi would formally propose the name. But at the 4:00 P.M. meeting, the Governing Council reacted enthusiastically to Allawi's name, applauding in approval. Then Mahmud Othman, a Sunni Kurd and council member who loved talking to the press, ran out of the room and informed the media that Allawi was the chosen prime minister.

When Brahimi arrived at 5:00 P.M., he had such a good discussion about the choice that a vote on Allawi was not even carried out. But nobody in the room, including Brahimi, knew that the media was already reporting the news of Allawi's selection as a result of Othman's personal announcement. So it then appeared as if the Governing Council had forced Allawi's designation, with American lobbying behind the scenes (in effect, ultimately Allawi was the American choice).

For the presidency post, the field quickly narrowed down to two candidates. On one hand, Brahimi and CPA administrator Bremer leaned toward Adnan Pachachi, former foreign minister and member of the Iraqi council, and on the other, many in the same council supported Sheik

Ghazi al-Yawar, also a member of the council. Both were Sunni Muslims.

Meanwhile, Brahimi had moved forward on achieving a balanced composition for the thirty-six-member government, reaching accords on key cabinet posts for several new faces. Negotiations that continued frantically well past midnight on Monday, May 31, were finalized the morning of June 1, 2004.

As for the presidency, Pachachi had practically garnered a consensus when some Kurd leaders started a campaign against him, hoping that such a move would open the field for someone other than a Sunni Arab. After an intense meeting with Brahimi, al-Yawar accepted Pachachi's name as the final choice. But when the press slandered Pachachi, painting him as too moderate and someone who had sold out to the Americans, Pachachi withdrew his name and Brahimi rushed back and asked al-Yawar to accept the presidency. Al-Yawar, a graduate of Saudi and U.S. universities and a tribal sheik of the Shammar—a tribe that included Sunnis and Shiites among its members—would now be the Iraqi interim president.

Brahimi defined the interim sovereign government as "as good a government as possible in Iraq under present circumstances." The thirty-two-member cabinet of ministers chosen by Brahimi and his colleagues included twenty-one individuals with PhDs. In addition, the selection meant that at least two corrupt ministers of the Governing Council were out; three others, about whom suspicions existed, also were excluded. The Governing Council would dissolve immediately, and a new phase in Iraq's history would begin.

On Tuesday, June 1, American television cable networks opened with the last-minute news from Iraq: the interim government that would assume the exercise of sovereignty on June 30 had finally been named, with the post of prime minister going to Iyad Allawi and president to Sheik Ghazi al-Yawar. In the end, only four persons out of the new thirty-six-member administration had served on the U.S.–designated Governing Council, which dissolved itself that very same day. Most of the ministers appointed by the Governing Council were removed.

The announcement of the new administration was conducted entirely in Arabic before four hundred Iraqi and foreign guests in a monumental building once known as the Saddam Clock Tower. Allawi's first public statement in his new post centered on practical problems: the need for international military forces "to help in defeating the enemies of Iraq" and his inclination to discuss security arrangements with the coalition allies.

The Security Council met for urgent consultations on the afternoon of Tuesday, June 1. There the formation of the caretaker government in Iraq received mixed reviews. Most ambassadors coincided in their views that it was not the "ideal" government; there were "lights and shadows." As one representative stated, "Several new faces, six women in the cabinet but, on the other hand, the top two posts are occupied by ex–Governing Council members." It was recalled that Brahimi had sought a compromise when it came to the composition of the new government, however, and so it was decided that further analysis of the government formation would have to await Brahimi's return to New York and Foreign Minister Zebari's upcoming presentation to the council. That same afternoon, the United States and the United Kingdom distributed a new draft of the transfer of sovereignty resolution.

Despite some criticisms from Iraqi sectors, a big shot in the arm for the new Iraqi government's legitimacy came from Grand Ayatollah Ali al-Sistani who, after weeks of silence, issued a statement on Thursday, June 3, 2004, endorsing the government led by Prime Minister Allawi and urging it to lobby the Security Council for genuine sovereignty and the removal of "all traces" of occupation. Al-Sistani added that while the appointed government lacked "the legitimacy of elections," he "hoped that this government will prove its efficiency and integrity and show [the necessary] resolve to carry out the enormous tasks that rest on its shoulders."

The Allawi government was also welcomed by several Arab neighbors. Saudi Arabia, Kuwait, and Jordan formally recognized the interim government, while Egypt, through its foreign minister, hailed Allawi's designation as a "step on the road to sovereignty." The United States' return to the multilateral road was paying off in terms of concrete international endorsements of the newly chosen Iraqi government.

On the same morning as the announcement of the new government in Iraq, President Bush addressed the press corps from the White House Rose Garden. He seemed buoyant as he enthusiastically backed the thirty-six Iraqi appointees of the government announced in Baghdad. According to observers, Bush's jovial mood may have arisen because "With the introduction of both a new Iraqi government and a new UN draft resolution, the Bush administration [sensed] the beginning of the end to its controversial costly intervention in Iraq."[16] It was Bush's first international success after many months of bad news from Iraq. And this success was owed to a multilaterally conceived and led solution.

Bush informed the press that he had spoken earlier in the day to Kofi Annan to "congratulate him on the UN's role in forming this new government." He also told reporters about positive conversations he had had with several world leaders. Asked about the role of the Governing Council when it came to the main designations in the new government, the president responded, "Brahimi made the decisions and brought their names to the Governing Council. As I understand it, the Governing Council simply opined about names. It was Mr. Brahimi's selections, and Ambassador Bremer and Ambassador Blackwill were instructed by me to work with Mr. Brahimi. As we say in American sports parlance, he [Brahimi] was the quarterback."

During the Rose Garden press conference, President Bush stated that American troops would follow the chain of command "to a U.S. military commander." Then he added, "There may be times when the Iraqis say, 'We can handle this ourselves; get out of the way,' ... and then there may be times when they say, 'You know, we've got our hands full; why don't you join us in an operation?' And [America] will collaborate closely with the new defense ministry."

Senior U.S. military commanders reported a major policy shift. They began writing orders to modify the focus of the military's mission from "offensive combat operations to protecting a new Iraqi government and parts of the economy while building up Iraq's own security forces."

The international focus was now on the Security Council resolution. During the Rose Garden conference, Bush expressed his "hope that the new government sends somebody to New York soon."

On Thursday, June 3, the Security Council convened in closed consultations (and also in a previous briefing open to the public) to hear Foreign Minister–designate Hoshyar Zebari, who had just arrived in New York from Baghdad.

The open session generated great public interest: the media showed up in large numbers, and the Security Council chamber was packed in anticipation of the foreign minister–designate's presentation and a report from the secretary general about Brahimi's work. Brahimi, at that moment, was still in Baghdad.

During the council's open session, Minister Zebari seemed animated and satisfied. He concurred with Brahimi and Kofi Annan in that "the selection of the interim government was based on merit and qualification, with an element of political and social balancing." The foreign minister also focused on what the Security Council resolution should contain. He said clearly, "We seek a new and unambiguous resolution that underlines the transfer of full sovereignty to the people of Iraq and their representatives. This resolution must mark a clear departure from previous UN Security Council resolutions that legitimized the occupation of our country."

On the key security issue, the Iraqi minister stated that his country would continue to require "assistance and partnership" of international troops; but he also added that such presence would have "to be regulated under arrangements that compromise neither the sovereignty of the interim government nor the right of the multinational force to defend itself. Iraqi forces must be under Iraqi command but operate in liaison and partnership with the multinational force … the new Iraqi government must have a say in the future presence of these forces, and we urge that this be reflected in the new resolution."

That weekend, the members of the Security Council met with the secretary general during a retreat at Greentree Estate in Long Island, New York. The museumlike country mansion in bucolic surroundings accommodated all fifteen ambassadors and their wives, the secretary general, his top advisors, and a late arrival: Lakhdar Brahimi, who was coming from Baghdad via Paris.

Work conducted in this convivial atmosphere touched on urgent matters such as the recent combat in the Democratic Republic of Congo and a council visit to West Africa. But the focus of the council's attention inevitably centered on Iraq.

Brahimi detailed the tripartite working group's selection process for the new government and how it had culminated in the selections of Allawi as prime minister and al-Yawar as president. He observed, "This is not old wine in a new bottle" and argued that the two chosen individuals were competent and honest. Brahimi also explained that he had involved Iraq's political parties in the consultation process because otherwise, they could become "a nuisance" to the selection process.

As the meeting at Greentree Estate came to a close, the ambassadors of the United States and the United Kingdom distributed copies of two letters Prime Minister Allawi and Secretary Colin Powell had just sent to the Security Council that focused on key security aspects to be considered in the resolution. Earlier, during a break, John Negroponte informed me that he had requested the Security Council presidency to call for closed consultations on the following day, Sunday, June 6, at 5:00 P.M. It was also decided that Brahimi would formally report to the Security Council on Monday, June 7, at 4:00 P.M. The idea was to accelerate the negotiation of the Iraq resolution.

Since Chile, Brazil, and Spain had worked jointly on some amendments to the draft, we agreed to meet with the American ambassador and the British envoy, Sir Emyr Jones Perry, an hour before the closed consultations on Sunday.

But as we left the country mansion that Saturday evening for Manhattan, the ambassadors of Brazil, Spain, and I decided to meet before going to the U.S. mission. We would get together at 3:00 P.M. at the Spanish mission on Forty-Sixth Street, just around the corner from the American embassy.

The tripartite group—Chile, Brazil, and Spain—had emerged out of presidential talks held in Guadalajara, Mexico, at the Europe–Latin America and Caribbean Summit on May 29, 2004. On that occasion, presidents Chirac of France, Zapatero of Spain, Lula da Silva of Brazil, Lagos of Chile, and Fox of Mexico had actually discussed the draft resolution on Iraq and agreed to continue talks as a "like-minded group."

After the agreement in Guadalajara, I called President Lagos and said, "Mr. President, I hope you are not intending to pursue discussion on the Security Council resolution at the presidential level." "Oh, no!" Lagos responded. "What happened was that Chirac suggested we look at the status of the resolution; we talked about it, but obviously, it is up to you guys in New York to gather as a 'like-minded group' and contribute constructively to the elaboration of the resolution."

I followed the president's instruction, and we held a meeting at the Chilean mission on Wednesday, June 2, 2004, at 5:00 P.M., with the ambassadors of France, Brazil, Spain, and Germany. We then agreed that if the Mexicans decided to contribute ideas, we would take those on board, but that we would limit our work to the current Security Council members.

The ambassadors of the five countries were in full agreement on what should be improved in the draft resolution: reinforce the transfer of sovereignty, clarify the security relationship between the caretaker government and the multinational force, reinforce the language on human rights and international humanitarian law, and underscore the UN's role. But since France and Germany had just handed over their own suggestions to the United States and the United Kingdom, we decided that Chile, Spain, and Brazil would proceed separately with their own ideas, although in coordination with France and Germany.

So at 3:00 P.M. on Sunday, June 6, we gathered at the Spanish mission. There was not a soul present in the building or on the streets of the United Nations Turtle Bay neighborhood. There was only the presence of huge trucks and equipment for the movie *The Interpreter*, directed by Sidney Pollack and starring Nicole Kidman and Sean Penn. It was being filmed at the UN. Coincidentally, in January 2004, as president of the UN Security Council, I had authorized the movie to be filmed in the council chamber after receiving a positive recommendation from Secretary General Kofi Annan.

The ambassadors of Spain, Brazil, and I, and our assistants, went through the amendments we would present to the Americans and the British. This time, the Spaniards were on our side of the bargaining table. The strategy would be to fight only the critical paragraphs and drop those that were not essential.

We then walked to the U.S. mission, arriving at 4:00 P.M. sharp at the main entrance on First Avenue, only to find it closed. A Secret Service officer led us to a side door on Forty-Fifth Street. As we wound our way past piles of boxes, furniture, and moving carts, we recalled that in a matter of hours the whole building would be vacated, to be demolished and replaced by a new and larger U.S. mission on the same site. While temporary offices were already set up and functioning nearby, the United States' top officials had yet to move. As we moved through the building, Brazilian ambassador Ronaldo Sardemberg whispered in my ear, "This is the real end of occupation." I laughed and told him I would borrow his witty remark and repeat it to Negroponte. I also remarked that at least the U.S. mission's withdrawal from its First Avenue address was a genuine "end of occupation," but it was yet to be seen if the same would occur in Iraq.

We finally reached the office of the American ambassador. Having received our proposed amendments ahead of time, our hosts had already started including some of them in a new draft. Specifically regarding the addition of a paragraph on international law, they had accepted our request. The sponsors also agreed to insert our proposed wording, "full responsibility and authority," regarding the nature of the assumption of power by the interim government, and our proposed date for that to occur: "by June 30, 2004." In another paragraph, they included the date of the end of the transition period: "by December 31, 2005." They had also accepted our suggestion to reduce the U.S. briefings to the Security Council on behalf of the multinational force from the originally proposed six months to a quarterly basis. So we concentrated on the pending points.

A key paragraph had to make it clearer that the interim government should have control of the Iraqi military and police forces, because the original draft only made reference to "security forces." The sponsors of the draft explained that they understood the term security forces to include the military. We insisted this was not evident to everyone, so they agreed to add the word military. In addition, we changed the vague wording regarding the control of the military and security forces by the Iraqi government. We also wanted a new phrase inserted about the application of international humanitarian law and the respect for human rights. Our colleagues refused this suggestion, their argument being that they had already accepted a similar suggestion to the introductory section of the draft and that both the letters of Prime Minister Allawi and Secretary Powell made clear commitments in this regard. Furthermore, they said that the United States and the United Kingdom would request that both letters be annexed to the resolution as an integral component of it. We insisted on the change nonetheless. In turn, they reiterated their position, the end result being no new paragraph on the matter. I sensed that Washington and London had already made near-final pronouncements on our amendments and on those of others.

Another paragraph spoke of establishing a "partnership" between the MNF and the Iraqi government. We did not like the broad sense of the phrase and had demanded that "in security matters" be added in reference to the partnership. Our colleagues got the point, and we settled on "security partnership." Yet another paragraph welcomed the efforts of member states in support of the Iraqi government, but we felt it was important to specify the involvement of "international organizations" to underline a multilateral approach. This suggestion was also accepted. Several other drafting suggestions that emphasized the role of the "sovereign government of Iraq" were also incorporated.

All in all, we considered the outcome of our meeting to be very positive. The United States and the United Kingdom had accepted about 70 percent of our amendments. In addition, prior to our trilateral effort, the cosponsors of the draft had incorporated Chile's suggestions to add an introductory paragraph reaffirming "the right of the Iraqi people to freely determine their own political future and control over their natural resources" and a reference to a "leading role" for the UN under the principal tasks to be accomplished in Iraq.

So, when the hour was up, we closed out the meeting and were ready to cross over to the UN building for the consultations of the Security Council. Ambassador Negroponte descended with us to the first floor and escorted us out. As we passed boxes and moving equipment, I commented, "So, this is the end of occupation by the U.S." Negroponte laughed heartily and told us they were selling everything, since the building would be torn down. He mentioned that the ambassador's chair, which had been occupied by Adlai Stevenson, among others, had generated the greatest interest.

The consultations meeting began late, as our negotiation had held up the United States and British delegations.

It began with Ambassador Negroponte formally presenting the letters sent by Prime Minister Allawi and Secretary Powell. He emphasized the prime minister–designate's request for assistance from the international community so that the exercise in Iraqi sovereignty would succeed. The U.S. envoy stressed that this occurrence was a genuine transfer of sovereignty and that the coalition countries should be respectful of this new condition and phase in Iraq.

Negroponte then suggested a work program. A new draft of the resolution would be presented the next day, Monday, around noon. In the afternoon, the council would hear Brahimi's official report in an open session. Immediately thereafter, the council would hold closed consultations to discuss the new draft. The objective of the draft's cosponsors was to "put the text in blue," that is, to prepare it to be voted on, by the evening of Tuesday, June 8. Everyone agreed with this schedule. However, several ambassadors insisted on amendments and suggestions to be incorporated into what appeared to be the upcoming final draft.

During the consultations meeting, Russia insisted that an international conference be held on Iraq. The French ambassador manifested that it was necessary to clarify the relationship between the interim government and the MNF—something the three ambassadors had posed to the cosponsors but had left to France and Germany to argue—including the requirement of a prior "agreement" on any sensitive offensive military operation. He then presented a new paragraph that said precisely that.

The new resolution had to convince not just the lawyers, experts, and government officials, but principally the people in the streets of our capitals and, most of all, the people of Iraq. They had to believe that a new stage would begin on June 30, with the inauguration of a sovereign government.

The new version of the resolution was circulated by the United States and Britain on Monday, June 7. It incorporated all the revisions agreed upon with Spain, Brazil, and Chile. The other changes accommodated those suggestions made by France, Germany, Pakistan, and Algeria (newly elected member of the council in 2004). It also incorporated references to the letters by Prime Minister Allawi and U.S. secretary Powell, which were annexed to the resolution. After the distribution of the new draft, Lakhdar Brahimi began presenting his official report in the council's open session.

Although Brahimi gave fewer details than he had in previous private consultations, he underlined an important fact. The Transitional Administrative Law adopted by the Governing Council of Iraq and the occupying forces on March 8, 2004, stated in article 2(b) that the interim government to assume power on June 30 would be "constituted in accordance with a process of extensive deliberations and consultations with cross-sections of the Iraqi people" led by the Governing Council and the CPA. This provided for only a marginal role on the part of the UN, since the language included these words: "possibly in consultation with the United Nations." Circumstances on the ground had changed, and, in the end, the Americans had come to accept that the UN was the only credible body to conduct the selection of the new Iraqi government.

During the council session, Kofi Annan delivered a significant statement outlining the difficult moments the UN had endured during the unilateral Iraq invasion and its aftermath, which later led to the American reversal toward multilateralism. The secretary general affirmed that "since the outbreak of the Iraq crisis, the role of the United Nations has been difficult, often dangerous, hedged about with constraints and controversy." Against this background, continued Annan, "it was inevitable that agreement on the role to be played by the United Nations in the aftermath of the war, especially in the political process, would also be elusive." That role "was never specifically defined," said the secretary general, and it was only through an exchange of letters with the Governing Council and the CPA, wherein assistance was formally requested from the UN, that Annan had asked Special Advisor Lakhdar Brahimi to play the facilitator role in the political transition process. Annan reminded the council audience that Brahimi and his team had left Baghdad with their job done on June 2, 2004, one year to the day after Sérgio Vieira de Mello and his UN team had arrived in that city.

At a rare joint appearance in Paris back on June 5, Chirac and Bush had anticipated that an agreement was imminent on the resolution. President Chirac had declared that negotiations on the text had "moved forward positively" and that "we should be able to put the finishing touches on this text very shortly." According to Secretary of State Powell, the pending issues could be resolved "in a couple of days." He added that "with the receipt of the Allawi letter, this puts us much closer to the finishing line." The predictions were right on target.

On that June 7 day, the Americans introduced new language to accommodate France and Germany on the military operations issue, although not in the exact drafting proposed by France. In addition, the Russian idea of the international conference on Iraq was conditionally accepted. And the secretary general's suggestion to mention the formation of the Independent Electoral Commission of Iraq was incorporated into the text.

That Monday night, Russian president Putin declared, "There is every reason to believe that this work can produce a positive result." The next morning, German foreign minister Fischer announced that his country could vote yes on the sovereignty resolution. French foreign minister Michel Barnier likewise announced his intention for an affirmative vote, saying that "many of our ideas are in this text" and adding that the document was proof "that there was a real dialogue for the first time in this affair [Iraq]. ... The Americans clearly understood, after months and months of military operations, that there was no way out by arms, by military operations in Iraq." The Chinese foreign minister, in turn, signaled his affirmative vote in a Tuesday-morning declaration.

The positive response the draft resolution elicited led the Americans to seek a vote that same Tuesday afternoon. Before that occurred, I received a phone call from Santiago. It was the president. Early in the morning, I had left messages for both the president and the foreign minister to explain the final negotiations and changes in the resolution. President Lagos was glad to hear of the acceptance of the proposals by Chile, Spain, and Brazil, and of the receptiveness toward the amendments offered up by France and Russia. He gave me the green light to vote yes.

The Security Council unanimously approved the text that would become resolution 1546. Kofi Annan and Lakhdar Brahimi were present, and most ambassadors took the floor to express the "historical significance" of the resolution. This marked the "start of a new era" for Iraq and opened the way not only for the genuine exercise of sovereignty by the Iraqis, but also for the construction of democracy. Unlike one year before, the Security Council had achieved consensus on a polemical matter. Attitudes toward multilateralism had changed as the war on the ground had also changed.

After the session concluded, I spoke privately to Ambassador Negroponte, who would soon be heading for Baghdad as the first U.S. ambassador to come before the interim sovereign government. We congratulated each other on the negotiating flexibility shown during the past weeks.

Then he said, "You know, this resolution actually represents the instructions for my diplomatic mission in Iraq. Everything is [in] here that I have to do and promote."

The End of Occupation?

International reaction to the acceptance of the sovereignty resolution was varied. *The Washington Post* reported, "U.S. bends to France, Russia on UN Iraq Resolution," emphasizing "last-minute concessions" to incorporate French and Russian demands to the text. Russian president Putin declared,

"Without any exaggeration, I would state that it [the resolution] is a major step forward." Prime Minister Blair provided a historical perspective: "We all now want to put the divisions of the past behind us and unite behind a vision of a modern and stable Iraq." President Bush hailed the 15 to 0 vote as "a catalyst for change ... a very important moment." Kofi Annan, in turn, declared moments after the adoption of the resolution that it was "equitable and fair," and that "all sides should be able to work with it."

The Economist underlined the change from unilateralism to multilateralism that had taken place in one year regarding Iraq: "If you had said, after the United Nations refused to back America's invasion of Iraq, that not much more than a year later the UN Security Council would unanimously endorse America's handover to a sovereign Iraqi government, you would have seemed optimistic." In an editorial piece, the same journal concluded that President Bush had "acknowledged, in the face of earlier misplaced advice, that the UN has a crucial part to play in helping Iraq along the road to some kind of democracy."[17]

Early on June 28, the international television networks reported some surprising news: in a five-minute ceremony at 10:26 A.M. local time, the coalition authority in Iraq, led by Administrator Paul Bremer, had transferred power to the interim sovereign government, led by Prime Minister Allawi and President al-Yawar. The event took place two days before the planned June 30 handover.

Bremer handed over a blue portfolio containing a signed document—in which he identified himself as the "ex-administrator"—that delivered political authority to the chief judge of Iraq's high court, Mahdi Mahmoud, in the presence of Prime Minister Allawi, President al-Yawar, Deputy Prime

Minister Barhan Salih, and British envoy David Richmond. Bremer also delivered to Allawi a letter from President Bush requesting the establishment of diplomatic ties with the interim government.

Hours later, all the members of the new Iraqi government took oaths of office, placing a hand on the Koran. Bremer then flew in a Black Hawk helicopter to Baghdad International Airport, where he boarded a C-130 military transport plane that would take him back to his home in Vermont. He was leaving behind the full control and authority he had held over Iraq for nearly fifteen months.

The decision to hasten the transfer of power by two days had been made by Prime Minister Allawi. It was intended to deprive the radical sectors of any opportunity to mount attacks to spoil the handover. The U.S. government had had several days' prior knowledge of the possibility of pushing ahead the schedule. But Allawi made the final decision only the night before, on June 27.

On June 28, President Bush was in Istanbul at the NATO summit. It was there that he learned the news. He received a handwritten note from National Security Advisor Rice, which was delivered by Secretary Rumsfeld: "Mr. President, Iraq is sovereign. Letter was passed from Bremer at 10:26 A.M. Iraq time—Condi." As cameras rolled at the summit, the president smiled and scrawled a response on the same piece of paper: "Let freedom reign." Then he looked at his watch to check that the transfer had occurred and whispered the news to Prime Minister Blair sitting beside him. The two men shook hands.

After the transfer, a larger ceremony was held in Iraq to celebrate the change. Polls showed that the Iraqis were openly supporting the new administration.

President Bush stated that June 28 constituted "a day of great hope for Iraqis and a day that terrorist enemies hoped never to see. ... Fifteen months after the liberation of Iraq and two days ahead of schedule, the world has witnessed the arrival of a full sovereign and free Iraq." Prime Minister Blair was more subdued: "This is an important staging-post on the journey of the people of Iraq toward a new future." German chancellor Schroeder offered his country's "trusting collaboration" to the Iraqi government and added that since Berlin was "interested in an early transition to sovereignty, now that this has happened earlier, I can only welcome it." NATO leaders issued a declaration during their Turkey summit on June 28, saying, "We are united in our support for the Iraqi people and offer full cooperation of the new sovereign interim government as it seeks to strengthen internal security and prepare the way to national elections in 2005." The statement added that NATO had decided to "offer assistance to the government of Iraq with the training of its security forces." The multilateral organizations were responding positively to the United States' pragmatic shift to multilateralism and its requests for assistance.

As was to be expected, Iraq's Middle Eastern neighbors were more cautious. Egypt's foreign minister called the transfer "a positive step on the right road, leading to Iraqis taking control of their own affairs and total sovereignty." Syria said the handover was a positive step that hopefully would lead to "full sovereignty and an end to the Iraqis' suffering." Jordan's king Abdullah II proved more supportive when he said that the transfer of power was "a landmark in the history of Iraq" and that his country would assist Iraq in "regain[ing] its position as an independent and democratic nation enjoying freedom and prosperity."

In the final declaration of the Sixth Conference of the Ministers of Foreign Affairs of States Neighboring Iraq, held in Cairo on July 21, 2004, the ministers "welcomed the transfer of authority to the sovereign Interim Government" and considered it a "step toward the formation of an elected and fully democratic representative government." They also welcomed UN Security Council resolution 1546, "which provides for the end of occupation." A few days later, Prime Minister Allawi went on a weekend tour of Iraq's neighboring countries to consolidate support for his country.

Despite observations that the new interim Iraqi government was not a "normal" sovereign government, since it would not fully control some areas—such as the administration of ports and airports, which had been awarded by contracts to foreign firms—some major symbolic changes were immediately noticed. For example, at the celebration ceremony organized by Prime Minister Allawi, Iraq's old red, green, and black flag presided over the event. The Iraqi flag agreed on after an artistic competition organized by Bremer, a flag that had come to identify the Governing Council and the "liberated Iraq," was gone. In addition, a virtual curtain of flags, some even with the inscription God Is Great—which Saddam Hussein had added after the 1991 Persian Gulf War—flew behind the seats of the principal officials of the new government.

A national CNN–*USA Today*–Gallup poll found that three in four Americans favored the handover of power to the Iraqis. According to the survey, 75 percent of Americans overall favored the transfer of authority plan (82 percent of Republicans, 72 percent of Democrats), and only 22 percent opposed it. But when asked whether the transfer reflected the success or failure of U.S. policy in Iraq, 60 percent viewed it as a sign of failure and only 32 percent as a manifestation of success, with strong differences in perceptions along partisan lines.

One day after the handover, Ambassador John Negroponte presented his diplomatic credentials as official U.S. envoy to President al-Yawar and Foreign Minister Zebari. This indicated that a sovereign government was in place. It was a new phase for the American presence in Iraq, with the State Department's authority beginning to prevail over that of the Pentagon. While Bremer had reported daily to Condi Rice at the NSC, Negroponte would report to the secretary of state. Negroponte, an experienced career diplomat, had joked before going to Baghdad as the first post-occupation U.S. ambassador: "When you are ambassador to the UN Security Council, you either go on to become the secretary of foreign relations of your country or they send you to Baghdad!" In previous months, such UN colleagues as Russian ambassador Sergei Lavrov had been named foreign minister, while British ambassador Sir Jeremy Greenstock had been sent to Baghdad as Bremer's counterpart.

Negroponte was replaced as ambassador to the UN by former U.S. senator John C. Danforth, who had served three terms in the Senate before deciding not to run again. Danforth, known as a moderate Republican and a nonideological individual, resigned only a few months after his appointment and was replaced temporarily by John Bolton who, lacking Senate confirmation, had to leave his post in 2007. Rounding the circle, Bolton was replaced by the former U.S. envoy to Iraq, Ambassador Zalmay Khalizad.

The International Monetary Fund recognized the new interim government, a decision that opened the way to financial assistance for Iraq's reconstruction. The country would be eligible for at least $100 million in loans. In addition, various nations restored diplomatic relations with Iraq, including France, on Monday, July 12. The French foreign ministry announced that the two countries would exchange ambassadors as soon as possible. By mid-July 2004, the new Iraqi foreign ministry had sent 250 diplomats to nineteen countries and announced the imminent appointment of forty-three ambassadors abroad as it reopened diplomatic ties with a growing number of nations.

The new situation in Iraq was further reflected in the formal arraignment of Saddam Hussein in an Iraqi courtroom on Thursday, July 1, 2004. The arraignment set in motion the trial against him and eleven of his top associates; the charges were having committed crimes against humanity. The interim Iraqi government had also assumed full legal, although not physical, custody of Hussein. With the end of U.S. occupation, prisoners of war such as Hussein were no longer detained under the norms of the Geneva Conventions, and with the subsequent transfer of legal custody, POWs had to be charged or released.

The televised court appearance of Saddam Hussein would command worldwide attention. In the long and complex trial, the ex-dictator contemptuously denounced the court—a special tribunal established in December 2003 to try crimes against humanity—by calling it "a theater by Bush, the criminal." The scene would be repeated, with less melodrama, in October 2005, and in new appearances by Hussein and his collaborators before the tribunal. (The ex-dictator was sentenced to the death penalty and was executed on December 30, 2006.)

In his first days in office, Prime Minister Allawi focused his efforts on improving the security situation. One of the initial undertakings of the new government was to begin transforming the Iraqi Civil Defense Corps—a paramilitary force—into a national guard. Allawi's strategy was to have the approximately one hundred thousand armed individuals from the disbanded militias enter Iraqi security forces. All those who joined the new national force would be treated as army veterans with corresponding benefits, and any independent militias not joining would be declared "illegal armed forces."

On July 6, 2004, a government decree gave Prime Minister Allawi authority to exercise martial law powers to quell the insurgency, a decision seen by some as a sign that democracy could be stifled before it even started.

After an initial decline in rebel attacks, the acts of violence against the U.S.–led multinational force and the Iraqi security forces mounted considerably. Military conflicts and the assassination of abducted foreign nationals rose significantly from August to December 2004. Fighting in Najaf involving the MNF and the al-Sadr militia was particularly serious, while combat in Fallujah and bombings in Baghdad highlighted the enduring security challenge the new government faced, as well as the tense moment approaching with the UN–organized January 2005 elections.

The 2005 Elections and the Nouri al-Maliki Government

The United Nations continued to work with the Allawi government to prepare for the January elections, even though Allawi had suggested that perhaps the elections could be postponed—an idea he came to quickly withdraw. The UN's election chief, Carina Perelli, went ahead with the necessary technical preparations after the establishment of the electoral commission and basic rules. The difficulties she encountered were eased by the decision to use a system of proportional representation for a single national district when it came to electing the national assembly. The assembly would then hold the responsibility for choosing a transitional government. Recognizing that it was impossible to adopt a completely new voter registration system, the UN opted to use the ration card system, a decision that was subsequently adopted by the electoral commission.

But a debate began on whether or not elections would be possible in 2005, given the worsening security situation. Defense Secretary Rumsfeld declared on September 26, 2004, that elections might not be held at all in 20 to 25 percent of Iraq due to security impediments. In contrast, at about the same time Colin Powell told *Fox News Sunday* that "for elections to have complete credibility and stand the test of international scrutiny, what we have to do is to give all the people of Iraq an opportunity to participate. Just as we would have difficulty with partial elections here in the United States … I think [in Iraq] it has to be throughout the country."

The UN electoral effort, in cooperation with the Iraqi Independent Electoral Commission, continued throughout the second half of 2004. At a commencement address at the U.S. Air Force Academy in Colorado Springs in June 2004, President Bush thanked the UN for its role in assisting Iraq in preparing for its national elections. It was not an easy task, as members of the Independent Electoral Commission were targeted for assassination, and terrorists threatened to attack polling stations and exact retribution against any Iraqi who dared to cast a vote.

As the date of the election approached, new discussions among Iraqis about the postponement of the voting did not help to create the climate of confidence that the UN and Iraqi organizers of the electoral process desired. The UN had deployed electoral experts inside Iraq, despite the security risks, plus a support group stationed in Amman, Jordan, and another small contingent in the New York headquarters.

Yet, in the end, Iraqis went to the polls in massive numbers—well beyond what was expected. About 8.5 million votes were cast, with a significant percentage of women voters. Most of the world leaders commended the Iraqi people on their courage, and Secretary General Kofi Annan stated that the successful voter turnout demanded an effort at national reconciliation.

The election established the 275-member national assembly that would draft the new, permanent constitution. As anticipated, the Shiite parties, known as the United Iraqi Alliance, won 48.2 percent of the votes with 140 seats, followed by the Kurds with 25 percent and 75 seats, and the Iraqi list of Prime Minister Allawi with 13 percent and 40 seats. The Sunni candidates were barely represented in the new parliament, since many Sunni parties boycotted the election. (The constitutional process had a built-in de facto veto: The constitution could be blocked if 75 percent or more of the voters in at least three provinces opposed it. So, conceivably, if they joined together, the Kurds, Shiites, and Sunni Arabs could obstruct the new law of the land.)

Iyad Allawi later suggested that Iranians had pumped in millions of dollars to support the candidates' United Iraqi Alliance coalition of Shiite religious parties, while a covert operation by the CIA to channel money to moderate Iraqi candidates had been reversed after initial implementation. Iraqi democracy had been born "tainted," it was suggested.[18]

In April 2005, the national assembly elected Kurdish leader Jalal Talabani as the president of Iraq; he was the first non-Arab president in a country predominantly Arab. In turn, he chose, after intense negotiations, Shiite Muslim politician Ibrahim al-Jaafari as prime minister, to replace Iyad Allawi.

President Bush publicly thanked the United Nations for its contribution to the Iraqi elections, and U.S. officials also expressed their hope that the UN would oversee the next stage. Secretary General Annan, during a speech on February 10, 2005, at the Banqueting House in Whitehall, London, declared that the UN was "very proud of the assistance it was able to give [to the Iraqis], both in developing the political base for elections, and in the technical preparations," and he assured that the UN would also help in "the very delicate [act] of building a constitution," in organizing "the referendum on the draft constitution, and the subsequent parliamentary elections."

Assisted by the UN, the national assembly elaborated the new constitution, approved by a narrow margin in October 2005. Although 79 percent of the population voted in favor of it, three provinces—predominantly Sunni—turned it down, two of them by more than two-thirds, coming close to the rules for blocking the constitution if three provinces voted against it by a two-thirds majority or more. The October referendum paved the way for parliamentary elections held in December and for eventual negotiated modifications to the constitution. In April 2006, newly reelected President Talabani asked Shiite compromise candidate Nouri al-Maliki to become prime minister and form a government, thus ending four months of political deadlock.

As the Iraqi transition continued to face severe problems, the Pentagon and its neoconservative advisors lost control. Rumsfeld's resignation as defense secretary—announced one day after the November 7, 2006, congressional elections, amply won by Democrats—placed control of Iraq policy in the hands of the State Department, now led by Condoleezza Rice, who was appointed secretary of state in January 2005.

Paul Weyrich, founder of The Heritage Foundation, summed up some of the costs of what he called "the neocons adventure" in Iraq: "America is stuck in a guerrilla war with no end in sight; our military is stretched too thin to respond to other threats; and our real enemies, non-state organizations such as Al Qaida, are benefiting from the Arab and Islamic backlash against our occupation of an Islamic country."

The emphasis on the spread of democracy gained a "second wind" in Secretary Rice's agenda due to the impressive turnout in the January 2005 Iraq elections. However, a meeting of Muslim nations attended by Secretary Rice in Bahrein in mid-November 2005 demonstrated that the expansion of democracy in the Middle East continued to be a difficult challenge, as Egypt refused to endorse a final declaration on democracy. At about the same time, as part of the so-called Broader Middle East and North Africa Initiative, the Bush administration established a government-financed, semi-independent foundation and a Fund for the Future for democracy promotion tasks.

The United States summoned the United Nations on Iraq once again during late 2006 as it prepared a long-sought international compact with Iraq, an agreement to channel aid from donors throughout the world under the condition that the Baghdad government would implement an array of political and economic reforms. The compact materialized in 2007, coordinated by the United Nations and the World Bank, although its concrete results had been meager given the problems on the ground.

In 2007, the al-Maliki government faced political paralysis and was very far from becoming the model of democracy in the Middle East originally envisioned. Under strong international pressure to address the concerns of the disaffected Sunni minority, the al-Maliki Shiite-led administration announced in late August 2007 that former Baathists would be allowed to return to government jobs. But Sunnis, who had earlier quit the government, saw this reconciliation deal as too little, too late since they had sought, unsuccessfully, equitable distribution of oil revenues and tough measures to curb Shiite militias. Iraq remained torn by sectarian tension among Kurds, Sunni Arabs, and Shiites (and among rival Shiite groups) as the economy stagnated.

The Bush administration had changed its policy regarding its ties with Iraqi political parties, groups, and individual players. After the invasion, Bremer, the Coalition Provisional Authority chief, ordered the firing of the top four tiers of the ruling Baath party—around thirty thousand members—and disbanded Hussein's security forces. The massive purge of Baathists in government posts, in line with the regime-change doctrine, meant that thousands of civil servants were dismissed from key jobs. An editorial by *The Wall Street Journal* concluded that "The biggest U.S. mistake, virtually everybody now seems to agree, was not trusting [Iraqis] with the keys to their own country very much sooner."[19]

In 2007, Bremer disclosed an exchange of letters with Bush to refute an assertion by the president that American policy should have been to keep the Iraqi army intact. According to Bremer, "The decision to recall Saddam Hussein's army was thoroughly considered by top officials in the American government," and, he insisted, "it was the right decision."[20] Bremer also criticized the Bush administration for not having sent enough troops to secure Iraq. He confided that he had often raised the issue of more troops with Bush's administration, to no avail. Bremer's version was anonymously confirmed by Washington senior officials.[21]

To confront the security crisis in Iraq, in mid-2007, President Bush had decided on a "surge" in U.S. troops and operations in the hope of achieving military momentum. In the closing days of the summer of 2007, General David Petraeus, commander of the multinational forces, and Ryan Crocker, American ambassador to Iraq, testified in Congress on the war and political developments in the country, asserting that, despite setbacks, improvements could be perceived in the security environment since the surge in offensive operations started in June 2007. In September 2007, President Bush made a brief surprise visit to Baghdad and, anticipating domestic political pressure, suggested that a troop reduction was possible if what was described as recent military successes and stability would endure, thus allowing American forces to pull back. Some Sunni tribal leaders' followers in the provinces had begun to fight alongside the American-led forces to oppose Al Qaida insurgent activity. In November 2007, the Iraqi government credited Iran with helping to rein in Shiite militia violence and stem the flow of arms into the country, thus contributing to improve stability.

Critics of the war argued that now American troops could not be pulled out of Iraq because they were vital for a security situation that had supposedly improved, while before they could not be withdrawn because the conditions were bad. On Monday, November 26, 2007, President Bush signed, via video link, a Declaration of Principles with Iraqi prime minister al-Maliki, to guide negotiations on broad relations between the two countries, including the legal status of American military forces that would eventually remain in Iraq for the long run.

Meanwhile, the Iraqi Parliament had passed a resolution demanding a timetable for the withdrawal of foreign troops. Prime Minister al-Maliki, irritated by American pressure to make progress on reforms, warned that the Iraqis could "find friends elsewhere." To complicate matters, controversy grew in Iraq and in the United States over the role of private contractors such as Blackwater USA, which billed the State Department $1,222 a day for each security guard (six to nine times what it would cost to have an army sergeant do the same work) and liberally shot and killed innocent Iraqis, including a bodyguard of Iraq's vice president. (Federal contracts performed with private contractors in Iraq from 2003 through the first half of fiscal year 2007 surpassed $44 billion.)

Former secretary of state Madeleine Albright reflected in an op-ed piece in the summer of 2007 that only an international effort actively involving the United Nations could bring peace to Iraq, just as the organization had done—together with the United States and the European Union—in the Balkans. Patrolling borders, aiding reconstruction, further training the Iraqi army and the police, stimulating a power-sharing arrangement that recognizes majority rule but protects majority rights, argued Albright, could be attainable so long as the UN, as the main expression of the international community, was involved.[22] Coincidentally, the Bush administration's U.S. ambassador to the United Nations wrote a similar op-ed piece in mid-2007, arguing for "a larger United Nations role" in Iraq, which no other actor could perform to stabilize the country.[23]

Once again, the UN was being visualized as indispensable in assisting with a historic political process that could open at least a window of hope and opportunity in Iraq.

Chapter Five

Worlds Apart:
The Alienation of Allies

President Bush's unilateral decision to invade Iraq in March 2003 caused a deep transatlantic rift between the United States and European allies such as France and Germany. It also froze ties with its hemispheric partners Mexico and Chile. The differences over Iraq endured well past the time both the United States and its allies had turned the page on the invasion.

The Iraq war dealt a hard blow to the already questionable "American exceptionalism" belief: that the United States is qualitatively different from all other nations, should be treated differently, and, consequently, if Washington sidesteps multilateral agreements or international law, it is because the United States can be trusted to act wisely due to the high moral goals it has always instigated.[1] The Iraq invasion and its aftermath—including the false evidence on WMD and the United States' double standard of judging others on their human rights records but not abiding by human rights norms in Guantánamo or Abu Ghraib—demonstrated, in the eyes of many Europeans and Latin Americans, that such exceptionalism was essentially rhetoric used by policymakers to justify unilateralist behavior. America as the "City upon a Hill"—to use Puritan leader John Winthrop's metaphor—that holds a special place as a model for the rest of the world thus paid a heavy toll on Iraqi soil.

On the other hand, the lack of widespread international support for the Iraq war reinforced, at least during an initial period of time, the "go-it-alone and dismiss unwilling allies" streak present in U.S. foreign policy and in the traditional exceptionalist ideology. Security Council members that did not support the use of force were stigmatized as unfriendly by Washington. Allies or partners were redefined as only those few that had unconditionally agreed with America's unique vision and policies. The conclusion seemed to be that a U.S.–led "coalition of the willing" could replace established multilateral institutions such as the UN or NATO. Multilateralism seemed temporarily dead, and important countries previously considered close allies were shunned or antagonized outright.

The questions that immediately emerged were, Why would the United States alienate allies it might need for other important foreign-policy challenges? Why such a black-and-white approach to multilateralism and international cooperation?

France and Germany could prove to be key players, along with Great Britain, in attempting to negotiate a deal with Iran over its nuclear program. Russia and China could prove significant partners, along with others, in containing the development of WMD in North Korea. Did it make sense, then, to put them in a category of countries to be ignored because of their stance toward the Iraq war?

When talk by neoconservatives of punishing those in the Security Council that had opposed the American stance became louder, the question raised in Latin America was, Who are the natural U.S. partners for the promotion of free trade, democracy, and stability in the region? If an "axis of virtue" (as opposed to the so-called axis of evil) existed in Latin America of countries committed to democracy, free trade, multilateralism, dialogue, and constructive leadership, then clearly Chile under President Ricardo Lagos and Mexico under President Vicente Fox qualified. Why antagonize these strategic partners when they could be needed as trusted allies beyond the situation in Iraq?

Unfortunately, the Iraq war put France, Germany, Russia, Mexico, Chile, and others into a category of "distant friends," at least for an important period of time. Days before the Iraq invasion, Bush told President Aznar of Spain—according to secret Spanish records leaked in the fall of 2007—that friends should realize the costly consequences of opposing the American drive to war. "[President Ricardo] Lagos should know that the Free Trade Agreement with Chile is pending confirmation in the Senate and that a negative attitude on this issue might endanger that ratification," said Bush. Then he added, "Angola is receiving funds from the Millennium Account and these also could be compromised if they do not show a positive stand. And [President Vladimir] Putin should know that with his attitude he is endangering Russia's relations with the United States."

As a result of the war, transatlantic relations experienced the greatest damage in half a century. Yes, the Western alliance had been split before: over the Suez crisis in 1956 when President Dwight Eisenhower intervened with UN backing to force Great Britain and France to relinquish control of the canal; over France's resistance to integrate the military component of NATO; and over the U.S. war in Vietnam. But those crises had been overcome because, in the end, the East-West conflict always realigned the Western bloc. Without the Cold War stimulus, the rift over the American-led war became much more serious than all previous crises.

In addition, since some European countries, including the United Kingdom, Spain, and Italy, sided with Washington, the European Union integration process suffered an internal crisis of major proportions. So did NATO, the principal security instrument that provided cohesion among Western nations under U.S. leadership.

• • •

In the Western Hemisphere, the inauguration of President Bush in 2001 had promised the beginning of a bright new period of U.S. interest in Latin America based on promotion of democracy and free trade. Bush even broke with a long-standing tradition and visited Mexico, instead of northern neighbor Canada, on his first international trip, in February 2001. But the Iraq war differences between the United States and the Latin American members of the UN Security Council, Mexico and Chile—countries considered from the outset as "sure votes"—pushed Washington's positive attention away from the region. Actually, Bush, who at the beginning of his administration had promised to "look south not as an afterthought, but as a fundamental [U.S.] commitment," had shifted his attention to Central Asia and the Middle East after the 9/11 attacks.

Most Latin American countries, or at least the larger ones, joined the opposition over the use of force in Iraq. Traditionally, Latin Americans have favored international law, the pursuit of consensual solutions to international controversies, and the exhaustion of multilateral diplomacy in response to crises. For two hundred years, countries of the region had known "Pax Americana," preemptive military action, and regime change.

Fulfilling the doctrine of Manifest Destiny, and beginning with the 1823 Monroe Doctrine, which declared that the Latin American and Caribbean region was within the United States' sphere of influence, Washington had invaded or intervened in, among others, Nicaragua, Cuba, Puerto Rico, the Dominican Republic, Honduras, Panama, Colombia, Haiti, Guatemala, and Grenada. The Platt Amendment, inserted in the Cuban Constitution, had granted the United States the right to intervene in the Caribbean nation's internal affairs, while the Roosevelt Corollary to the Monroe Doctrine, proclaimed by President Theodore Roosevelt, declared the U.S. right as a civilized nation to exercise an "international police power" in the Western Hemisphere to stop "chronic wrongdoing."

The 2003 Latin American Security Council members knew well what foreign intervention meant. Mexico had been occupied by foreign powers, including the United States, on several occasions and as late as World War I, and had lost one-third of its territory to the United States, a fact deeply ingrained in the mind-set of the Mexican people and the country's political elite. Chile, a long-standing democracy, had been the target of a CIA–supported coup d'état attempt and a furious destabilization campaign by the Richard Nixon administration due to the 1970 democratic election of Socialist candidate Salvador Allende as the nation's president. A better reading in Washington of the painful history of U.S.–Latin American relations would have shown that endorsement of the Iraq invasion by countries of the region would not be the sort of "slum dunk" that some Bush administration officials assumed.

In the end, of the five countries in Latin America singled out as "special partners" by the Bush administration, only Colombia supported the U.S. stand on Iraq. The budget the

White House initially proposed for the Iraq war contained an additional $100 million for Colombia's internal war effort. But up to the last minute before the invasion, Colombia, too, favored a peaceful outcome to the Iraqi crisis.

Canada suffered similar consequences as Chile and Mexico. Canada, if you recall, had also presented a proposal to disarm Iraq peacefully that was similarly dismissed by Washington. After the invasion, President Bush cancelled a long-planned trip to Canada scheduled for May 6, offering the explanation that he was too busy with the war effort—this despite the fact that combat was declared over on May 1.

During the early months of the Bush administration, policymakers called attention to the fact that the United States exported more to Latin America than to the European Union and that, in recent years, American exports to Latin America had grown twice as fast as exports elsewhere. Prior to the war, a State Department high official, in a statement to the Western Hemisphere Subcommittee of the Foreign Relations Committee of the House of Representatives, identified Mexico and Chile as U.S. partners in the promotion of democracy and stability in the region.[2]

Yet it would take painstaking efforts and time to fully recompose the damaged ties with Latin America and Europe over Iraq.

Chile: The Distant Neighbor

On Monday, March 17, 2003, at 11:30 A.M., as the United States prepared to invade Iraq, the Chilean foreign ministry in Santiago received a non-paper that formally communicated that the United States, the United Kingdom, and Spain would not seek a vote on the so-called second resolution. It stated, "This phase of Security Council action has come to an end." The memo indicated that the time for further inspections was over, and that it was "time to put the debate behind us." The informal paper expressed the "hope that you will instruct your delegation to the United Nations to work with us, not against us, in order to meet the challenges ahead." It ended with the desire "to avoid further damage to Security Council credibility."

A few days before, on March 11, and prior to the withdrawal of the second draft resolution, White House spokesman Ari Fleischer had declared that if Chile and Mexico voted against it, President Bush "would, of course, feel disappointed." It is a question of "principles and a matter of diplomacy," Fleischer had concluded.

When Bush placed his last telephone call to President Lagos before the invasion, the Chilean president insisted that negotiations with concrete benchmark requirements for Saddam Hussein should be pursued to avert war. Chile was not available to support a resolution authorizing the use of force at that moment, Lagos said, adding that there was still time to disarm Iraq peacefully. Bush disagreed.

Many journalists and pundits predicted that Chile's position would entail heavy costs for the country. "Payback time" could come in the form of endangering the free trade agreement that Chile was then negotiating with Washington. This hypothesis was given more credit when the first American official to criticize the Chilean posture on Iraq after the invasion was Robert Zoellick, the U.S. trade representative. On Thursday, April 10, 2003, he voiced the administration's disappointment with Chile: "We worked very closely with our Chilean partners. We hoped for their support in a time when we felt it was very important." Zoellick added that no concrete date had been determined yet for signing a trade agreement between the two countries. A few days later, on April 25, Secretary of State Powell repeated that his government had felt "disappointed" by the lack of diplomatic support given to the United States on the Iraq question by Chile, Mexico, and Canada.

However, under the Bush administration, Chile and the United States had actually developed a smooth and constructive relationship that went well beyond trade matters.

In early January 2001, before George W. Bush was inaugurated, the first contact between government officials of the two countries took place between Condoleezza Rice, as national security advisor–designate, and myself, as deputy foreign minister of Chile. It was the first meeting that Rice held with a foreign official in her upcoming position.

We had been in touch a few times during the 1999 American presidential campaign, when Condi was Bush's foreign policy advisor. She even suggested that I drop by to see her during the campaign if I happened to travel to the United States, but I was unable to make such a trip at the time. So I told her that we would have to get together if her candidate won and she became national security advisor or secretary of state. She laughed and promised a meeting if that proved to be the case. When Bush was finally proclaimed president and Condi designated national security advisor, I called to congratulate her and reminded her that a visit between the two of us was pending. She said, "Come on over to Washington, and we will have a lunch or a breakfast meeting." President Lagos backed the idea and told me to go to Washington. My trip to the American capital was very low-key, far from the curious eyes of the press.

At the time, my agenda was tight, and Condi's even more so. We agreed to have a working breakfast at the restaurant of the Washington, DC, hotel where she was staying. It was a good meeting. After exchanging a few memories of our graduate student years at the University of Denver and updating each other on mutual friends, we mostly talked about Latin America. I stressed the importance of a free trade agreement with Chile that had been postponed over the years and only finally launched during the last months of the Clinton administration: "If the Bush administration is serious about promoting democracy and free markets in the region, then a free trade deal with Chile will be a powerful political signal and the easiest one to achieve." Condi agreed with this analysis. I also added, "We should get the two presidents together as soon as possible, within the constraints that you will have in the next few months." She thought a Lagos-Bush meeting would be a good idea.

To my surprise, Condi's questions went straight to Venezuela; I had put Colombia at the top of my briefing list. I said President Bush had to attempt to work with President Hugo Chávez. She listened without making any comment. Brazil proved another topic of discussion; Cuba never came up. Condi mentioned Bush's special interest in Latin America, and particularly Mexico.

Many other meetings between U.S. and Chilean officials ensued, which attested to good bilateral relations. Foreign Minister Soledad Alvear developed a fluid relation with Colin Powell, as did the two presidents. Chile was behind important initiatives to foster U.S. ties with other Latin American countries, such as when President Lagos personally convinced Bush to give International Monetary Fund support to a weakened Argentina under President Fernando de la Rúa. Or when, on September 17, 2002, during a visit to Condi Rice's West Wing office at the White House, I suggested that, with Luiz Inácio Lula da Silva being the most likely winner of the presidential election in Brazil, Washington should not play its customary game of wait and see, but instead should be proactive and invite President-elect Lula da Silva to the White House. She liked the idea, and it later materialized, thus opening a constructive relationship between Washington and Brazil. President Lagos also visited Bush at the White House on April 16, 2001, after which a senior U.S. official stated, "President Lagos is a leader in promoting economic reform, free trade, and democracy, and the state of relations between the two countries. He is quite good." Three weeks later, President Bush remarked before a gathering of the Council of the Americas at the State Department that "the United States has few better friends, for example, than the Republic of Chile," and he complained that Canadian goods were displacing American products in the Chilean market because "the U.S. has left its trade talks with Chile unfinished."

In this context, the Iraq war's negative effects on Chile seemed disproportionate to the quality of the Chilean-American ties.

Yet complaints about Chile came not merely from official sources. A *Wall Street Journal* columnist wrote that "threats by supposed friends Mexico and Chile" to oppose the U.S.–led resolution on Iraq in the UN Security Council stood "in stark contrast to the statesmanship of Britain's Tony Blair and Spain's José María Aznar." Mexico and Chile, continued the analyst, "have been a disappointment to those of us pulling for mature Latin leadership." In a not-so-veiled warning, the opinion piece concluded, "Let Mr. Lagos peddle Chilean wine in France."[3]

I personally witnessed the degree of tension that existed in the bilateral post-Iraq relationship during a visit to

Washington, DC, in late March 2003. I was to lecture at the distinguished Inter-American Dialogue located on Connecticut Avenue. As is customary, invitations to such lectures are sent to government officials as well as members of Congress, academics, nongovernmental organizations, and so on.

Even though I had not requested any official contact with the White House during my visit, for I had recently left my post as minister secretary general of government, I nonetheless received a call from Ambassador John Maisto, director of Inter-American Affairs of the National Security Council, inviting me to have a coffee at the White House.

Unlike other times when I met with Condi Rice and entered the White House from the Pennsylvania Avenue entrance or the south gate, this time I went in from Seventeenth Street, the regular and direct access to the NSC at the Old Executive Office Building.

Maisto was as friendly and cordial as always. We talked for a while about our families and the hardships of public service, and then we crossed over to the White House. He introduced me to the cafeteria, which was, to my surprise, fronted by a simple door divided in the middle, with the bottom half closed and topped with a surface for placing cups. The upper half opened to a not-very-large kitchen. The "cafeteria is not much to speak of," Maisto said, "but the cappuccinos are good." As we walked back to the Old Executive Office Building, Maisto motioned toward some vehicles parked along the inside street between the White House and the NSC building and remarked, "Cheney is in."

Back in his comfortable office, Maisto went straight to business. He wanted to pass along an important message to the Chilean government, and he considered me to be an efficient conduit. "There is deep disappointment with how

Chile stood on the Iraq question at the UN," he began. "President Bush is truly disappointed with Lagos, but he is furious with Fox. With Mexico, the president feels betrayed, with Chile, frustrated and let down." The American president felt personally and politically close to his Mexican counterpart, while his relationship with President Lagos and Chile was not as close. Besides, from the very beginning, the Chilean president had made it unequivocally clear to Bush that Santiago would not go along with the use of force against Iraq without certain prerequisites agreed to in the Security Council.

I listened without interrupting.

"I am afraid that particularly in Congress, Chile's position on Iraq may lead to delays of the bilateral free trade negotiations. There is already talk of separating the Singapore negotiations from those with Chile to the detriment of Chile. ... And the war in Iraq, particularly if it drags on, will fill the U.S. political agenda. It will be harder to get on that agenda, and Chile has lost some influence."

At that moment, I responded that Chile's position on Iraq at the UN Security Council was based on sound international law and sensible political reasons. The invasion was not the only way to disarm Iraq. Unilateralism was dividing the international community, I added. Then I said that the bilateral negotiations for a free trade deal were a totally different matter. They would be an important signal for the region if successful, and a bad one if interrupted or delayed, particularly for an unrelated issue like Chile's position on Iraq, a position shared by most of the region's countries.

Maisto reacted to my words. "Let me tell you, for President Bush, multilateral and bilateral matters are inextricably linked. You cannot separate one from the other." Then Maisto touched on a controversy that had just exploded in

Chile: "Your government told us officially that the Chilean mission in Geneva would vote against the motion to convene a special session of the Human Rights Commission to address the Iraqi situation, given that this is a matter under UN Security Council jurisdiction, but your Chilean ambassador there abstained instead. Your friend Condi," Maisto stated, "has said, 'Well, what will the Lagos administration do now after it did not honor its word?'"

At that time, the mini–diplomatic crisis was all over the Chilean media. Ambassador Juan Enrique Vega, a Socialist political appointee close to President Lagos, had disobeyed Lagos's decision that, since the UN Security Council was discussing the humanitarian dimensions of the war in Iraq, the Chilean government would oppose a proposal to convene a special session of the UN Human Rights Commission in Geneva to explore the same matter. Instead, Vega abstained. In contrast, Mexico and twenty-five other states had voted against the Geneva initiative.

Chilean foreign minister Soledad Alvear then confirmed that the Chilean ambassador to Geneva had "precise instructions" that were not followed. The ambassador explained that he felt he had a "margin for action" and suggested that there was a moral question at stake in the vote.

I told Maisto, "I cannot speak for the Chilean government, but knowing President Lagos, I can predict that Ambassador Vega will not last in his post. Chile's credibility is on the line, and whatever reasons may be given to cast a vote different from the one decided and communicated by the foreign ministry, I believe that President Lagos might consider it as a challenge to his authority and to Chile's good name." Maisto remained silent for a few seconds and then said, "Here at the White House, everything that is said about us by key foreign ambassadors and authorities is analyzed. Words have an impact; President Bush gets daily briefings with declarations by foreign leaders and, certainly, Condi Rice. She reads them. And now you can imagine the impact of the Geneva vote when we had different information."

We shifted to lighter subjects and soon concluded our conversation. I returned to my hotel on M Street and contacted a secure conduit to discreetly and urgently convey my conversation with Maisto to President Lagos.

Yet Lagos had already made his decision. On Sunday, March 30, Ambassador Vega was recalled to Santiago, after which he promptly submitted his resignation. The next day, President Lagos declared, "The instructions of the president of the republic must be followed, and that is the reason why the [ambassador's] resignation was accepted immediately. There are no moral imperatives when one is acting in representation of the nation." A new bilateral tension with Washington had been surmounted.

Relations between the two countries had not been made easier when the British press disclosed in early March 2003 that eavesdropping was occurring at the Chilean mission and at the residence of the ambassador, as well as on the office telephones and e-mails of other UN Security Council delegations that were actively involved in the Iraq resolution negotiation. A leaked memo, allegedly written by the U.S. National Security Agency and dated January 31, 2003, asked British counterparts to step up surveillance operations "particularly directed at UN Security Council members (minus United States and GBR, of course) to provide intelligence on the voting intentions of those members regarding Iraq." Katherine Gun, a translator at the British Government Communications Headquarters, had supposedly leaked the memo; she was arrested and prosecuted, but one year later, the charges against her were dropped. Chile quietly protested the spying after finding evidence of wiretaps and other eavesdropping devices, and eventually the issue died down.

Yet former British cabinet member Claire Short's comments that she had read transcripts of Kofi Annan's presumably private conversations made the situation more complex. On Thursday, February 26, 2004, the spokesman for the secretary general referred to the alleged taped phone conversations, saying, "We would be disappointed if this were true" since "such activities would undermine the integrity and confidential nature of diplomatic exchanges." The declaration concluded, "The secretary general, therefore, would want this practice stopped, if it indeed exists." Eventually, the case became low profile.

The wiretapping episodes should not have come as a surprise. At the 1945 San Francisco conference that saw the birth of the United Nations, the U.S. Army Signal Security Agency, forerunner of the National Security Agency and the Federal Bureau of Investigation, wiretapped the cable traffic of forty-three out of forty-five delegations attending the meeting. Among those spied upon was the foreign minister of Chile, including his messages opposing the granting of special veto privileges to the five permanent members of the Security Council.[4]

The greatest cost that Chile suffered over the Iraq episode came to be the relative slowdown of the ongoing free trade negotiations with the United States. In comparison, free trade negotiations proceeded swiftly between the Bush administration and the Central American governments, most of which had contributed symbolic support to the Iraq war effort. Fortunately, however, decoupling the Singapore and Chile negotiations only meant that the Chilean trade deal would be signed after the Asian one, and by late March/ early April, there was an agreed-upon text between Washington and Santiago that would be sent to the White House for President Bush's signature and then to Congress.

Bush first announced his decision to sign the pact with Singapore in a speech at Camp Lejeune in North Carolina. The small but economically powerful Asian city-state had been a strong advocate of the U.S. position on Iraq while it was an elected member of the Security Council, up to December 31, 2002. Prime Minister Goh Chok Tong even interceded with some heads of government of the undecided group of countries on the council in 2003 to lobby for the U.S.–U.K. stance. Hence, it was no surprise that the Singapore prime minister signed the free trade agreement at a ceremony in the White House on Tuesday, May 6, 2003. At the signing, President Bush praised Singapore as "a steadfast friend in the fight against global terrorism and a member of the coalition on Iraq."

The day after the Singapore pact was signed, I was announced as the new Chilean ambassador to the United Nations. That very same day, President Bush offered a positive signal for congressional approval of the free trade agreement with my country: "We have an important free trade agreement with Chile that we will move forward with." He added that Chile and Mexico "continued being good friends," despite discrepancies over Iraq. About the same time, Colin Powell, in a television interview with the Canadian Broadcasting Corporation, dismissed the reprisals idea: "We are not conspiring in some State Department, Pentagon, or White House basement about how to take revenge on these three friends [Canada, Chile, and Mexico]."

Exactly one month after the Singapore ceremony at the White House, Chile signed its free trade agreement with the United States at a ceremony at the Vizcaya Museum in Miami. Chilean foreign minister Alvear and U.S. Trade Representative Zoellick were present; the presidents of their respective countries were not. For Chile, the ceremony marked the culmination of a process that had started in the early nineties. While clearly the political level, format, and location were different from that of the Singapore ceremony, what mattered from the Chilean standpoint was the substance of the ceremony.

For President Lagos, Iraq policy and free trade ran on entirely separate tracks. Free trade involved Chile's interests as well as those of the United States, and Washington's canceling trade negotiations with Chile over the Iraq controversy would have sent a bad signal to the region's economic players who knew that Chile was the country best poised to complete an accord with the United States. Such an event would have been a very high price to pay: if there was to be no trade deal with Chile, then with which other country in the region? And what about all the rounds of negotiations that had already been completed, short of the goal? What about the political capital that the Bush administration and USTR Robert Zoellick had invested in the trade agreement with Chile since early 2001? The United States did not have much leverage to apply on Chile.

The conclusion in Chile was that the country perhaps would have to pay a small price for its position on Iraq in the Security Council, but that price would not be substantial. On the other hand, the Chilean posture regarding Iraq justified the costs, since it would be a long-term gain as regards foreign policy consistency in affirming multilateralism and international law.

Clearly, supporting the Iraq war benefited some countries. The military alliance formed for Iraq convinced Bush to favor negotiations of a free trade agreement with coalition member Australia, a move that many observers saw as virtually impossible a few years before.

Unlike Australia, New Zealand opposed the Iraq war and so experienced Washington's cold shoulder. In early April 2003, Helen Clark, the New Zealand prime minister, had to apologize to U.S. authorities for saying that the United States would not have invaded Iraq had Democratic contender Al Gore become president instead of George W. Bush. Still, Clark stuck to the posture of adhering to international law, condemning unilateralism and arguing that the Iraq war had set "very unfortunate precedents for the future."

Given the existence of a free trade agreement between Australia and New Zealand for almost twenty years and the fact that the two economies are closely integrated, New Zealand had indicated its strong desire to pursue a pact with the United States as well. At one point, the possibility of a free trade agreement was even explored between the United States on the one hand, and Chile, Australia, New Zealand, and Singapore on the other. However, after the Iraq invasion, the Bush administration pushed forward free trade negotiations with Australia. Its leaving aside New Zealand was seen as economic revenge.

As regards Chile, on May 22, the Bush administration gave the green light to selling ten fighter F-16 jets to Chile for its air force. The Pentagon had lobbied Chile for the sale, as well as the governments of France and Sweden, which were promoting competitive planes. Relations between Santiago and Washington seemed to be normal.

Post-Iraq ties between Chile and the United States had

been largely repaired when Secretary Colin Powell attended the June 2003 General Assembly of the Organization of American States in Santiago. Powell declared that "disappointment" with Chile was a thing of the past, but requested that the Lagos government support future resolutions in the UN Security Council on the reconstruction of Iraq and collaborate in the fight against terrorism. Both governments also agreed to push for congressional ratification of the just-signed free trade agreement between the two nations.

Lagos and Bush met and had a lively and informal chat during the Asia-Pacific Economic Cooperation (APEC) Summit at the Queens Imperial Hotel in Bangkok, Thailand, on October 20, 2003. They spoke about personal matters and the trade agreements completed both with Chile and Singapore, whose heads of government, coincidentally, flanked Bush on either side—a fact that Bush jokingly attributed to advanced planning. It was a relaxed meeting that allowed the Chilean and American leaders to reconstruct their personal ties.

The presidents met again at the Special Summit of the Americas held in Monterrey in January 2004. The affinity now existing between Lagos and Bush could clearly be perceived in their body language. In one instance, Bush placed his arm around Lagos's shoulder as if they were old and close friends. Both laughed at the lighthearted banter, including Lagos's comment that Bush's Spanish was improving. At the time, Lagos did not need to lobby Bush on the free trade agreement, which by then was ratified by both congresses (although the agreement was mentioned as a concrete bilateral achievement). Finally, the two men could concentrate on other regional and world issues, with Lagos perceived as a serious and reliable interlocutor of the region.

The two presidents had a talk at the Intercontinental Hotel on January 12, after which Bush referred to the Chilean president as "a strong leader who believes in human dignity and human rights and in freedom. I am grateful for [his] strong voice here in our neighborhood." He was impressed by Lagos's speech in which the Chilean leader stressed that Latin America "is not the poorest continent, but it is perhaps one of the most unequal" in socioeconomic terms. When, at the formal Monterrey closing ceremony, the president of Bolivia made an inopportune appeal for his country's aspirations to gain sovereign access to the Pacific Ocean through Chilean territory, Lagos delivered a firm reply on the need to respect international law and not to disregard boundary treaties dating more than one hundred years. Lagos called for bold integration rather than division, and Bush was impressed and supportive of the Chilean president. He later joked to Lagos, "Now I know I must always have you on my side on any fight."

The Monterrey summit proved an occasion for mending fences with neighbors. While there, Bush had breakfast with Canadian prime minister Paul Martin, during which he announced a shift in a U.S. policy linked to Iraq: he said that now Canada would be eligible for second-round reconstruction contracts in Iraq. And in a get-together with President Fox, he invited the Mexican leader and his wife to visit him in March at his Texas ranch.

Chile was the first Latin American country to deploy troops in Haiti, in March 2004, contributing to the Multinational Interim Force created by the UN Security Council (resolution 1529) to secure a stable environment in that nation in the aftermath of Jean-Bertrand Aristide's resignation as president. The White House was very appreciative of the Chilean military peacekeeping contribution at a critical moment of crisis in Haiti. President Lagos made it clear that Chilean forces could be sent to Haiti because, unlike Iraq, this operation was backed by a UN Security Council resolution. Chile's forces opened the way to the first UN Stabilization Mission, established by the Security Council on April 30, 2004, and dominated by Latin American military forces.

Bush invited Lagos for a visit to Washington on Monday, July 19, 2004. The Chilean president arrived with nothing to request from Washington and an open agenda; the actual discussion ranged from an evaluation of the bilateral free trade agreement to the Middle East conflict and the situation in Haiti, where Chile had sent more than six hundred troops under a UN Security Council peacekeeping operation. After the meeting with Lagos at the Oval Office, which was followed by a luncheon, Bush declared that the Chilean leader was a "wise man who understands the politics of South America very well and is very worldly, so I always enjoy visiting with him. He is a man of good advice and sound counsel." The next day, President Lagos paid a visit to Kofi Annan at the United Nations in New York to underscore Chile's multilateral commitment.

•••

The Iraq page had been fully turned when Condi Rice called me on September 1, 2004, as I prepared to board a plane for Chile for consultation meetings with President Ricardo Lagos and other government officials.

A U.S. and French initiative to pass a resolution on Lebanon (shaken by a crisis when the president announced that, contrary to the constitution, he would run for reelection) calling for fair elections and demanding the withdrawal of Syrian troops from Lebanese territory was facing possible defeat. A vote count had secured just eight votes in favor, one short of the necessary nine to approve a resolution in the absence of a veto. Brazil, Algeria, China, Pakistan, the Philippines, and the Russian Federation had signaled that they would abstain. In turn, I had also received written foreign ministry instructions to abstain, but we had not announced our decision publicly.

Condi requested Chile's help. "This is an important resolution and we would like Chile's support," Condi said, underlining that this was a joint American-French initiative. "Look," I said, "I will discuss the issue directly with President Lagos within a few hours." I added that I personally agreed with the thrust of the resolution's democratic and sovereign intent, but that there were problems with the current draft. Condi assured me that the cosponsors would be willing to amend the text, depending on the suggestions.

The next morning, I briefed the president at his office and we agreed to vote in favor of the draft if the specific reference to Syria was removed and replaced by a call "upon all remaining foreign forces to withdraw from Lebanon." President Lagos had received insistent phone calls from Syria's president, Bashar al-Assad, which he had delayed answering until our conversation. I phoned our representative in the Security Council from President Lagos's desk to convey the proposal and new instructions. We had a deal, and moments later, resolution 1559 was approved by the minimum nine votes required. The resolution had a powerful mobilizing effect in Lebanon, and soon after, Syrian troops pulled out from Lebanon in accordance with resolution 1559.

The new climate of repaired friendship between the

United States and Chile was apparent during the November 20 to 21, 2004, APEC summit in Chile, when President Bush stayed over for a bilateral visit and lauded President Lagos's leadership in Latin America. Bush told Lagos that Chile was "the model for Latin America." Asked by reporters about the Iraq war differences between the two countries, Bush replied, "President Lagos didn't agree with my decision, and I respect that. He's still my friend." President Lagos, in turn, praised the "modern and mature" relationship between the United States and Chile.

Secretary Rice visited Chile in April 2005, when she attended the Third Ministerial Meeting of the Community of Democracies. The trip was followed by stopovers in Brazil, Colombia, and El Salvador. More significantly, Rice, in a demonstration of pragmatism, threw U.S. support behind the Chilean candidate José Miguel Insulza for the Organization of American States secretary general post. While Insulza was not the original choice of Washington, lending him support allowed reaching a consensus, thereby avoiding a division within the hemisphere. Secretary Rice returned to Chile in March 2006 to attend the inauguration of the first woman president of Chile, Michelle Bachelet. The new Chilean president was hosted by President Bush at the White House in June 2006, where they discussed the ongoing UN peacekeeping operation in Haiti, bilateral trade, educational and health reform, and regional issues such as energy. Iraq was not on the agenda.

Mexico: "So Far from God, So Close to the United States"
The relationship between presidents Fox and Bush had begun to develop quite well even before they became heads of state. As governors of Texas and Guanajuato, respectively, Bush

and Fox had met in 1996. This paved the way to what would soon become unprecedentedly close ties between Mexico and the United States.

When President-elect Fox visited Washington in August 2000 to meet with President Clinton and presidential candidate Al Gore, he proposed a "NAFTA plus" scheme that would involve not merely the movement of products and services across borders, but also of labor. It was a delicate issue to raise in an electoral year. After Washington, Fox traveled to Dallas to visit Republican candidate George W. Bush in his home state. The two had a good meeting, and Bush showed openness to Fox's determination to tackle the issue of immigration.

The two men had a lot in common. Both were ranchers and wore cowboy boots; both served as governors before their respective elections to the presidency; both had business experience in the private sector prior to becoming president; both were religious; neither was an intellectual, in contrast to their predecessors; and both instead considered themselves men of action.

Six months after their encounter in Dallas, Fox and Bush met again, in February 2001, this time as presidents. This led the way to a higher stage in the bilateral relationship.

In fact, President Bush's first trip abroad, on February 16, 2001, broke a long tradition, as it was not to northern neighbor Canada, but to visit boot-wearing President Fox at his Ranch San Cristóbal in Guanajuato. On the occasion, the two heads of state offered a joint press conference during which they announced a new era of relations focused on trade, security, energy issues, immigration, combating drug trafficking, the extension of democracy, and education. There was a clear message from the White House that Mexico, and Latin

America, would count high in the U.S. foreign policy agenda. Mexican foreign minister Jorge Castañeda, a good friend of many years, phoned me in my capacity as Chilean deputy foreign minister to tell me that he had advised Condoleezza Rice and Colin Powell to work closely with Chile as a partner for democracy promotion and to attain a free trade agreement.

Bush felt at ease during this first visit to Mexico, spoke a few phrases in broken Spanish, and expressed his intention of building a strong partnership. Bush underlined that Mexico was the first country he visited as president, and he said he had "intended it to be that way. ... Our nations are bound together by ties of history, family, values, commerce, and culture. Today, these ties give us an unprecedented opportunity. We have a chance to build a partnership that will improve the lives of citizens in both countries."

But the Guanajuato summit between Bush and Fox ended with a bad omen. Saddam Hussein's antiaircraft missiles had violated the no-fly zone, and Bush rushed to *Air Force One* to order an air strike against Iraqi forces and installations. Fox's advisors were outraged because the news from Guanajuato would not be the new U.S.–Mexican relation, but Iraq.

Following the third Summit of the Americas, held in Quebec on April 21, 2001, both presidents met again and offered another joint press conference, during which they announced Fox's state visit to the White House in September. Bush declared that relations between the two nations went beyond bilateral issues, and he thanked Fox for offering him "good advice and counsel on hemispheric relations." The presidents met again on May 3, 2001, when Fox visited Washington in response to an invitation by the American Jewish Committee.

On September 5, the Mexican president became the

first foreign head of state to visit the White House during the Bush administration. It was another powerful political signal, although at the time, it was rumored that some top advisors did not share Bush's marked interest in Mexico and Latin America. But Bush had linked Mexico to some of his favorite political themes: it was "family values," he said in 2001 in San Antonio, Texas, that prompted Mexicans to cross the border to find work in the United States. Hence, it was in the national interest to help Mexico succeed.

Thus it came as no surprise that during Fox's state visit to the White House from September 5 to 7, 2001, Bush enthusiastically affirmed that there was no country more important to the United States than Mexico. Both presidents then announced a Partnership for Prosperity, an alliance that included both the public and private sectors.

President Fox pragmatically believed that to agree on a comprehensive American-Mexican immigration reform would take four to six years. But, unexpectedly, during the welcoming ceremony at the White House, Fox stated that the immigration accord would have to be completed by the year's end—in short, within four months. Bush cautiously abstained from commenting on Fox's deadline.

Fox's remarks were described in *The Washington Post* as an "unwelcome surprise" to the Bush administration, and observers noted that the White House had been caught off guard. Apparently, the Mexican authorities had reasoned that such an excellent bilateral relationship had to be seized as an opportunity to move difficult issues forward quickly and that those issues should be solved while the honeymoon lasted. *Time* magazine elected Fox the Person of the Week at the end of the state visit, expressing that "the tenor of this week's discussions in Washington suggest a sense of common destiny and shared responsibility unparalleled in the troubled history of U.S.–Mexican relations."

These words would soon be forgotten.

Unfortunately for Mexico, all of this happened just days before the attacks on 9/11, and the world's harsh new reality would radically change those declared goals, priorities, and wishes.

Ties between the two countries deteriorated further after 9/11, not only because Washington took on other priorities. In August 2001, Washington had delivered a message to the Fox administration suggesting a gradual approach to the immigration issue: first a guest-worker program then, in due time, regularization of the undocumented Mexicans in the United States. The Mexican government rejected the idea. Moreover, a few days before the terrorist attacks against the Twin Towers and the Pentagon, Mexico had announced that it would withdraw from the 1947 Rio Treaty, considered a relic of the Cold War. But immediately after 9/11, Washington had no other collective security mechanism at the hemispheric level to coordinate a common strategy against terrorism except the Rio Treaty. Yet Mexico opposed utilizing it, calling instead for the elaboration of a new hemispheric security scheme, with security viewed as a phenomenon beyond the military dimension. The Bush administration had expected unconditional solidarity at that moment and was not pleased by Mexico's posture.

While the Canadian prime minister phoned Bush immediately after 9/11, offered assistance and solidarity, and made a quick visit to Washington, Fox was not as quick to react and stayed away from Washington for several weeks. Eventually, on October 4, 2001, the Mexican president visited Bush in Washington to express his solidarity for the

9/11 attacks. He also talked about international security and border control, and later went on to visit Ground Zero in Manhattan to express sympathy for those who had died there, including many Mexicans.

Although priorities had changed for Washington, relations with Mexico on the whole continued to be positive, although not as intensely as before. Therefore, Fox went out of his way to accommodate his friend Bush during the March 18 through 22, 2002, UN Summit on Financing for Development held in Monterrey, Mexico.

Unfortunately, attending this meeting wound up creating an embarrassing situation for the Mexican president, one involving Fidel Castro and causing a crisis in Mexican-Cuban ties.

A few weeks after the Monterrey summit, on April 22, 2002, Fidel Castro revealed a tape of a conversation held on March 19 with Fox in which the Mexican leader asked the Cuban to leave earlier so as not to cross paths with Bush during the retreat part of the summit, when the presidents, unaccompanied by their delegations, would engage in dialogue.

The background to the story is this: Castro said that he knew that Washington would put pressure on Mexico to impede his participation in the summit. The Cuban leader therefore had sent a letter to Fox informing him that he would stay in Mexico only "for the minimum time possible," meaning two days out of the five-day conference. Then Fidel recalled that he had received an urgent phone call from Fox prior to his departure for Monterrey. As is recorded on the tape, Fox requested that the ensuing conversation remain "private" and "between friends."

In the tape, Fidel asked President Fox to repeat the offer that became known in Mexico as "you have lunch and leave";

then he made Fox agree to get Kofi Annan to move Cuba's speech up to an earlier time slot, and, in turn, Fidel agreed to arrive near midnight on Wednesday. During the conversation, Fox also offered Fidel a privileged seat at the official Thursday luncheon and requested his Cuban counterpart "not attack the U.S. or President Bush."

In the end, Castro did not attend the luncheon and, instead, held bilateral talks, departing Mexico at around 5:00 P.M. on Thursday the twenty-first, just as President Bush arrived at the Monterrey airport.

The Mexico-Cuba incident had been preceded by a first-time-ever Mexican vote in favor of condemning Cuba for human rights violations, at the UN Human Rights Commission on April 20. Moreover, during a visit to Havana by President Fox on February 26, Foreign Minister Jorge Castañeda had made a conceptual distinction that "relations with the Cuban revolution had ceased to exist and that they had started with the Republic of Cuba." Later, in Miami, Castañeda asserted that "the doors of the Mexican embassy in Havana [were] open to all Cuban citizens, the same as Mexico." The distortion of these declarations led to forced entry attempts by Cubans at the Mexican diplomatic mission in Havana, as well as to other serious incidents, all of which created tension between the two countries prior to Monterrey.

Indeed, Mexico's relations with Havana had actually reached their lowest point ever. Mexico, the country that had never suspended relations with Fidel Castro—not even at the worst moments of the Cold War—was now facing a bilateral crisis with the island. This far-reaching expression of friendship and courtesy on Fox's part risked Mexican ties with Cuba and proved to be internationally embarrassing to Mexico, although ultimately this carried no weight with the

White House when it came to bilateral differences over the Iraq war.

In September 2002, as the discussions on Iraq heated up at the UN Security Council (Mexico had entered the council as a nonpermanent member the previous January), the Mexican government decided to withdraw from the Rio Treaty, and the U.S. State Department expressed disappointment at Mexico's decision to abandon this Cold War–era, hemispheric, reciprocal-assistance defense pact.

The Fox administration had modified Mexico's role in world affairs, which formerly emphasized relations with its northern neighbor and international trade agreements. The first clear departure from this approach was the Fox administration's announcement that it would seek a place as a nonpermanent member of the UN Security Council for 2002 to 2003. This changed Mexico's long-held posture of avoiding participation in the Security Council so that Mexico would not risk confrontation with the United States over matters of vital national interest to its neighbor.

Mexico had been a nonpermanent member of the UN Security Council only twice before: in 1947, when it occupied a seat for one year, thanks to a drawing, and in 1980 to 1981. But for Fox, one of the cornerstones of the new democratic Mexico meant a highly visible role in multilateral affairs and, specifically, in the UN Security Council.

On October 26, 2002, Bush and Fox met again, during the APEC summit held in Los Cabos, Mexico. Immigration was on the agenda, but this time Bush declared that the long-term solution was to encourage "commerce on both sides of the border, so people can find jobs here in Mexico, for starters." Iraq was a centerpiece of their talks, as Bush urged the UN Security Council to pass a resolution to hold

Saddam Hussein accountable. "If the UN won't act," Bush said in Los Cabos, "if Saddam Hussein won't disarm, we will lead a coalition to disarm him."

During 2003, relations between the two neighbors continued to suffer over the Iraq issue. Mexico-bashing took various forms, including a website entitled "Vicente, el Meddling Presidente," designed to attack President Fox and his new foreign minister, Luis Ernesto Derbez, and Mexican foreign policy, particularly on issues such as Iraq, migration and undocumented workers, and Mexican relations with border states.

Articles appeared in the American press citing anonymous government officials who made serious accusations or revealing intelligence about the dangers Mexico posed to U.S. security. On April 7, 2003, *The Washington Times* published a report entitled "Terrorism Said to Seek Entry to U.S. via Mexico." The article stated that "At least 14 Al Qaida members are said to be in Mexico, said officials who spoke on the condition of anonymity. The Al Qaida members are working with Mexican organized crime groups … the officials said." According to the piece, the terrorists were "attempting to infiltrate the United States from Mexico to conduct attacks in the country." Yet the Department of Homeland Security had no information on such a plan, and the story never resurfaced.[5]

In February 2003, Fox spoke candidly about Mexico's relations with Washington in light of the Iraq discussions: "We have committed ourselves to mutual understanding; for the first time, we have differentiated positions and … I do not expect by any means reprisals or pressures from the American government."

In his memoir, *Revolution of Hope*, President Fox recalls

that Bush insisted on getting support for the use of force against Iraq while Mexico believed that there was no need to rush to war without sufficient evidence of WMD.[6] "We got strong hints from second-tier U.S. diplomats that it would be awfully difficult for Congress to back an immigration bill if Mexico opposes the United States in a time of need," Fox asserts. But the United States did not have many carrots or sticks to pressure Mexico.

Fox complained that President Bush never consulted with his partners, perhaps with the exception of Tony Blair. The Mexican president said, "With the rest of us, it was never, 'What do you think we should do about Iraq, Vicente?'— rather, it was, 'Here is what we intend to do, and we really need to have Mexico with us.' This was not a leader of the new global democracy listening to his allies, soliciting our views, and then building a multilateral consensus to take action. ... Bush and his top aides presented the war plan as a unilateral fait accompli, not a subject for multilateral debate."

After the Iraq war began on March 19, it became evident that the Mexico–U.S. relationship had declined dramatically. Bush was actually angry at his friend Fox. His last phone call to the Mexican president on Wednesday, March 12, to lobby for the U.S.–led resolution had not produced the desired commitment from his amigo. "The vote at the United Nations is tomorrow. ... We need your vote, President Fox." It was no more "Vicente," the Mexican president noticed, just as Bush had shifted from the familiar "Ricardo" to "President Lagos" when he had phoned the Chilean leader on the same issue. Fox responded that more evidence and time were needed. Fox informed his colleague that he was going to undergo back surgery that very same day. Foreign Minister Derbez would respond to future calls from Bush while Fox was hospitalized at the Central Military Hospital. The operation's timing raised ironic comments in Mexico, and annoyed Bush.

Reinforcing his words to Bush that he was not going to support the use of force, Fox delivered a public message soon after his operation affirming that "Mexico's voice was being listened to by the whole world" and that his commitment was "to achieve a peaceful outcome to the Iraq conflict." He also argued that it was necessary to "continue to pursue solutions that comply with the letter and spirit of the United Nations Charter," adding that Mexico "insists upon the multilateral road for conflict settlement and regrets the road of war."

After the Iraq invasion began, Bush no longer returned President Fox's calls. On April 22, Fox candidly admitted he had not had any contact with the White House in recent weeks and said that he wanted to "send a greeting" to Bush through the journalists to whom he was speaking.

More than a month later, the Bush administration gave the first sign of lukewarm rapprochement with Mexico. On Tuesday, May 13, former president George H. W. Bush arrived in Mexico City as a special envoy of George W. Bush. He was taken immediately to the Los Pinos presidential residence, where a smiling President Fox greeted him. After the closed-door meeting, there was no joint statement to the press, although Foreign Secretary Derbez described the visit as a clear recognition of the deep friendship between the two presidents. Bush Senior's visit indicated that, despite strong differences over the war in Iraq, relations between the two countries had to regain a normal track. One week earlier, Minister Derbez and Colin Powell had met to resume discussions on drug trafficking and immigration. Derbez had also visited Condi Rice and members of the U.S. Congress during that time.

The ice was broken on October 10, 2003, when Bush called Fox to discuss the agenda of the bilateral talks at the APEC summit in Thailand. Fox reported that the phone call lasted twenty minutes, which showed that "there is on Bush's part a true intention to reconstruct the relationship, to return to rapprochement, to return to having enough time to talk not only about the bilateral agenda, but also the global one." This phone conversation took place six days before the voting of resolution 1511 on Iraq (which was approved unanimously) and as the 2004 American presidential campaign began to unfold. Not surprisingly, when the two presidents met on October 20 in Thailand, Condi Rice informed the press that among the top issues to be addressed were border matters and humanitarian immigration policies.

In January 2004, Fox presided at the Fourth Summit of the Americas in Monterrey, Mexico, with Bush attending. At that point, a Zogby poll in Latin America deemed Bush as the hemisphere's most unpopular president. For the first time in long years, anti–United States feelings were surging in the region. Yet Fox congratulated Bush on the capture of Saddam Hussein and stressed immigration in the bilateral talks, with the Mexican leader expressing support for Bush's program on immigration reform. The program would allow Mexicans to enter the United States legally under a guest-worker program, whereby they could serve as temporary laborers in jobs not in demand by American workers for a renewable period of three years, provided they had sponsorship by an employer. At a press conference, Bush denied that his immigration proposal was a response to electoral pressure to gain the Latin vote and argued it was simply "the right thing" to do.

As a sign of the renewed ties, President Bush invited Fox and his wife, Marta Sahagún, to visit his ranch in Crawford,

Texas, in early March 2004. Fox, responding to press inquiries, stated, "Some want to see things from the wrong side and claim that Fox has submitted to Bush, that Fox is already Bush's lackey." He then underlined the importance for Mexico of an immigration agreement with Washington.

In mid-November 2003, Mexican ambassador to the UN Adolfo Aguilar Zinser, an outspoken critic of U.S. policy toward Iraq, remarked while lecturing at the Ibero-American University, in Mexico City, that the United States had always treated Mexico as its backyard and that such treatment would continue "so long as there would be someone in Mexico who thought it necessary to *tragar camote* [swallow a bitter pill]." The ambassador was publicly reprimanded by President Fox, and on November 17, Aguilar Zinser was given until January—the end of Mexico's term on the Security Council—to vacate his post.

Colin Powell called Aguilar Zinser's comments "outrageous. ... Mexico is a partner of the United States, a neighbor of the United States, a great friend. We never, ever, in any way would treat Mexico as some backyard or as a second-class nation."

"We have problems with your ambassador at the UN, Mr. President," Bush had told Fox in front of several witnesses during the APEC summit at Los Cabos in late 2002. Fox had remained silent on that occasion. This time, the Mexican president was upset. When Fox referred to the controversy again, stating that Aguilar Zinser had "offended the Mexican people and their president," the ambassador decided to resign immediately, without waiting until January 1.

Aguilar Zinser told me at the Friday, November 21, luncheon of the Security Council members with the secretary general, "I have no other option." Attending the lunch would be his next-to-last activity at the council before his official farewell in the council hall.

That day, Aguilar Zinser drafted a handwritten letter of resignation, addressed to President Fox, which he showed me. I was shocked—it amounted to a public denunciation rather than a private resignation. So I offered a couple of suggestions to soften it, which he accepted. Within twenty-four hours, he had left the United Nations. A year and a half later, in June 2005, Adolfo Aguilar Zinser died tragically in a car accident. He was honored by all relevant political forces and actors in Mexico, including President Fox.

A 2005 summit of the U.S., Canadian, and Mexican leaders in Crawford, Texas, helped to consolidate the fence-mending process after Iraq. Some interpreted the brief, cordial, and unpretentious summit as "surprisingly productive," for it addressed questions about the implementation of NAFTA and the development of trilateral work plans. Prior to the Crawford summit, Bush had flown to Canada for his first international trip during his second term in office. This was to support the process of rebuilding frayed alliances. Another sign of policy change in the post–Iraq invasion context had been Condi Rice's visit to Mexico early in the second Bush administration. There, the secretary of state lauded Mexico's case as a "remarkable story" of "great progress." During her visit, Mexican officials discussed immigration, water, and farming, and afterward, they opined that Rice's visit had been "friendly" and "positive." Normal contacts at the presidential level continued in 2006 with a trilateral summit in Cancun, which included Canadian prime minister Stephen Harper; a visit to the White House by Mexican president-elect Felipe Calderón in November 2006; and a bilateral meeting in Mérida between Calderón and Bush.

Iraq had become a past bitter chapter in the rich bilateral agenda between Mexico and the United States.

The Transatlantic Divide with the "Old Europe"

In September 2002, a group of foreign ministers met for dinner at the classic hotel Pierre on Fifth Avenue and Sixty-First Street in New York, across from Central Park. Secretary of State Colin Powell was present, as was French foreign minister Dominique de Villepin. At that dinner, Powell advised de Villepin, "Be sure of one thing: don't vote for the first [resolution] unless you are prepared to vote for the second." In other words, Washington was telling Paris that if Iraq was found in "material breach" of its obligations, under what later would become resolution 1441, France would have to vote for another resolution approving the use of force against Hussein. Not only did that never happen, but it was France, in fact, that would lead the antiwar coalition within the Security Council.

In Washington, everyone was aware that at a January 20, 2003, Security Council session organized by the French presidency on fighting terrorism, France had used the occasion to criticize the U.S. push for war. The night before, French minister de Villepin had met with Secretary Powell at his suite at the Waldorf Astoria, where, during a friendly chat, the French official communicated his country's misgivings about the perceived bellicose direction of U.S. policy. Powell mistakenly thought that the issue would not be pursued further.

The next day, the Security Council session focused on terrorism. American diplomats had obtained assurances from their French colleagues that only terrorism would be discussed on that occasion. After the meeting ended, Powell left for a luncheon, held at the residence of the French ambassador on Park Avenue and Seventy-Second Street, while de Villepin, as president of the council, stayed at the UN to offer a customary after-session press conference. Although the meeting had been on terrorism, the French minister took advantage of a question on Iraq to state, "We will not associate ourselves with military intervention that is not supported by the international community. Military intervention would be the worst possible solution." Powell was unaware of what had occurred until after the lunch ended.

Even worse, once de Villepin arrived at the lunch and sat down, the dining room doors were shut and the French foreign minister announced, to Powell's surprise, that the subject of discussion would be Iraq, not terrorism. Powell was clearly displeased as he received what he considered to be extensive "lectures" from the foreign ministers of France, Germany, Russia, and, to a lesser extent, China on what they saw as a misdirected U.S. policy on Iraq. Colin Powell reiterated the position of his country regarding Iraq, and toward the end, when he was obviously quite irritated, said that many of those who were "criticizing the United States on Iraq had also protested the American invasion of Panama to get rid of Noriega, only to later congratulate the White House on having reestablished democracy" in the Latin American nation. Powell added that he suspected the same thing would happen on Iraq.

Colin Powell was truly annoyed about this unexpected debate on Iraq. He later commented he had been set up and "betrayed." This was the first clear moment of publicly aired sharp differences between France and the United States over Iraq.

Everyone therefore took due note when, with a combination of belligerence and disdain, Pentagon chief Donald

Rumsfeld framed the transatlantic issue, arguing that France and Germany represented the "Old Europe," meaning these nations were outdated and interesting merely for tourism's sake, and not the "New Europe," which was composed of countries formerly belonging to Eastern Europe that supported the United States on Iraq and would supposedly be the vital force in shaping Europe's future. The "center of gravity is moving east," Rumsfeld added. Rumsfeld may have also had in mind what occurred the day before in Brussels, when France, Germany, and Belgium had blocked a U.S.–led initiative to give NATO's support to Turkey if Iraq tried to retaliate against that country in the event of a war.

In anticipation of the war against Iraq, conservative columnists concentrated their ire on the UN and France. Many simply forgot, or did not want to remember, that France was the United States' oldest European ally since the time of independence.

...

In *The Wall Street Journal*, Paul Johnson wrote an op-ed entitled "Au Revoir, Petite France" in which he claimed, "France is a second-rate power militarily. But because of its geographic position at the center of Western Europe and its nominal possession of nuclear weapons, which ensures its permanent place on the UN Security Council, it wields considerable negative and destructive power. On this occasion, it has exercised such power to the full, and the consequences are likely to be permanent." Johnson went even further: "The Security Council will now be marginalized and important business will be transacted elsewhere. Indeed, it may prove difficult to keep the United States within the organization at all." In the new ad hoc coalition's context, Johnson predicted, "France will become irrelevant. We will see then what Germany will do."[7]

For conservative columnist George Will, the one appropriate role for France would be to assist the United States in reading the Iraqi archives that described the collaboration between France and Saddam Hussein over the prior twelve years. William Safire, in turn, argued that U.S. postwar policy "should be to reward friends and to remind others that actions have consequences. ... As America rewards freedom's friends, future leaders in Berlin, Paris, and Moscow will get the message that shortsighted political actions have long-term consequences."[8]

American officials also bitterly criticized France and its antiwar European partners. On March 13, Ari Fleischer, the White House press secretary, accused the French of "poisoning" the diplomatic process launched by the British to seek a last-minute compromise, adding that it was "extraordinary" that France had closed all doors to support a new UN Security Council resolution. At the time, French foreign minister de Villepin had replied that the British-American proposal only sought to delay the war by a few days, not avert it.

A soon-to-be-famous phrase, attributed to Condi Rice, began to circulate in Washington circles. The U.S. policy toward the antiwar European countries in the Security Council would be "to isolate France, ignore Germany, and forgive Russia." The idea was to divide the bloc and implement a case-by-case approach that would also consider American interests. Thus, it was clear that America would work more intensely with some countries than others while extending red-carpet treatment to the allies in the "coalition of the willing."

France was America's main target in terms of "payback." Discussions centered on concrete punitive measures, such as reducing or impeding certain sales to France of sensitive software and other defense-related materials that require federal approval. Yet doing so would certainly entail a cost for U.S. exporters as well. Others felt that intelligence cooperation between the two countries would have to decline, as France had proven itself to be an "untrustworthy ally."

Reflecting the anti-French sentiment, Deputy Secretary of Defense Paul Wolfowitz asserted in April 2003 that "France is going to pay some consequences, not just with us, but with other countries." In addition, Wolfowitz told the Senate Armed Services Committee that Russia, Germany, and France could be of service to the reconstruction by forgiving Iraq's debt: "I hope they'll think about the very large debts that come from money that was lent to Saddam Hussein to buy weapons and to build palaces and to build instruments of repression." Iraq's debt with France and Russia was estimated at $8 billion each, and Germany's was estimated at $4.3 billion. Neoconservative commentators went as far as suggesting that Iraq should declare a unilateral moratorium on its foreign debt, especially those amounts corresponding to weapons purchases under Hussein, since it was assumed there would be no official American objection, given that two of Iraq's main creditors were Russia and France.[9] The U.S. administration's unilateral call for the elimination of international claims on Iraq (since Washington was owed very little by Iraq) was thus defined by an observer as being equivalent to "seeking to spend other people's money."[10]

In the U.S. Congress, reactions to the European opposition to war were particularly harsh. Representative Henry J. Hyde, chairman of the House International Relations

Committee, deplored "the callous attitude of other countries whose interests we are also defending. ... We do have a right to expect more from old allies, especially those whose freedom has been purchased with American lives. So it is with great pain and regret that we have seen some turn their backs to us. It is at difficult times that we can assay the true weight of their friendship and reveal the easy promises of the past as so much fool's gold."

Asked by reporters in Paris whether the United States intended to punish France, Secretary of State Powell—who had visited the French capital to meet with seven other foreign ministers to prepare the G-8 meeting in Evian in June 2003—replied, "No ... but you take note of those who disagree with you, and you try to find out why and if it is appropriate to draw some conclusions. And consequences follow those conclusions."

President Bush aired his displeasure with France in an NBC news interview on Thursday, April 24, 2003, when he conveyed that in his administration, the prevailing perception was that "the French position was anti-American." He then added, in reference to President Chirac, "I doubt he'll be coming to the ranch anytime soon." In Bush code, an invitation to his Texas ranch was the highest form of red-carpet treatment.

Relations between the two countries worsened when accusations—backed by anonymous U.S. administration sources—surfaced in both American and British newspapers about shady deals between France and the Saddam Hussein regime.

For example, *The Sunday Times* of London reported on April 27 that France had regularly informed Hussein about private meetings between European representatives and American officials on Washington's war plans, which, according to the paper, could have helped Iraq prepare for war. This information was supposedly based on documents found in the debris within the Iraqi foreign ministry.[11]

In March, columnist William Safire linked France to a complex scheme whereby a French intermediary had presumably facilitated Iraq's acquisition, via Syria, of chemical components for missiles.[12] In its April 21 issue, *Newsweek* reported a "possible" discovery in Iraq of Roland Z French missiles manufactured in 2002, although Roland Z production had ceased in 1993.[13]

The Washington Post and *The New York Times* went on to print stories with loose conjectures rather than hard facts about supposed European connivance with Saddam Hussein. *The Times*, for example, alleged that as tensions had risen in the UN in September 2002, France and Germany had supplied Iraq with high-precision switches that could be used for nuclear weapons.[14] One month later, *The Post* published that France, along with Russia, Iraq, and North Korea, possessed human smallpox strains prohibited by the World Health Organization.[15]

In turn, *The Washington Times* reported on May 6, 2003, that French diplomats in Syria had assisted in the escape to Europe of "an unknown number" of Hussein regime leaders by providing them with travel documents. It cited "U.S. intelligence officials" as the basis for the story and quoted "a senior Bush administration official" declaring, "Now you have the French helping the bad guys escape from us."[16] Even though the French embassy in Washington denied the story, chairman of the House Judiciary Committee James Sensenbrenner ordered an investigation and opined that France should be excluded from the U.S. visa waiver arrangement that allows tourists from developed countries, including France, to visit the United States without a visa. Interestingly, an investigation by the Department of Homeland Security concluded that the French passports story was false.

In view of such articles, the French authorities complained formally to the White House, State Department, and Congress that France was the target of a "campaign of repeated disinformation allegedly fed by Bush administration sources." A spokesperson for the French embassy in Washington declared at the time that France could "only assume that journalists were being truthful when they cited unnamed sources in the administration."[17]

As the war advanced on the ground in Iraq during April and May, the criticisms of the antiwar Europeans grew particularly virulent. A website, francestinks.com, was created to gather critical articles against Old Europe and mock the French—including in situations such as France's deficit in 2003 and the summer heat wave that cost the lives of hundreds of elderly people. Supposedly, the website was visited by more than 4 million first-time visitors in a one-year span. French exchange students going to the United States were rejected on account of their nationality when in the past, no such problem had arisen. A representative of Loisirs Culturels à L'Etranger, an exchange program based in Paris, reported that reaction among U.S. families to their exchange student was fine until they found out the visiting student would come from France, which would simply "end the conversation."[18] Even French wine exports were affected by a postwar boycott in the United States.

In the first four months of 2003, French nonmilitary exports to the United States fell 21 percent as compared to the same period in 2002, while nonmilitary exports from the United States to France dropped 24 percent, a marked fall considering the cheap dollar and expensive euro, which favored American exports. In late March 2003, a Swiss-American investment bank had arranged a complex financial deal with close to one hundred potential institutional investors, and in an unprecedented move, ten of the buyers declined to participate because the company raising the funds was French.[19] These were the very real costs for concrete exporters and investors of a unilateralist war.

• • •

France was not the only country to receive America's scorn. In May 2003, a White House high official privately stated that the United States would ostracize Chancellor Gerhard Schroeder, even though efforts would be made to improve ties with Germany at other levels. "The Bush-Schroeder relationship will never be what it was and what it should be" was a phrase heard at the White House. And in fact, Hesse state premier Roland Koch, a conservative and potential challenger to Schroeder's Social Democratic Party in the 2006 German elections, was given an interview with President Bush while visiting the White House.[20]

Bush was angered by Schroeder's reelection campaign, which was based on opposing the war in Iraq—a highly popular position among Germans—and his calling the Iraq war a "military adventure." The American president felt this was "cynical electioneering" and took it personally because allegedly he had been given direct assurances by Schroeder in a private conversation in May 2003 that the chancellor would not exploit the war issue. Personal relations between the two leaders had thus become "poisoned," since—according to a

White House source—President Bush "believes the character of a person is known by whether he keeps his word."

Chancellor Schroeder felt the sting when his request for a one-on-one meeting with Bush at the June 2003 G-8 Economic Summit in Evian, France, was refused by the White House. Yet Germany did not change its position. On October 9, 2003, Foreign Minister Fischer criticized American policy in Iraq: "The American domino theory under which a liberated Iraq was supposed to stabilize the Middle East and democratize one country after another has not proven right." For transatlantic ties to improve, he added, "we must approach one another as partners." An Allensbach poll in late April 2003 showed that Germans and Americans had increasingly negative opinions about each other. Only 11 percent of Germans now considered America to be Germany's best friend.

With time, and as the war in Iraq worsened, relations with Germany improved. On February 27, 2004, Bush and Schroeder met at the White House and issued a joint statement entitled "The German-American Alliance for the 21st Century." It focused on improving transatlantic relations based on common values and a common agenda, ranging from Iraq and terrorism to the Middle East and NATO.

Some smaller European countries, such as Belgium, allied with the French and German position on Iraq. Belgium also felt the heat. On August 1, 2003, the Belgian senate gave final approval to a moderate war crimes bill that the government hoped would mend relations with the United States. The bill changed a law that gave Belgian courts the power to try foreigners for war and human rights crimes regardless of where they had been committed. In fact, a number of claims were already being processed against

President Bush and Prime Minister Blair, and tensions had risen so high over the law that on June 19, Defense Secretary Rumsfeld had threatened to move the NATO headquarters out of Belgium unless the country scrapped the law.

The other side of the coin was that, at the time of the Iraq invasion, European opinion of the United States dropped to unprecedentedly low levels. One year after the invasion, a poll conducted by the Pew Research Center found that opinions of President Bush had an 85 percent negative rating in France; 85 percent in Germany; 60 percent in Russia; and 57 percent in Great Britain. The same poll demonstrated that most European respondents believed that U.S. and British leaders generally lied in claiming Iraq possessed WMD: in France, 82 percent; Germany, 69 percent; Russia, 61 percent; and Britain, 41 percent.[21]

By midyear 2003, as the war in Iraq intensified, some voices began to advocate a European-American rapprochement. In June 2003, a conference entitled "Desperately Seeking Europe" was organized in Berlin by the Deutsche Bank to address the collapse of the transatlantic alliance and ways to mend fences. An op-ed in the *Financial Times* at about the same time called for "Europe and America to put off their divorce."[22]

The official European position was to insist on a multilateral approach to addressing the Iraqi conflict. At a mid-April 2003 meeting in Saint Petersburg, the leaders of Russia, France, and Germany advocated that the Iraq war should be "resolved as quickly as possible in accordance with the UN Charter," in the words of Russian president Putin. Chirac, in turn, stated that the common goal of the three countries was to "create conditions that will give back to the Iraqi people their dignity and an opportunity to be masters of their own fate … only the United Nations has the legitimacy to do that."

By late April, there was a thick layer of frost between the White House and the Elysée Palace. Chirac and Bush had not spoken on the phone since February 8. But by May, Chirac called Bush, conceded the NATO approval for the military posting that Poland needed for sending troops to Iraq, and voted in favor of the reconstruction resolution 1483 in the Security Council.

The differences between some European countries, such as France, Germany, and Belgium, and the United States and Britain were not limited to the Iraq conflict. There were also discrepancies over the broad conception of European defense. Prime Minister Blair favored a European rapid-deployment force working under NATO to build "one polar power" across the Atlantic, led by the United States. Instead, Chirac, Schroeder, and others wanted a rapid-deployment force as the military arm of a distinct European Union foreign security policy.

During a summit held in Berlin on September 13, 2003, the leaders of Germany, France, and Great Britain could not agree on a common policy on Iraq. That made a common European foreign policy merely a dream.

One expression of the intra-European division had emerged in early 2003 when Spanish president José María Aznar and another seven European leaders signed a key letter supporting the American position regarding Iraq. As Spain and Great Britain had secretly promoted the idea of this European declaration of support for the United States, the letter made it clear that Europe was divided on the war. France and Germany did not reflect the views of the whole of Europe.

The Letter of Eight, as it became known, aroused anger

in Europe. Javier Solana, the EU commissioner for foreign policy, heard about it first on the radio. According to colleagues, he was "furious and disappointed." On January 27, 2003, Solana had won from Europe's foreign ministers an agreement to forge a common European policy on Iraq. In preparing the Letter of Eight, London and Madrid had therefore violated all procedures—neither the Greek presidency nor Solana had been informed, much less consulted.

The idea of the document had been posed to several European governments by a journalist. At the time, the only enthusiastic response had come from Aznar's staff. And in the end, it was Aznar who had convinced 10 Downing Street about the initiative.[23] On the day of the letter's publication, French foreign minister de Villepin canceled a trip to London to meet colleague Jack Straw for dinner at his official country residence at Chevening. On hearing of the letter, de Villepin excused himself, arguing he had an overload of work for a forthcoming Franco-African summit. President Bush, in turn, was delighted. According to a Spanish diplomat, he sent Aznar a handwritten note in capital letters: "José María, God bless you and Spain. George W."

But the letter was only the first part of the plot. On the day the Letter of Eight was published, ten countries from Central and Eastern Europe—all candidates to join NATO and the EU—received a draft to use in issuing a similar statement. It had been prepared by an American lobbyist close to the Pentagon. There was a dual purpose behind issuing such a draft: first, to reveal the differences between Old Europe and the New Europe of the candidates seeking entry into NATO and the EU, and second, to show solidarity between the ten and Washington, and thus favor the upcoming vote in the U.S. Congress on accepting seven of the ten into NATO.

Furthermore, the plan was to publish the Eastern and Central European letter on February 5, the day Secretary Powell would deliver his speech on the WMD evidence to the Security Council. In fact, the letter even referred to Powell's "compelling evidence," although no one had yet seen or heard that evidence. The Bulgarians, nervous about the EU reaction, consulted the night before with the French, who were appalled at the suggestion of Powell's compelling data. Aznar and Blair had led a master move ... but one that would have serious intra-European consequences.

Despite the differences over Iraq, European countries agreed on other important foreign policy matters. An example of such a collaborative agreement occurred on April 14, 2003, when foreign ministers meeting in Luxembourg called on Washington to "tone down its confrontational rhetoric toward Syria" in the aftermath of the fall of the Saddam Hussein regime. German foreign minister Fischer added, "We should concentrate on winning the peace and not get into another confrontation." Even Foreign Secretary Jack Straw saw fit to reassure the public, saying that "as far as 'Syria next on the list,' we made clear that it is not." It was a rejection of the regime change doctrine.

However, for Tony Blair, unilateralism would become a permanent reality if Europe did not recognize U.S. world primacy. In a controversial interview with the *Financial Times* in late April 2003, Blair went to the heart of the transatlantic angst when he noted that the world needed "one polar power which encompasses a strategic partnership between Europe and America." Insinuating a criticism of President Chirac, Blair added, "Those people who fear unilateralism should realize that the quickest way to get that is to set up a rival polar power to America." The prime minister did not oppose a stronger Europe "more capable of speaking with a unified force," but he clarified that that did not mean setting itself in opposition to the United States.[24]

•••

The existing transatlantic differences did not stem merely from the disagreements in the UN Security Council over the Iraq war. There were deeper causes behind the transatlantic controversy, and also behind the intra-European dispute regarding the relationship with Washington.

With the end of the Cold War, opposing perspectives arose in Europe about how to relate to the United States. There was a beneath-the-surface struggle between "Atlanticists" and "Gaullists": an integrated Europe cautious about the degree of national power to be yielded to the European Union and allied with the United States versus a united Europe creating its own defense structure and forces, with a common foreign policy and independent from the United States.

The vanishing of the Soviet threat with the fall of the Berlin Wall naturally loosened the tight transatlantic alliance symbolized in NATO. As a result, Europe intensified its own economic and political integration, viewing its role—at least in the French-German perspective—as a counterweight to the sole remaining superpower in the post–Cold War era. The end of the Cold War meant, for the first time since 1950, that Washington no longer worried about European integration. U.S. high officials now saw Western Europe as economically stagnant, as being in demographic decline, and as militarily irrelevant.

For some, the divide between the United States and Western Europe had become much deeper. Neoconservative thinker Robert Kagan discards outright the notion that "Europeans and Americans share a common view of the world." Europe is "turning away from power," he says, and moving toward a "self-contained world of laws and rules and transnational negotiation and cooperation." In the meantime, he believes, the United States focuses on the exercise of "power in an anarchic Hobbesian world where international laws and rules are unreliable, and where true security and defense and promotion of a liberal order still depend on the possession and use of military might." Between Americans and Europeans, there is only agreement on their present disagreement: they no longer share a common strategic culture. The problem today—if this is a problem, according to Kagan—is that "the United States can 'go it alone' ... [But] for the Europeans, the UN Security Council is a substitute for the power they lack."[25]

In September 2003, during the opening session of the UN General Assembly, the differences between the United States and Western Europe, as symbolized by France, were more than evident. Bush said that there was no "neutral ground" in the "clearest of divides—between those who seek order and those who spread chaos," and he then explained the objectives for Iraq: "The primary goal of our coalition in Iraq is self-government for the people of Iraq, reached by an orderly and democratic process. That process must unfold accordingly to the needs of Iraqis, neither hurried nor delayed by the wishes of other parties." Bush's speech was applauded politely by a full chamber of the General Assembly.

Later, it was President Chirac's turn. He stated that the UN had "just emerged from one of the most serious challenges in its history. Respect for the charter and the use of force were at the heart of the debate. The war, which was launched without the Security Council's authorization, has undermined the multilateral system." He went on as everyone listened in deep silence: "In an open world, no one can live in isolation, no one can act alone in the name of all, and no one can accept the anarchy of a society without rules. There is no alternative to the United Nations. ... In Iraq, the transfer of sovereignty to the Iraqis is essential. ... It is up to the United Nations to lend its legitimacy to that process." It was a pristine multilateralist response to Bush's discourse. When Chirac ended, the General Assembly crowd erupted in an ovation.

Relations between the United States and Europe did not improve until much later. Signals of cordiality emerged in a featured cover interview with President Bush in the weekly magazine *Paris Match* in which he stated that he had "never been angry at the French. France has been a longtime ally." Asked about the statement one year before that Chirac would not visit his Texas ranch soon, Bush responded, "If he wants to come and see cows, he's welcome to come out here and see some cows." Bush was probably unaware that the French president, as a former minister of agriculture, was an expert in cows. In fact, Chirac owned a country house in a farming community in Corrèze and was known to enjoy inspecting cows at agricultural fairs. Hence, when he was told about Bush's remarks during an NBC interview, the French president responded, "It is obvious that if the president invites me to his ranch, I will go with pleasure, gladly, especially since I seem to have understood that he raises cows."[26]

In 2004, President Chirac had given his own initial signals of reconciliation when at a news conference at the Elysée he remarked that he had never been angry at Bush, despite their "divergence of views" on Iraq. On June 5, 2004,

President Chirac hosted a dinner for Bush at the Elysée Palace; it was what many considered a "reconciliation encounter." The next day, Bush, Chirac, and other heads of government gathered at Normandy for the commemoration of D-Day.

European-American relations improved in the wake of President Bush's February 2005 European "listening tour," a visit preceded by Secretary Rice's ice-breaking European trip. During a speech in Brussels on February 21, 2005, Bush declared that in "a new era of transatlantic unity" the United States and Europe should work together to rebuild Iraq, seek peace in the Middle East, and impede Iran from developing nuclear weapons. That evening, Bush had dinner with President Chirac. The U.S. president stressed that this, his first dinner on European soil since being reelected, was with the French president. When President Bush was asked by a journalist if he now would invite the French president to his Texas ranch, Bush dodged the question.

By going to Brussels, President Bush more importantly, signaled that the European Union, and not only select European powers, was considered a negotiating partner. The new climate of U.S.–European relations was strengthened by their common approach to Ukraine's popular uprising in 2005, which evolved into a transition to democracy in that country, and by the cooperation between France and the United States over Lebanon.

It was clear that the presidents of France and the United States had arrived at the mutual conclusion that they had to work together on Iraq. As for Washington, it had not only reversed its course regarding France and other European allies as well as the UN, it did so in relation to NATO. After 9/11, NATO had ceased to be the locus for transatlantic security consultations and coordination, a trend further affected by the United States' deep differences with European powers such as France and Germany over the Iraq war. The uses for what the Bush administration considered outdated multilateral institutions were very limited when considering the flexibility of the "coalitions of the willing." NATO had been dismissed as an insignificant institution in the unilateralist mood following the invasion. But at the G-8 summit on Sea Island, Georgia, in June 2004, President Bush and Prime Minister Blair discussed the possibility of a greater NATO involvement in Iraq. At the closing of the summit, Bush commented, "I do not expect more troops from NATO to be offered up." But he then added that "what we are suggesting is for NATO perhaps to help train." A few days later, at the NATO summit in Istanbul on June 28, the Iraqi forces training deal was officially approved.

At the Istanbul meeting, Bush decided that it was time to mend differences with the host country. Tensions with Turkey had risen after its parliament's refusal to permit American troops to pass through its territory for the Iraq invasion. Bilateral relations reached their lowest point when Deputy Secretary of Defense Wolfowitz criticized the Turkish armed forces for not delivering on their commitment of support, and even called on Turkey to apologize for the parliamentary decision. Bush now extended the country an olive branch by publicly advocating for the start of talks on the accession of Turkey into the European Union. In turn, President Chirac responded that the American president had no business interfering in what was a European matter.

American-European differences would linger on, as demonstrated by the November 2005 transatlantic tension over allegations of secret CIA renditions of terrorism suspects and their transfer to detention camps on European soil and over the proposed use of military force to stop Iran's nuclear development program.

...

The inaugurations of center-right leader Angela Merkel as Germany's chancellor in November 2005 and of conservative Union of Popular Movement Party candidate Nicolas Sarkozy as president of France in May 2007 were well received in Washington. Both were new leaders, moderate conservatives, and friendly toward Washington. But on Iraq, their policies did not change significantly.

President Sarkozy, a declared admirer of America—who even spent a two-week vacation in U.S. territory during his first summer holiday—made an extraordinary about-face in France's approach to the United States, reflected in a highly visible and warm visit, in November 2007, to meet with Bush at the White House and Mount Vernon and to address a joint session of Congress, where he received a standing ovation. President Sarkozy charmed Washington by pledging continued support for the United States in Afghanistan, agreeing with the American stand on the Iran nuclear issue, and promising to resume a full military role in NATO. But on Iraq, differences remained, as Sarkozy had made clear previously during a gathering with the diplomatic corps in Paris, in August 2007. "France was and remains hostile [to the American war in Iraq]. History proved us right," Sarkozy said. He added, supporting his predecessor Jacques Chirac, "It is clear now that the unilateral use of force leads to failure." The French president asserted that "to be an ally does not mean alignment, and I feel perfectly free to express our disagreements, without complacency or taboos." With the frankness that characterizes him, Sarkozy demanded a concrete deadline for the withdrawal of troops from Iraq and described the Middle Eastern nation as one "that is falling apart in a merciless civil war."[27]

Likewise, German chancellor Merkel announced the day after her inauguration that her government would not change her predecessor Gerhard Schroeder's policy of refusing to become involved militarily in Iraq. In a visit to the NATO headquarters, Merkel stated: "We made it clear that we will continue not to take part in training inside Iraq, but that we will continue to conduct training in neighboring countries. So there will be continuity with the previous policy."

When Angel Merkel visited President Bush at the White House on January 13, 2006, the American president admitted that in his talks with the German leader, there had been "disagreements." "It's been a difficult issue in our relationship and I fully understand that. But in spite of disagreements, we share the desire for the Iraqi people to live in freedom. I want to thank the German government for help with reconstruction," Bush said. An editorial in *The Wall Street Journal* online observed that the German chancellor had "mostly changed the tone of the Schroeder foreign policy. Yet, minus his anti-American posturing, much remains the same today. Berlin's position on Iraq is unchanged."[28]

Despite the political affinities between Washington and the new leaders in Paris and Berlin, Iraq continued to be a highly divisive transatlantic issue.

Less-Than-Willing Allies and the Failed Evidence to Go to War
Not only trusted allies were alienated because of the Iraq war. Also shunned were those that, having joined the "coalition of the willing," eventually withdrew or reduced their

forces from the ground. The war in Iraq remained a highly controversial issue for most countries throughout the world.

When the premise for the use of force against Hussein—that he possessed, or was actively seeking to produce, WMD—proved false, disappointment spread among the few allies with troops on the ground, causing them domestic political problems.

Some of America's staunchest allies, such as Poland, diminished their military presence, precisely because of the false evidence regarding WMD in Iraq. Polish president Aleksander Kwaśniewski stated in 2004 that he felt "misled" by the Bush administration in terms of evidence of illicit weapons of mass destruction: "Naturally, one may protest the reasons for the war action in Iraq," the Polish president said. "I also feel uncomfortable due to the fact that we [Poland] were misled with the information on WMD." By 2007, only 900 Polish troops remained in Iraq from the 2,350 that it had in 2004.

The strongest expression of the Bush administration's belief in Iraq's WMD was Secretary of State Colin Powell's memorable February 5, 2003, presentation to the UN Security Council. Later, Powell recognized that the "sourcing" for much of the information for that presentation "was inaccurate and wrong and in some cases misleading." In September 2005, Powell told Barbara Walters in an interview that the Security Council speech had been a painful moment that would be a permanent blot on his record. On the other side of the Atlantic, former Spanish president José María Aznar, a strong supporter of the Iraq invasion, admitted in early 2007 that there were no WMD in Iraq, adding that he had not been "smart enough to have known that earlier."

A defining moment on the polemic was the release of

the U.S. Senate Select Committee on Intelligence report, a 511-page hard-hitting, unanimous document that concluded there had been a "global intelligence failure" by the CIA and other U.S. agencies to accurately assess Iraq's WMD. The intelligence community's evaluation of Hussein's alleged possession of WMD had not only turned out to be "wrong," the Senate report said, but it was "also unreasonable and largely unsupported by the available intelligence," according to Republican senator Pat Roberts, the committee's chairman.

A British report coincided with the U.S. Senate's Select Committee on Intelligence investigation. Lord Butler's report evaluating British intelligence used to justify participation in the Iraq war found no evidence that Saddam Hussein had significant, or any, stocks of chemical or biological weapons before the war or that Iraq had cooperated with Al Qaida. On the other hand, the report found "no evidence to question [Prime Minister Blair's] good faith" and no "deliberate attempt on the part of the government to mislead." The disclosure, in June 2005, of a 2002 British official memo portraying the Bush administration as obsessed on war with Iraq and unprepared for post-invasion problems caused considerable tension between London and Washington.

The presidential commission on Iraq's WMD concluded in a scathing report, published in 2005, that American intelligence agencies had been "dead wrong" in most of their judgments before the war about Iraq's WMD, that President Bush had received "flawed intelligence briefings," and that even now, those agencies responsible for the briefings knew "disturbingly little" about WMD threats to the United States. The panel thus recommended a major overhaul of the U.S. intelligence community. In the end, the most damaging fact was that American inspectors had found no WMD anywhere in Iraq, thus confirming the caution, and even skepticism, shown by many in the United Nations.

Another reason behind the U.S. intervention in Iraq was the supposed link between the Hussein regime and Al Qaida. Yet CIA director George Tenet—who resigned in 2004—disclosed that, in August 2002, senior Pentagon officials had briefed aides of President Bush and Vice President Cheney with disputed evidence of ties between Iraq and Al Qaida. Cheney had assured the public that "there was a relationship between Iraq and Al Qaida that stretched back through most of the decade of the nineties, that it involved training, for example, on biological weapons and conventional weapons, that Al Qaida sent personnel to Baghdad to get trained on the systems that are involved. The Iraqis provided bomb-making expertise and advice to the Al Qaida organization."

Three days later, President Bush seemed to contradict Cheney when he affirmed, "No, we've had no evidence that Saddam Hussein was involved with September 11." The debate that ensued was focused on the difference between a "relationship" between the terrorist movement and Iraq, and a concrete linkage to the 9/11 attacks.

On June 16, 2004, a staff report by the 9/11 Commission concluded that there was "no credible evidence" that the Saddam Hussein government had collaborated with the Al Qaida terrorist network on any attacks against the United States and that a purported April 9, 2001, meeting between an Iraqi intelligence officer and Mohamed Atta, leader of the 9/11 hijackers, never occurred, thus contradicting statements made only days before by Cheney that Iraq had "long-established ties" with Al Qaida. A day later, in a CNBC television interview, the vice president said that there was a "general relationship" between Iraq and Al Qaida and he "probably" had information that the 9/11 Commission had not seen. The commission's reply was a one-sentence declaration issued by Chairman Thomas H. Kean and Vice Chairman Lee H. Hamilton of the bipartisan commission: "After examining available transcripts of the vice president's public remarks, the 9/11 Commission believes it has access to the same information the vice president has regarding contacts between Al Qaida and Iraq prior to 9/11 attacks."

The voluminous final report of the National Commission on Terrorist Attacks upon the United States (567 pages), issued in 2004 after a nineteen-month investigation, exposed the failures of the intelligence agencies to prevent the 9/11 attacks. Furthermore, the document revealed that Deputy Secretary of Defense Wolfowitz and Undersecretary of Defense Douglas J. Feith had written memos to Secretary Rumsfeld on the days following 9/11 arguing that Iraq should be hit because of the assumed ties between Al Qaida and Saddam Hussein. (Feith resigned his post before Bush was inaugurated to his second presidential term; Wolfowitz became president of The World Bank, but was forced to resign in June 2007 over an ethics controversy.) The report also dismissed the allegation that one of the masterminds of the 1993 attack on the World Trade Center was an Iraqi agent.

In 2007, the link between Al Qaida and Iraq was reaffirmed by the Bush administration. According to the president, Al Qaida in Iraq had become the principal cause behind the country's severe violence. He referred to Al Qaida "as the same people" responsible for the 9/11 attacks. However, American military officers on the ground identified Shiite militias as potentially "the longer term threat to Iraq."[29]

The role of Vice President Cheney in the Iraq debate came

under increasing fire from late 2005 onward, as his chief of staff, I. Lewis Libby Jr., was indicted by a special prosecutor, and charged with obstruction of justice, perjury, and making false statements in the leak of a CIA operative's name. She was married to an American diplomat opposed to the Iraq war. Libby, later found guilty of the charges, was the author of a controversial memo for Powell's presentation on WMD before the Security Council. Powell had rejected the memo for exaggerating the accusations against Hussein.

The contrasting perspectives over the connection between Iraq, WMD, and Al Qaida led to deep differences between the United States and its allies. The final evidence not only confirmed the allies' doubts, it created a feeling of bitterness about the divisiveness resulting from the Iraq war and a sense of frustration about the missed opportunities for a peaceful outcome.

•••

Toward the end of 2004, Spain made a radical shift in its Iraq policy, withdrawing its thirteen hundred soldiers as a consequence of a change of government. In March 2004, the Spanish-American alliance over Iraq had broken after the election of Socialist candidate José Luis Rodríguez Zapatero as president of the government. Aznar's party's candidate was defeated days after the biggest terrorist attack in Europe, when, on March 11, three separate trains in Madrid were hit by explosions that killed nearly two hundred people and injured more than fifteen hundred. Some argued that terrorists had influenced the elections by playing on the antiwar sentiment. Actually, it would appear that Spaniards turned out en masse to the polls because they felt the Aznar government had misled them about who was really responsible for the terrorist attack. Foreign Minister–designate Miguel Ángel Moratinos denounced in an op-ed in *The Wall Street Journal* "the irresponsible manner in which Prime Minister José María Aznar handled the flow of information to the public [which] only reinforced the people's electoral inclinations."[30]

The new president, Rodríguez Zapatero, announced that the Spanish troops would be pulled out of Iraq. Vice President Dick Cheney accused Spain of abandoning the war on terrorism, and Secretary of Defense Rumsfeld inferred in a meeting with the new Spanish minister of defense, José Bono, that the troop withdrawal would be seen as an act of cowardice and an appeasement of terrorism. Bono rebutted this view, saying that it was a policy question, not one of cojones, which Spain, the minister added, indeed had.

Rodríguez Zapatero and President Bush had a phone conversation on the subject on Monday, April 19, 2004. It was brief and cold, lasting a mere five minutes. Bush told the new Spanish president that he was disappointed about the troop withdrawal. Rodríguez Zapatero answered that he understood Bush's position and respected it. Bush continued to complain, expressing that he viewed the decision as an untimely one, given the "difficult times" in Iraq. Rodríguez Zapatero replied that he could not go back on a promise, on a "commitment to the Spanish people," but that Spain was still an ally of the United States and "completely committed to the fight against terrorism." The end result of the conversation was that the United States had lost valuable troops and a staunch European ally.

The Rodríguez Zapatero–Bush dialogue put relations between the two countries on a less-than-lukewarm track. Many still recalled that President-elect Rodríguez Zapatero had candidly declared in mid-March 2004, "Mr. Blair and Mr. Bush must do some reflection and self-criticism. One cannot bomb a people by chance, one cannot lead a war with lies ... the war in Iraq was a huge disaster. It only generated more violence and hatred, and lessons have to be learned." Tensions remained high as Rodríguez Zapatero suggested in September 2004 that other countries with troops in Iraq should follow the Spanish example and withdraw their forces. The statement drew protests from Washington, including a strongly worded letter from Bush.

With a tone of amusement, Rodríguez Zapatero told the press an anecdote that symbolized the new directions of Spanish foreign policy. When he arrived at his new desk in the office of the president of the government, he said "there was [the] Spanish flag there ... but the EU flag has only been there for 24 hours." Spain "is going back to Europe," Rodríguez Zapatero declared. Aware of Tony Blair's close ties with Aznar, Rodríguez Zapatero noted that he had told the British prime minister on repeated occasions, "Tony, I'm going to beat those friends of yours, you know." On hearing this, Blair would look back at him in disbelief. After the elections, Rodríguez Zapatero told Blair the first time they met, "Tony, you see!" According to Rodríguez Zapatero, his British colleague retorted, "Well, I always liked you, really!"[31]

On September 13, 2004, Rodríguez Zapatero met with his counterparts from France and Germany, where he outlined Spain's intention to return to a more European-oriented foreign policy. Iraq was on the mind of the three European leaders when President Chirac said, "We have opened a Pandora's box in Iraq that we are unable to close." Rodríguez Zapatero later summarized the trilateral talks, picking up on Donald Rumsfeld's reference to the Old Europe by asserting that "the 'Old Europe' is as good as new."

Soon after leaving La Moncloa presidential palace, Aznar went on a visit to America. In California, he had an interview with actor and governor Arnold Schwarzenegger. He wound up privately meeting with President Bush and Colin Powell at the White House on May 17. White House press secretary Scott McClellan declined to comment on the conversation, stating only, "Mr. Aznar is a good friend of the president, but now he is a private citizen; he is the former president of Spain, and I will make no further comments." Moreover, during his stay in Washington, Aznar held an unusual meeting for a former head of government: he met with Defense Secretary Rumsfeld at the Pentagon.

When in November 2004 President Bush again invited José María Aznar to the White House for a private forty-minute talk, it provided yet another demonstration of how official ties had deteriorated between Spain and the United States, for Bush had yet to return President Rodríguez Zapatero's courtesy call congratulating him on his reelection victory.

A visit by King Juan Carlos to President Bush at his Crawford ranch in late November 2004 did soften bilateral tensions. But Spain was excluded from Secretary of State Condoleezza Rice's European tour in February 2005 and President Bush's "goodwill" European visit a few days later. An attempt on February 22 to materialize a formal meeting between Rodríguez Zapatero and Bush in Brussels failed and ended up being limited to a seven-second greeting. Though ministerial-level contacts continued, in October 2005, the American ambassador in Madrid declared that a possible meeting between Bush and Rodríguez Zapatero was not "in the agenda," adding that bilateral ties were "dialogue-oriented" rather than "strong."

In 2005, U.S.–Spanish relations suffered a new setback over Madrid's sale of weapons to the Hugo Chávez government in Venezuela. According to the Spanish authorities, the sale, for U.S. $1.8 billion, involved reconnaissance and transport aircraft as well as coastal patrol vessels, which are not considered combat material. But the Bush administration eventually vetoed the transfer of American technology components in the planes to be purchased by Venezuela. To make things worse, in November 2005 a new polemic broke out between Washington and Madrid after it was made public that the CIA could have used Spanish airports to transport suspected terrorists without the knowledge or consent of the Rodríguez Zapatero government. The controversy diminished in 2006 once the Spanish government reported that it was convinced that the American flights had not violated any law. In June 2007, U.S. Secretary of State Rice visited Madrid and had a cordial conversation with President Rodríguez Zapatero. A formal Bush–Rodríguez Zapatero meeting, however, was still pending.

The frosty state of relations between the two countries certainly was, in large part, due to the withdrawal of Spanish troops from Iraq. But those ties failed to be positively affected by the fact that President Rodríguez Zapatero contributed more than five hundred troops to Afghanistan to provide security for the October 2004 presidential elections and had sent forces to assist in the stabilization of Haiti, a Caribbean country important to the United States. In June 2007, Secretary Rice recognized that "Spain has done a lot of good work in Afghanistan."

After Spain, Honduras followed suit and withdrew its 370 troops. The Dominican Republic also ended its deployment of 302 forces; the Philippines withdrew its 90 troops ahead of schedule, on July 19, 2004; Nicaragua pulled out its force of 115 troops in February 2004; and Thailand recalled its 880 troops in late August 2004. Acting in a similar fashion, Singapore reduced its contingent of troops first from 191 to 33 and then fully withdrew them in March 2005; and three countries—Norway, New Zealand, and Kazakhstan—withdrew their military engineers. Other countries, including Portugal, Ukraine, the Netherlands, Slovakia, Bulgaria, and Hungary, executed complete withdrawals of their forces from Iraq during 2005 and 2006.

Even some countries that did not send forces to Iraq but had joined the "coalition of the willing" requested to opt out. Just about the time President Bush thanked "the soldiers of many nations who have helped to deliver the Iraqi people from an outlaw dictator" in his September 2004 speech to the UN General Assembly, Costa Rica asked to exit the U.S.–led coalition, since its highest court had ruled it illegal to support military action not authorized by the UN. Costa Rican president Abel Pacheco explained, "The Court has ordered me to get [my] country's name off that list, and that's what I'm doing."

By 2007, even Australia's contribution to the war had become largely symbolic. After having sent two thousand combat troops in 2003, the Australians began their pullout in May 2003, dwindling troops to less than one thousand. In October 2004, the Australian government quietly refused a UN overture to contribute a military force to protect UN officials in Iraq. Foreign Minister Alexander Downer flatly declared, "We don't have any intention of sending more troops" to Iraq. The November 2007 defeat of John Howard, Australia's prime minister, at the hands of Labor Party leader Kevin Rudd, announced significant changes in foreign policy. Incoming prime minister Rudd, a former diplomat, stated unequivocally after his victory that, though Australia would remain a U.S. ally, he intended to push for the ratification of the Kyoto Protocol on global warming, pay more attention to the UN, and withdraw Australia's 550 combat troops from Iraq, leaving a small support force on the ground to protect the embassy compound in Baghdad and perform other logistics chores. According to observers, Australian prime minister Howard's staunch backing of the Iraq war and of President Bush had contributed to his electoral downfall.

In November 2005, during President Bush's visit to Seoul in the context of an APEC leaders summit, the South Korean government announced that it was pulling out one thousand troops stationed in Erbil, thus reducing its contingent in Iraq to twenty-six hundred, still remaining the third largest force after the United States and Great Britain. The Korean troop reduction decision was particularly hard for the White House because it was made public during President Bush's official visit, and because it came in the midst of a heated debate in Washington about the withdrawal of U.S. troops from Iraq. By 2007, South Korea had only fifteen hundred troops deployed in Iraq.

Japan, a staunch supporter of the U.S. invasion of Iraq, deployed troops on the ground between 2004 and 2006. But by 2007, Tokyo had withdrawn all its forces, providing only logistical support for the U.S.–led operation. Italy, another initial strong supporter of the war, pulled out all its troops from Iraq by the end of 2006.

The European and Latin American allies on the UN Security Council that did not support the Iraq invasion suffered some cold-shoulder treatment and even some aggressive conduct from the White House. This changed as the Bush administration needed its reticent allies to help cope with an increasingly chaotic ground situation in Iraq and as the political costs of the war to the United States began to rise.

Reflecting on the question of America's allies in Iraq, author and political scientist Francis Fukuyama wrote that while the behavior of Germany and France in actively opposing the war was "deeply disappointing," the quality of some of the U.S. partners in Iraq was equally disappointing. Fukuyama concluded that, in the end, the United States needs "like-minded allies to accomplish both the realist and idealist portions of [its] agenda and should spend much more time cultivating them."[32]

Chapter Six

Conclusions: The U.S. War Backtrack
and the Future of Multilateralism

The Costs of a War without Friends

The United States relied on UN Security Council endorsement to confront Iraq in the Persian Gulf War of 1991, but it tossed aside multilateralism in its pursuit of Saddam Hussein in 2003, only to re-embrace it later in the chaotic wake of the Iraq war. The return to the UN was a tactical decision forced by a military conflict gone wrong. War is always about attaining political objectives at acceptable costs, and what the Iraq case demonstrated was that the United States had incurred heavy costs without securing the ambitious political goals that it had sought.

The United States has lost considerable ground in the world since the Iraq invasion. The terrorist attacks against the World Trade Center and the Pentagon generated a widespread outburst of solidarity and support for the American people and their government. But that political capital was eroded, initially by the international controversies over the way America began to conduct its war on terrorism and definitively by the deep international division over the Iraq invasion. The United States paid a significant price as a result of going to war without multilateral backing.

A gap has developed between how Americans perceive themselves and how the world sees them. There has been a marked decline of U.S. attractiveness worldwide, which has been reflected in numerous polls. Some dismiss such popularity drops as merely temporary. But, as in the aftermath of the Vietnam War, the attitudes could endure and become an obstacle to the pursuit of U.S. fundamental interests. According to a 2007 Marshall Fund survey, as compared to 2002, support for U.S. leadership in world affairs had plunged by 30 percent in Germany, 26 percent in Italy, 24 percent in Poland, 23 percent in the Netherlands, and even 22 percent in Great Britain. Overall, support for U.S. leadership, which was 64 percent across Europe in 2002, had declined to 36 percent in 2007. Worldwide anti-American sentiment may be difficult to reverse if the Iraq war drags on.

No country, especially the world's one superpower, needs to win popularity contests, but any nation going to war needs strong friends, willing allies, and the legitimacy of multilateralism. The irony of America's unrivaled military might is that it cannot solve many of the challenges of a complex world, one that is presently not following the U.S. lead.

In late 2007, well over four years after the invasion, the security situation in Iraq was still out of control. German prince Bernhard von Bülow's famous remark "One knows where a war begins, but one never knows where it ends" seems incredibly appropriate to Iraq. General John Keane, who served as the army's vice chief of staff during the invasion, told the House Armed Services Committee that the insurgency took the American military by surprise: "We did not see it coming and we were not properly prepared and organized to deal with it. Many of us got seduced by the

Iraqi exiles in terms of what the outcome would be."[1]

In August 2007, Defense Secretary Robert Gates candidly admitted that the United States had "underestimated the depth of the mistrust" and divisions among Iraq's political factions. Michael Ignatieff made a mea culpa that went much further. "The unfolding catastrophe in Iraq," he wrote, "has condemned the political judgment of a president. But it has also condemned the judgment of many others, myself included, who as commentators supported the invasion." According to the writer and member of Canada's Parliament, "the people who truly showed good judgment on Iraq predicted the consequences that actually ensued but also rightly evaluated the motives that led to the action. ... They labored, as everyone did, with the same faulty intelligence and lack of knowledge of Iraq's fissured sectarian history. What they didn't do was take wishes for reality."[2] Winston Churchill's remark about war comes to mind: "The statesman who yields to war fever must realize that once the signal is given, he is no longer the master of policy but the slave of unforeseeable and uncontrollable events."

Initially, President Bush expressed full confidence that the American-led forces would crush the nascent insurgency. "There are some who feel like the conditions are such that they can attack us [in Iraq]," he stated in July 2003. "My answer is, bring them on," dared the president. By the end of 2007, the number of American troops killed in Iraq approached thirty-nine hundred. Since the "Mission Accomplished" end-of-combat declaration of May 1, 2003, the number of dead soldiers exceeded thirty-seven hundred, almost twenty-five times those killed during the two-month combat operation period until victory was declared. United States military personnel wounded totaled more than twenty-eight thousand.

According to United Nations data, the rate of internally displaced Iraqis increased from one hundred forty-eight thousand between 2003 and 2005 to eight hundred thousand from 2006 up to early 2007, and 2 million civilians had fled Iraq seeking refuge in neighboring countries. As far as financial expenditures are concerned, in 2007, the Iraq war had surpassed—in 2008 dollars—the cost of the 1991 Gulf War ($88 billion, 90 percent offset by contributions of U.S. allies) and the Korean War ($456 billion), and 2008 year-end projections made it exceed the cost of the Vietnam War ($518 billion).[3]

Victory in removing Saddam Hussein from power was achieved at the expense of setbacks in the broader struggle for influence in the Muslim world, the postponement of the search for peace in the Israeli-Palestinian conflict, and at the cost of weakening the war against terrorism. In fact, according to the 2004 annual military report of the London International Institute for Strategic Studies, the war in Iraq increased the threat of terrorism, for it enhanced "jihadist recruitment and Al Qaida's motivation to encourage and assist terrorist operators." Moreover, the same report suggests that the Iraq war led to increased nuclear risk, as an overextended involvement in Iraq emboldened Iran and North Korea to resist Western pressures to rein in their nuclear aspirations.[4] It may be convincingly argued that the American invasion of Iraq without the UN blessing became a further justification for other nations—singled out by the United States as rogue states—to flout the norms and institutions of the world community.

The Economist summarized in late summer 2007 the dismal situation in Iraq as follows: "There were no WMD, the government is in chaos and the country is ravaged by violence. Under occupation Iraq has become both a recruiting-sergeant and a training ground for al-Qaida. The civilian death toll is contested, but almost certainly exceeds 100,000. More than 3,700 American soldiers (and nearly 300 other coalition soldiers) have died. The serious debate is therefore not between victory or defeat but over how to mitigate the consequences of a disaster that has already taken place."[5]

As American casualties rose, the patience of the American public and congressional leaders seemed to be wearing increasingly thin. "How long a war?" growing numbers of Americans asked, while even Republican members of Congress demanded that the Bush administration set a specific exit strategy for Iraq.

The Bush administration rejected several plausible compromises offered by its closest allies to disarm Iraq. One consequence was that many countries important to the United States refused to provide troops to the war effort, while several others actually withdrew or reduced their forces from the ground. The allies, ignored or rejected when they proposed alternatives to the war, were later urged to help when the war unraveled. The problem was that the divisions and mistrust lingered on, beyond the events in Iraq. An American observer lamented, "Countries that would once have supported American foreign policy on principle, simply out of solidarity or friendship, will now have to be cajoled, or paid, to join us."[6]

Even the patience of the staunchest U.S. allies ran out. By late 2007, key initial supporters of the U.S. invasion, including Japan, Australia, Italy, South Korea, and Poland, had either fully pulled out their troops from Iraq or considerably reduced the size of their forces on the ground.

Great Britain, which had sent forty thousand troops to Iraq in 2003, had drawn down its contingent to forty-five hundred toward the end of 2007. Furthermore, Prime Minister Gordon Brown had announced that he would withdraw half of the remaining troops by the spring of 2008, strongly suggesting that all British soldiers could leave Iraq at the end of 2008. Brown, unlike his predecessor Tony Blair, was keeping his distance from President Bush on Iraq and other foreign policy issues and also shifting away from the close personal camaraderie between Blair and Bush in favor of a more "businesslike approach." In the meantime, the most senior British military officer dealing with postwar planning stated in September 2007 that American policy in Iraq was "fatally flawed."[7] For one observer, Great Britain's "glide path out of Iraq" under Prime Minister Brown was oriented to fight 2008 parliamentary elections "free of the political burden of an unpopular war."[8]

In Europe, while a few U.S. allies tried to collaborate with Washington to bring the Iraq war to an acceptable conclusion, most governments continued to believe that the war was, according to specialists' perceptions, "a great mistake that has only stirred up a hornet's nest, and that [the Europeans'] basic interest is, in any case, to minimize the chances that Islamist networks will try to commit terrorist acts on their territory." In short, "most Europeans now believe that it has become dangerous to be America's ally."[9]

In December 2006, the bipartisan Iraq Study Group concluded in its final report, sent to President Bush, that circumstances in that country were "grave and deteriorating" and recommended "new and enhanced diplomatic and political efforts in Iraq and the region, and a change in the primary mission of U.S. forces in Iraq that will enable the United States to begin to move its combat forces out of Iraq responsibly." The bipartisan group found it indispensable to "immediately launch a new diplomatic offensive to build an international consensus for stability in Iraq and the region."

A Changing Attitude toward the United Nations

Since unilateralism in the form of a "coalition of the willing" proved insufficient at achieving success in Iraq, the White House administration went from accusing the UN Security Council of irrelevance to entrusting it with the authority to lead the delicate negotiations for transferring sovereignty to an interim government, one chosen largely by UN envoy Lakhdar Brahimi. Paul Wolfowitz, in a June 9, 2004, *Wall Street Journal* op-ed piece, recognized the "critical role" played by the UN in helping the United States in Iraq.[10] In contrast, in April 2003, Wolfowitz had dismissed any significant role for the UN in Iraq. Arthur Schlesinger described the situation bluntly: "Once the going got tough in Iraq, the Bush administration tried to dump the mess of its own making on the United Nations, heretofore an object of contempt in Bush's Washington."[11]

Looking back, multilateral sanctions worked, since Hussein's illegal income was insufficient to finance nuclear, chemical, or biological weapons systems. But, as has been noted, "only when U.S. troops invaded Iraq in March 2003 did these successes become clear: the Iraqi military that confronted them had, in the previous twelve years, been decimated by the strategy of containment that the Bush administration had called a failure in order to justify war in the first place."[12] Hussein was not able to import nuclear, biological, or chemical weapons, although he managed to buy conventional weapons and components and to evade the sanctions by selling oil outside the UN's allowed Oil for Food program by smuggling it to neighboring countries.

The scandal over the Oil for Food program seemed, at times, a political payback tool directed at the United Nations for its refusal to support the American stand on Iraq. Despite the merits of the accusations against the UN, the amount of money skimmed by Saddam Hussein in the program through a system of bribes and kickbacks ($1.7 billion)— investigated by former chairman of the Federal Reserve Paul Volcker, leading an independent inquiry committee set up by then secretary general Koffi Annan—were insignificant compared to the huge sums generated by Iraq through the smuggling of oil out of the country, principally to Turkey and Jordan. This information, however, had been available to key members of the UN Security Council, including the United States, and was seen as the price tag for maintaining the sanctions in order to keep WMD out of Hussein's reach. According to the Volcker report, the value of oil smuggled outside of the program was estimated at nearly $11 billion, and more than two thousand companies from sixty countries were identified as paying illicit surcharges and kickbacks to Saddam Hussein. When the Oil for Food scandal broke out, I asked my defense attaché (who attended meetings of Security Council 661 Committee, which monitored the Iraq sanctions regime) if he had detected any irregularities in the Oil for Food program; he responded that access to information about the operation by nonpermanent members such as Chile was highly restricted. "The five permanent members are truly in charge, and they know perfectly well what has been going on," he told me.

Occurrences of waste, fraud, and corruption in Iraq went well beyond the Oil for Food program and affected the American occupation authority under Paul Bremer. In 2005, the special inspector general for Iraqi reconstruction, Stuart

Bowen, accused Bremer's administration of not properly monitoring the spending of $8.8 billion in Iraqi money. Bowen issued a report in late October 2005 stating that the United States had "no comprehensive policy or regulatory guidelines" in place for managing postwar Iraq, and also noting increases in costs of planned projects and "possible funding anomalies" in the Iraqi reconstruction effort. Several contracting fraud scandals came to light in 2007, prompting Defense Secretary Robert Gates to dispatch the Pentagon inspector general to Iraq to investigate a huge ring of fraud and kickbacks involving the building and operation of warehouses and the purchase of weapons, supplies, and other military materiel.

On a particularly ironic note, only *after* the U.S. invasion did potentially dangerous nuclear materials disappear from sites in Iraq; before the war, these materials had been systematically monitored by the UN International Atomic Energy Agency (IAEA). Specifically, the IAEA reported that large quantities of sophisticated equipment were looted and removed from Iraq after the invasion. On October 25, 2004, the president of the UN Security Council received a communication transmitted by Kofi Annan; in it, the director general of the IAEA reported that Iraqi authorities had informed him of the loss of tons of high explosives—some of which could be used to trigger nuclear devices—from the Quaqua munitions depot outside Baghdad "after September 4, 2003." This loss was the result of theft and looting "due to [the] lack of security," according to Iraqi officials.

John A. Shaw, deputy undersecretary of defense for International Technology and Security, declared that "almost certainly" Russian troops working with Iraqi intelligence had removed the explosives before the American invasion. Shortly thereafter, senior Pentagon officials reported that

Shaw's remarks were unfounded. *The Wall Street Journal* suggested that the timing of the explosives-removal story was the "UN's revenge" or a way "to have cast its vote in the [2004] U.S. presidential election."[13] But long after the presidential election, it was reported that about ninety sites for unconventional arms materials in Iraq—sites that the UN had monitored—had been razed or looted since the American-led invasion.

In the end, the UN returned to play a crucial role at the explicit request of the United States. During 2004 and 2005, President Bush repeatedly referred on national television to the negotiations of UN envoy Brahimi and to the UN electoral assistance team led by Carina Perelli, thanking Secretary General Kofi Annan for what the president underlined as "important work." In the wake of the successful January 30, 2005, Iraqi elections, organized by the United Nations, and in view of the key UN role in the elections in Afghanistan and Palestine, Washington had reappraised the usefulness of the world organization. One columnist put it rightly: "First Vieira de Mello, then Brahimi, and now the elections had demonstrated the UN's irreplaceable political capacities."[14]

Although the United States had walked away from the solitary road, it did not truly embrace multilateralism. It should be recalled that the Bush administration came into office with a negative sentiment about multilateralism, rejecting the Kyoto Protocol on global warming, the Anti–Ballistic Missile treaty, and the International Criminal Court. Resorting to the UN was a pragmatic decision based on need, not strategic commitment. It was a shift to tactical multilateralism. For the United States administration, unilateralist options remained open. In a sense, there was a return to the traditional, though weakened, American exceptionalism foreign policy behavior that accepts collective action but is always accommodating a go-it-alone posture when needed. Moreover, UN bashing would not go away easily. On March 23, 2005, Vice President Cheney stated in an interview aboard *Air Force Two* that "there is ample evidence here at home a great many Americans are not happy with the performance of the United Nations."

Koffi Annan and the UN faced harsh American criticism when, pressed by a reporter, the secretary general branded the U.S.–led war in Iraq as "illegal." Similarly, when he sent a letter to Colin Powell in October 2004, two days before the American presidential election, questioning an imminent U.S. attack on the city of Fallujah that, in the secretary general's view, could stiffen Sunni opposition to the Iraq transition process (Annan declined advice to phone Secretary Powell instead), the letter was leaked, creating a situation that was portrayed by anti–UN sectors as a move to favor Democratic candidate John Kerry. Throughout Ambassador John Bolton's period at the UN, the organization was the target of permanent and bitter attacks, ranging from the Iraq Oil for Food scandal to accusations of lack of substantial administrative reform. It seemed that Washington, once again, had little use for the United Nations.

Kofi Annan had once told President Bush, "Don't bash the UN, Mr. President; you'll find you need us later." On August 10, 2007, the UN Security Council extended for one more year the mandate of the United Nations Assistance Mission for Iraq. This time, however, the United States sought and was able to secure an expanded role for the UN in Iraq. According to *The Washington Post*, "The U.S. push for a broader UN role in Iraq underscores Washington's reliance on the United Nations to strengthen international support for the war." The Bush administration's overtures to the UN, manifested in two visits by Secretary General Ban Ki-moon to the White House during the first half of 2007, contrasted, in the view of *The Post*, "with the disdain it held for the organization in the past years."[15]

In sum, the United States retreated from the ideological conception that in 2003 assigned little, if any, role to the UN and that sought to replace it with alternative groupings or ad hoc coalitions. It was the recognition, according to a *Wall Street Journal* columnist, that "the U.S. cannot pursue all national security objectives unilaterally" and that "the UN still has a valuable trademark, international legitimacy, and latent potential that should not be undervalued."[16]

Why the United States Should Care about Multilateralism

During election time in the United States, the UN often becomes the target of criticism from some politicians. The 2008 presidential election was no exception.

Republican presidential hopeful Mitt Romney dismissed the UN as "an extraordinary failure" and refloated the post–Iraq invasion idea of a "coalition of free nations" as an alternative to the world organization. The former Massachusetts governor stated, "We should develop some of our own—if you will—forums and alliances or groups that have the ability to actually watch out for the world and do what's right."[17] Likewise, former New York mayor and Republican presidential hopeful Rudolph Giuliani—the only New York mayor to have ever addressed the UN General Assembly, following 9/11—wrote, "The UN has proven irrelevant to the resolution of almost every major dispute of the last fifty years. Worse, it has failed to combat terrorism and human rights abuses." Giuliani did recognize that the organization "could be useful for some humanitarian and peacekeeping functions."[18]

Democratic presidential hopeful Hillary Clinton was less critical of the UN, arguing that United States should view "international institutions [as] tools rather than traps." Clinton wrote, "After 9/11 the world rallied behind the United States as never before. ... We had a historic opportunity to build a broad global coalition to combat terror, increase the impact of our diplomacy, and create a world with more partners and fewer adversaries." According to Clinton, that opportunity was lost "by refusing to let the UN inspectors finish their work in Iraq and rushing to war instead."[19]

In a similar vein, unlike his fellow running mates, Republican hopeful Michael Huckabee wrote that the United States is presently "more vulnerable to the animosity of other countries" and suggested that "American foreign policy needs to change its tone and attitude, open up, and reach out." Huckabee affirmed that the Bush administration's arrogant bunker mentality has been counterproductive at home and abroad.

In the coming times, the United States should reflect on the way it exercises its power globally and on the role of the United Nations if it wishes to be more in sync with the agendas of the rest of the world. The world organization sometimes is slow to react to crises and other times it simply fails. But there is nothing better than the UN to confront today's global challenges and threats.

After 9/11, the United Nations responded immediately. On September 28, 2001, the Security Council approved resolution 1373 creating the Counter-Terrorism Committee, oriented, among other things, toward increasing the capacity of states to fight terrorism, promoting the adoption of laws and regulations to combat terrorism, and stimulating adherence of states to the UN conventions against terrorism. The Al Qaida and Taliban Sanctions Committee of the Security Council—one of the best examples of "targeted sanctions" on individuals and entities, instead of nations—was strengthened and expanded. And in 2004, the Security Council created the Committee on the Non-Proliferation of Weapons of Mass Destruction (or 1540 Committee) so as to restrict member states' ability to share WMD technology with non-state actors. The UN General Assembly, in turn, adopted a global counterterrorism strategy and plan of action, in September 2006, that became a major step to fight terrorism.

My experience as chairman of the Al Qaida and Taliban Sanctions Committee convinced me that much has been achieved by the UN in the combat of terrorism but that the effectiveness of current and future actions depends on the degree to which countries implement the agreed measures to fight terrorism. The UN is not to blame if more is not done in this regard. It is up to the states that make up the UN to fulfill their obligations. Evidently, the United States cannot combat terrorism alone, since this is not only a military task, but also a diplomatic, financial, social, and educational task.

The UN has contributed to saving lives in many parts of the world, with more than one hundred and ten thousand military personnel serving on eighteen peacekeeping operations. The UN is the world's largest military force deployed, after the U.S. armed forces, with successes such as Liberia, Sierra Leone, or Haiti to offset the failures of Rwanda and Bosnia.

The United Nations is a comparatively efficient and cost-effective force provider. A study by Oxford University economists concluded that international military intervention under Chapter VII of the UN Charter is the most cost-effective means of reducing the risk of violent confrontation in post-conflict societies.[21] Moreover, a report by the U.S. Government Accountability Office estimated that "it would cost the United States about twice as much as the United Nations to conduct a peacekeeping operation similar to the current UN Stabilization Mission in Haiti"[;] that is, $876 million compared to the UN cost of $428 million for the first fourteen months of the mission.[22] The Haiti UN operation is being led by Latin American countries providing the military forces, with no U.S. troops on the ground.

When a tsunami struck the Indian Ocean on December 2004 killing at least one hundred and fifty thousand people and destroying the livelihood of millions, the U.S. government convoked a group of nations in the region with available resources to get relief started. But one week later, when all involved came together in Jakarta to plan and coordinate the multilateral effort, everyone, including the United States, agreed that the United Nations was indispensable and should take the lead because it had the technical skills, and, moreover, it had the legitimacy: everyone was willing to work with the UN. Thus the UN Office for the Coordination of Humanitarian Affairs efficiently led the international efforts to assist the victims of the Asian tsunami, gaining worldwide praise for its contribution to provide relief and assistance.

In today's interdependent world, a threat to one becomes a menace to all, and no state can defeat these challenges and threats alone. In many respects, the United Nations has turned into an imperative, even for the United States.

In an era of easy air travel and unprecedented intercontinental personal contact, pandemic diseases threaten us all and can only be confronted multilaterally. During 1918 to 1919, the Spanish flu killed some 50 million people, of whom five hundred thousand were Americans. By contrast, when SARS respiratory syndrome hit the world in 2003, the UN World Health Organization led the global effort to fight back, with the result that only seven hundred people died because of the epidemic. Combating borderless threats such as avian influenza without international cooperation is useless since, increasingly, the lines between external and domestic problems are being erased.

Global warming is one of the most serious threats that the world faces. This phenomenon is a scientific certainty, and we know it is the result of human-caused emissions. The consequences of global warming are not just environmental; the phenomenon has economic, social, and security repercussions that we witness daily throughout the world. World leaders have agreed that, despite differences on how to respond to the challenge—through a combination of mitigation, adaptation, technology, and financing—negotiations among countries should take place in the United Nations under the auspices of the UN Framework Convention on Climate Change, which has now been ratified by 191 states.

But even in the case of Iraq—as argued in this book—the United States needs the United Nations. When the Washington-led coalition realized that it required an Iraqi body to help it run the country, it turned to the UN for assistance in creating the Iraqi Governing Council. Later, when the United States decided that it was time to transfer power to the Iraqis but did not have the political capacity to engage Iraqi forces, Washington turned again to the UN, this time to materialize that provisional government. Then the UN provided critical help in organizing the January 2005 elections, in drafting the electoral and political parties' law, in advising on the overall electoral process, and in drafting the new constitution.

The UN brought something that the American-led coalition did not have: legitimacy in the eyes of the Iraqis. Kofi Annan put it thusly in a 2005 op-ed: "Precisely because the United Nations did not agree on some earlier actions in Iraq today it has much needed credibility. ... The UN can be useful because it is seen as independent and impartial."[23]

Approaching 2008, the UN again appeared as a key component of the solution to an enduring Iraqi crisis. An August 2007 Security Council resolution decided that the UN Assistance Mission for Iraq would, among other things, assist with political dialogue, and national reconciliation; help with constitutional reform; collaborate with regional dialogue, including on issues of border security, energy, and refugees; facilitate humanitarian assistance; help improve Iraq's capacity to provide essential services; and promote the protection of human rights and judicial and legal reform. This was a qualitative and quantitative surge of the UN role in Iraq. An observer warned about the heightened UN involvement in Iraq: "If any outside intervener can help Iraqis regain peace and stability at this late date, it's probably the United Nations. But if Iraqis and the Arab world see the United Nations as simply a tool for achieving the Bush administration's agenda for Iraq, the UN will fail as miserably as Washington has failed."[24]

On September 22, 2007, on the sidelines of the General Assembly, a ministerial-level meeting involving Iraq and the "expanded neighbors" took place, including the permanent members of the Security Council, the G-8, the League of the Arab States, the European Union, major donors, and others. Participants strongly supported the United Nations' key role in advancing inclusive political dialogue in Iraq and the need to enhance regional cooperation for a more stable Iraq.

Secretary General Ban Ki-moon expressed in a report to the Security Council on October 15, 2007, that the UN was prepared "to do more" in Iraq "in an effort to advance an inclusive political dialogue in the resolution of internal boundaries issues." He added that the UN was ready to assist in areas ranging from constitutional review to reconstruction and development assistance. The UN had assumed a larger task that faced formidable obstacles in the deep divisions among Iraqi actors regarding such controversial issues as the sharing of oil revenues, the reintegration of former Baathists, the relationship of the federal government and the provinces, and the demobilization of militias.

"Why is the UN alarm suddenly being rung?" asked columnist James Traub in October 2007. It was, in his view, because "every other pathway, whether political or military, looks increasingly like a dead end. ... Even a profoundly stubborn White House may have come to see the virtues of international diplomacy."[25]

Beyond Iraq: To Lead or to Impose

The United States is the most powerful nation on the globe, and its leadership, or active participation, is vital to address the current international security challenges. But such recognition entails the responsibility not to impose its will on the world, but rather to lead through collective action, thus making its actions predictable and acceptable to the rest of the international community.

In the end, "power is the ability to influence others." And, as Joseph Nye stresses, that can be done with "sticks, carrots," and through the enticement of "values and culture." Soft power, or the power to attract, "could save a lot in blood and treasure." According to Nye, both soft and hard powers are necessary to succeed in Iraq and in other countries of the Middle East.[26]

Agreement is necessary on consensual and credible ways to confront the threat of WMD, particularly as regards potential access to them by terrorists, but also to find effective responses to other high-priority threats, including the so-called soft security threats, such as humanitarian crises that spill across borders, pandemic diseases, global warming, or civil strife rooted in complex causes.

American public attention seems to be moving past Iraq to focus on other foreign policy priorities, including the need for the United States to improve its standing in the world. According to findings from focus groups and a national survey by Public Opinion Strategies and Hart Research, presented in New York City at a November 2007 event of the UN Foundation and The Century Foundation, a new cluster of issues, such as improving America's relations with other countries, global warming, and dependence on foreign oil, are beginning to significantly concern American citizens.[27]

These emerging trends show that the United States should begin looking beyond Iraq to repair the international fallout caused by the war. The researchers read the following statement to those polled: "America cannot face all of its enemies or solve the world's problems alone. We need help. But to gain help, we have to work closely with other countries around the world. We need to share the burden and not be the sole supplier of resources, finances, military forces and diplomacy for peace in the world." Asked if they would be more likely or less likely to vote for a candidate who would advance such a message, 81 percent responded that they would be more likely, while only 7 percent answered they would be less likely. Moreover, 52 percent of respondents expressed that they would much more likely vote for a candidate espousing such a view.

Terrorism continues to be on top of the American voter concerns (38 percent), followed by the United States' dependence on foreign oil (33 percent), improving America's relations with other countries (27 percent), and environmental issues such as global warming (25 percent). But to face these problems, Americans now seem to agree that the United States cannot go it alone and that it needs international cooperation and global partnerships. There is also a sober recognition that the United States' image worldwide and relations with other countries, even allies, have deteriorated and require repair. (Those responding that the United States was less respected by other countries jumped from 67 percent in July 2004 to 78 percent in September 2007.)

We live in a unipolar world. While the United States is sole among nations in the magnitude of its power, its destiny nowadays is more deeply intertwined with that of other countries than ever before due to the growing globalization and flow of information, ideas, goods and services, crimes, pollution, and people across borders. Such challenges suggest that acting alone is not the best or most efficient way for a superpower to achieve results. The reliance on coercive policies and the unilateral use of force are not likely to provide effective or durable solutions to old and new security threats. In fact, American citizens want the United States to be a leader in the world but not a bully or a policeman, preferring partnerships according to the public opinion polling just cited.

A common argument in Washington is that unilateralism is often needed so that multilateralism will kick in. But actions bring about consequences, and unilateralist discourse and behavior leads to disputes and even opposition by allies, with effects difficult to predict. Furthermore, such argument ignores the central problems of unilateralism. Unilateralism lacks international legitimacy, can be inefficient for the purposes sought, carries a greater possibility of error as compared to multilateral action, and runs counter to the logic of collective action in a community composed of numerous and diverse member states. Not listening to allies and partners when collective action is needed subsequently causes alienation and reticence on the part of friends—friends who can even become adversaries of the policies pursued.

Legitimacy is sometimes intangible, but one knows it when one sees it. Certainly it emerges from compliance with the UN Charter, but it goes beyond that: legitimacy is constructed through cooperative actions, through the joint promotion of self-interest as well as the interests of others. American leadership shown through a concert of world powers will likely produce consent, even for complex actions, thus gaining legitimacy. The temptation to go it alone, to disregard world rules and act in opposition to consensual approaches, will lead inescapably to lack of legitimacy.

Solitary action also can be inefficient and expensive. The neoconservative agenda of regime change would require not only long-term commitments, but also enormous resources. According to a Realpolitik view, the eventual overextension of U.S. capabilities through unilateral regime change and nation-building interventions could lead to battle fatigue and further world rejection. In addition, one may ask, could regime change be an option in cases of countries that possess WMD and that, for example, have tested nuclear weapons? Nations that already have WMD could escape regime change, as in the case of North Korea, where Washington has recognized the merit of the classic multilateral diplomatic approach. In this case, preventive diplomacy seems less dangerous and more realistic than preventive war.

The United States needs multilateral support and cooperation of allies where unilateralism simply will not work. Multilateral diplomacy initiatives by formerly estranged allies such as France and Germany—along with Great Britain—have played a key role in addressing Iranian nuclear development. Russia and China, in the six-nation talks, used their influence to seek, along with the United States, a freezing and dismantling of North Korea's nuclear arms program.

The lesson of Iraq is that American commitment to multilateralism ultimately benefits the United States as well as the rest of the world. Even tactical multilateralism, in the line of American exceptionalism, is much better than unilateralism. And from a realist perspective, perhaps the best that can be expected from Washington is instrumental or tactical multilateralism. According to one such view, "America's decision to cooperate in multilateral forums will be determined predominantly by the extent to which any specific organization is perceived by important U.S. domestic actors to be an effective and congenial vehicle for the promotion of America's objectives."[28]

The United States' attitude towards the UN cannot be defined through a sweeping characterization—at best, it may never be a full and unconditional commitment, but at worst, it may never reach a complete rupture with the organization. Yet some believe that, nowadays, to recuperate the international ground lost, what would be required is what Robert S. McNamara calls "genuine, as opposed to symbolic, multilateralism," which involves discarding notions such as that the UN is basically for "wimps." After Iraq, à la carte multilateralism may not be sufficient to regain a climate of trust and deep-seated commitment to international cooperation. If institutions are used only when they serve immediate practical goals—implicitly discounting some broader commitment to cooperation on any other term but one's own—they will be weakened.

Obviously, no country will exclude the possibility of acting alone or using force preemptively as a tool of last resort under truly exceptional circumstances. Former secretary general Kofi Annan reflected pragmatically on this challenge. "It is not enough to denounce unilateralism," he said, "unless we also face up squarely to the concerns that drive [countries] to take unilateral action. We must show that those concerns can, and will, be addressed effectively through collective action."

Yet a war of choice is quite different from a war of necessity. In the Iraq case, there was no serious and urgent threat to justify abandoning the normal constraints of international law. The employment of force must be a last-resource option, after nonmilitary means have been fully explored and exhausted. There is also the question of proportionality in the use of force to meet a threat. Moreover, elevating unilateral action or preventive strikes to a doctrine would not only go against international law, but also impede the possibility of building global governance. The use of force will simply not be effective in achieving the national interests of any single power if the issues concerned also affect the interests of other nations. The decision, in the end, is whether to create a predictable, cooperative world order, one based principally on prevention, dissuasive measures, and multilateral negotiations, with the UN at the center, or one based on the imposition of force.

There is much work to be done to achieve a more secure and stable world order, not least of all to complete the UN's institutional overhaul. To be feasible, a new, cooperation-based order would have to be seen as worthwhile and beneficial for all, one that certainly includes the most powerful nations. It would be naive to expect a stronger multilateral world without the United States behind this approach.

The United Nations does not have by itself the ability to lead; it is up to member states to play that role. For international cooperation to work, American commitment and leadership is a must. Multilateralism, evidently, cannot entail a veto power over America's pursuit of its own security, nor can it mean that others set aside their national interests to achieve consensus in favor of U.S. concerns and priorities.

In his book *After Victory*, about the attempts to establish international order by the victors of hegemonic struggles in 1815, 1919, 1945, and 1989, author G. John Ikenberry argues that even the strongest victor needs the willing cooperation of the defeated and other less-powerful states through an agreed-upon multilateral constitutional order. Ikenberry writes that if the United States "had not endeavored to build the array of regional and global institutions that it did in the 1940s, it is difficult to imagine that American power would have had the scope, depth, or longevity that it in fact has had. *International institutions can make the exercise of power more restrained and routinized, but they can also make that power more durable, systematic, and legitimate.* When American power holders bridle at the restraints and commitments that international institutions often entail, they might be reminded that these features of institutions are precisely what had made American power as durable and acceptable as it is today" (emphasis added).[29] In this same line, Morton

H. Halperin and Michael H. Fuchs observe that "a slow-moving UN Security Council or General Assembly is a small price to pay compared to the grave consequences of a world without an effective international forum for diplomacy, conflict resolution and action."[30]

History allows us to draw some useful lessons. The Romans in ancient times knew that unbound hegemony without allies and politics was doomed to failure, and, thus, during the best and most peaceful years of the empire, they combined domination with alliances. These are very different times. But the war in Iraq shows that military action does not suffice if it is not accompanied by substantial cooperation with friends and if it does not enjoy the multilateral legitimacy that the United Nations can provide. Today's challenge, therefore, is to move beyond Iraq to reconstruct international trust and global governance under a truly cooperative framework, where the United States will necessarily play a leading role.

Notes

Introduction

1. John Burns and Edward Wong, "Death of Hussein Aide Is Confirmed; Annan Visits Iraq," *The New York Times*, November 13, 2005, A10.
2. Zalmay Khalizad, "Why the United Nations belongs in Iraq," *The New York Times*, July 20, 2007, A23.

Chapter One: Early Warnings

1. George Bush and Brent Scowcroft, "Why We Didn't Go to Baghdad" in Micah L. Sifry and Christopher Cerf, eds., *The Iraq War Reader* (New York: Touchstone, 2003), 102.
2. James Mann, *Rise of the Vulcans: The History of Bush's War Cabinet* (New York: Penguin Books, 2004), 190–193.
3. Stephen Fidler, "A Test of Leadership," *Financial Times*, September 15, 2001, 14.
4. Barton Gellman and Dafna Linzer, "Afghanistan, Iraq: Two Wars Collide," *The Washington Post*, October 22, 2004, A1.
5. Brent Scowcroft, "Don't Attack Saddam," *The Wall Street Journal*, August 15, 2002.
6. Daniel Webster, quoted by Adam Roberts, "The Use of Force," in David Malone, ed., *The UN Security Council* (Boulder, CO: Lynne Rienner Publishers, 2004), 145.

7. Francis Fukuyama, "The Neoconservative Moment," *The National Interest*, Summer 2004, 63.

Chapter Two: War Games in the United Nations

1. William Kristol and Robert Kagan, "The UN Trap?" *The Weekly Standard*, November 18, 2002, 10–12.

2. Hans Blix, *Disarming Iraq* (New York: Pantheon Books, 2004), 74–80.

3. Quoted in CNN.com, April 3, 2004, and in *The New York Times*, April 3, 2004, A26.

4. Ashraf Khalil, "Arab Nations Deny Exile Proposal Brewing for Hussein," *Chicago Tribune*, January 11, 2003.

5. See "Acta de la Conversación entre George W. Bush y José María Aznar–Crawford, Texas, 22 de febrero de 2003," *El País*, September 27, 2007, 18–20. See also Ernesto Ekaizer, "Bush avisó a Aznar que estaría en Bagdad en Marzo con o sin Resolución de la ONU," *El País*, September 26, 2007, 18–19. The same day of the publication of the full text of the secret Spanish memo, on September 27, 2007, the White House refused to comment on the contents of the transcript of the Bush-Aznar dialogue. The White House press secretary asserted that the administration would not "comment on the details or talk about a private conversation between two world leaders and whether or not that happened."

6. Paul Heinbecker, "Canada Got It Right," *Globe and Mail*, March 19, 2004, A17.

7. David Sander and Felicity Barringer, "President Readies U.S. for Prospect of Imminent War," *The New York Times*, March 7, 2003.

8. Peter Stothard, *Thirty Days: Tony Blair and the Test of History* (New York: HarperCollins Publishers, 2003), 3–13.

9. Blix, *Disarming Iraq*, 248.

10. Stothard, *Thirty Days*, 20–21.

11. Richard Stevenson and Warren Hoge, "Threats and Responses,"

The New York Times, March 15, 2003.

12. Stothard, *Thirty Days*, 58–59. Also notes of the author in conversation with President Ricardo Lagos.

13. Bob Woodward, *Plan of Attack* (New York: Simon and Schuster, 2004), 342–345. This dialogue is also based on direct sources of the author.

14. Stothard, *Thirty Days*, 14.

15. Adolfo Aguilar Zinser, in *El País*, March 23, 2004.

Chapter Three: Unilateralism in Retreat

1. Richard Perle, "Thank God for the Death of the UN," *The Guardian*, March 21, 2003.

2. David Gelernter, "Replacing the United Nations," *The Weekly Standard*, March 17, 2003.

3. "Ulster Summit," *The Independent on Sunday*, April 6, 2003.

4. "UN Mustn't Obstruct New Iraq," New York *Daily News*, May 10, 2003.

5. "Views on Bush and the War," *Los Angeles Times*, April 5, 2003, A4.

6. "The UN and Iraq," *New York Post*, September 4, 2003, 28.

7. "A Bigger UN Role in Iraq," *The New York Times*, September 4, 2003.

8. "Wobbly on Iraq?" *The Wall Street Journal*, September 4, 2003, A18.

9. "Back to the United Nations," *The Washington Post*, September 4, 2003, A20.

10. Dana Milbank and Thomas Ricks, "Powell and Joint Chiefs Nudged Bush toward UN," *The Washington Post*, September 4, 2003, A1 and A12.

11. Steven Weisman and Felicity Barringer, "U.S. May Drop Attempt at Vote on Iraq in UN," *The New York Times*, October 8, 2003, A1 and A18.

12. *Newsweek*, November 30, 2003, 24–38.

13. Jeffrey Record, "Bounding the Global War on Terrorism," Strategic Studies Institute, U.S. Army War College, December 2003.

14. Charles Kupchen, quoted in Farah Stockman, "Annan Says UN to Help with Iraq Elections," *The Boston Globe*, January 28, 2004.

Chapter Four: Why Multilateralism Matters

1. Jean-Marie Colombani, "Are We Still All 'Americans'?" *The Wall Street Journal*, March 9, 2004.

2. "One Year After," *The New York Times*, March 19, 2004, A22.

3. "Sixty Years On," *The Economist*, June 5, 2004, 9.

4. "Il faut sortir de se trounoir qui est en passé d'aspirer le Moyen-Orient et, au-delà, le monde," *Le Monde*, May 14, 2004.

5. Ivo Daaler and Anthony Lake, "Transfer Power in Iraq to the UN and NATO," *The Financial Times*, May 13, 2004, 15.

6. Samuel P. Huntington in an interview with Federico Rampini, "Non possiamo vincere in Iraq è l'ora di ritirare le truppe," *La Repubblica*, May 17, 2004, 8.

7. "America Adrift in Iraq," *The New York Times*, May 15, 2004.

8. "Chalabi Reportedly Told Iran that U.S. Had Code," *The New York Times*, June 2, 2004, A1 and A19.

9. Howard LaFranchi, "Big Hurdles Loom with Handover," *The Christian Science Monitor*, May 24, 2004.

10. Steven Weisman, "Factions Jostle for Top Posts in a New Iraq," *The New York Times*, May 24, 2004, A1.

11. Farnez Fassihi, et al., "Early U.S. Decisions on Iraq Now Haunt American Efforts," *The Wall Street Journal*, April 19, 2004.

12. "The President's Speech," *The New York Times*, May 25, 2004, A24.

13. "A Framework for Iraq at Last," *Financial Times*, May 26, 2004, 14.

14. Interview in *El País*, May 18, 2004.

15. Alissa Rubin and Maggie Farley, "Iraqi Council Nominates a Prime Minister," *Los Angeles Times*, May 29, 2004, A10.

16. Robin Wright and Mike Allen, "Many Hurdles Ahead for U.S.," *The Washington Post*, June 2, 2004, A1.

17. "New Way Ahead" and "A Glimmer of Hope, At Last," *The Economist*, June 12, 2004, 14 and 43.

18. David Ignatius, "Bush's Lost Iraqi Election," *The Washington Post*, August 30, 2007, A21.

19. "An Iraqi Face at Last," *The Wall Street Journal*, June 29, 2004, A14.

20. L. Paul Bremer III, "How I Didn't Dismantle Iraq's Army," *The New York Times*, September 6, 2007, A13.

21. Elizabeth Bumiller and Jodi Wilgoren, "Bush Put on Defensive by Bremer's Remarks," *International Herald Tribune*, October 7, 2004. Bremer "clarified" his position in an op-ed piece where he only confirmed his disagreements with the administration on troop levels needed in Iraq. Bremer stated, "I had tactical disagreements with others, including military commanders on the ground. ... I believe it would have been helpful to have had more troops early on to stop the looting that did so much damage to Iraq's already decrepit infrastructure. The military commanders believed we had enough American troops in Iraq." Paul Bremer, "What I Really Said About Iraq," *International Herald Tribune*, October 9, 2004, 7.

22. Madeleine Albright, "How to Change Iraq: Bush Should Start by Admitting Fault," *The Washington Post*, June 9, 2007, A21.

23. Zalmay Khalizad, "Why the United Nations belongs in Iraq," *The New York Times*, July 20, 2007, A23.

Chapter Five: Worlds Apart

1. On this subject, see Michael Ignatieff, *American Exceptionalism and Human Rights* (Princeton, NJ: Princeton University Press,

2005). Also see Edward C. Luck, "American Exceptionalism and International Organizations: Lessons from the 1990s," in Rosemary Foot, Neil MacFarlane, and Michael Mastanduno, eds., *U.S. Hegemony and International Organizations* (New York: Oxford University Press, 2003). On the effects of the American war on terror on the image of the United States abroad before the Iraq war, see Edward C. Luck, "The U.S., Counter-Terrorism, and the Prospects for a Multilateral Alternative," in Jane Boulden and Thomas G. Weiss, eds., *Terrorism and the UN: Before and After September 11ᵗʰ* (Bloomington: Indiana University Press, 2003).

2. Testimony of J. Curtis Strubble, acting assistant secretary of state, WHA, House of Representatives, February 27, 2003.

3. Mary A. O'Grady, "Friends Don't Let Friends Fight Terror Alone," *The Wall Street Journal*, March 21, 2003.

4. Stephen Schlesinger, *Act of Creation: The Founding of the United Nations* (Boulder, CO: Westview, 2003), 93 and 100–101.

5. Bill Gertz, "Terrorists Said to Seek Entry to U.S. via Mexico," *The Washington Times*, April 7, 2003.

6. Vicente Fox, *Revolution of Hope* (New York: Viking, 2007), 281–290.

7. Paul Johnson, "Au Revoir, Petite France," *The Wall Street Journal*, March 18, 2003, A16.

8. William Safire, "Rewarding Freedom's Friends," *The International Herald Tribune*, May 18, 2003.

9. James Surowiecki, "A Clean Slate for Iraq," *The New Yorker*, April 16, 2003.

10. Edwin Truman, "The Right Way to Ease Iraq's Debt Burden," *Financial Times*, April 28, 2003.

11. *The Sunday Times*, quoted in *El País*, April 28, 2003, 6.

12. William Safire, "The French Connection," *The New York Times*, March 13, 2003.

13. Arian Campo-Flores, Kevin Peraino, and Mark Hosenball,

"Periscope," *Newsweek*, April 21, 2003.

. Tom Zeller, "Pssst … Can I Get a Bomb Trigger?" *The New York Times*, September 15, 2002.

. Barton Gellman, "Four Nations Thought to Possess Smallpox," *The Washington Post*, November 5, 2002.

. "France Gave Passports to Help Iraqis Escape," *The Washington Times*, May 6, 2003.

. Brian Knowlton, "France Protests 'Plot' by the U.S.," *International Herald Tribune*, May 16, 2003, 1 and 4.

. Alison Leigh Cowan, "French Exchange Students Get the Cold Shoulder," *The New York Times*, July 4, 2003, B6.

. Robert J. McCartney, "U.S., France Agree to Work on Trade Relationship," *The Washington Post*, June 17, 2003, A13. See also "The Dangers of War," *The Economist*, March 15, 2003, 60.

. Reuters, "Rice Quoted Saying U.S. to Ignore Schroeder," May 25, 2003.

. "The Pew Global Attitudes Project," The Pew Research Center, Washington, DC, March 16, 2004.

. Charles Grant, "Europe and America Put Off Their Divorce," *Financial Times*, July 23, 2003.

. Quentin Peel, et al., "The Plot That Split Old and New Europe," *Financial Times*, May 27, 2003.

. Interview with Tony Blair, *Financial Times*, April 28, 2003, 6.

. Robert Kagan, *Of Paradise and Power: America and Europe in the New World Order* (New York, Alfred A. Knopf, 2003).

. President Bush's red-carpet treatment afforded to close allies was to invite them for dinner and an overnight stay at his Prairie Chapel Ranch in Crawford, Texas. Included in this exclusive group were the leaders of Italy, Australia, Great Britain, Spain, Japan, and Russia.

. Elaine Sciolino, "French Leader Raises Possibility of Use of Force in Iran," *The New York Times*, August 28, 2007, A3. See also *El Mercurio*, August 28, 2007, A6.

28. "The Merkel Leadership Deficit," Opinion, www.wsj.com, November 11, 2007.

29. "U.S. Officials: Shiite Muslim Militias Are the Biggest Threat," *The Miami Herald*, August 3, 2007, 8A.

30. Miguel Ángel Moratinos, "Spain's New Course," *The Wall Street Journal*, March 30, 2004.

31. Interview with José Luis Rodríguez Zapatero in *The New York Times*, May 6, 2004.

32. Francis Fukuyama, "The Neoconservative Moment," *The International Interest*, summer 2004, 63 and 67.

Chapter Six: Conclusions

1. S. Hedges, "War Planners Did Not Expect Insurgency Says General," *Chicago Tribune*, July 16, 2004.

2. Michael Ignatieff, "Getting Iraq Wrong," *The New York Times Magazine*, August 5, 2007, 26.

3. ISN Security Watch, "U.S.: The Financial Costs of Warfare," Zurich, September 27, 2007, 2–3

4. See Reuter cable, "Iraq Has Increased Terrorist Risk: Report," October 19, 2004. See also Peter Spiegel and Mark Huband, "Iraq Conflict 'Has Led to Increased Nuclear Risk,'" *Financial Times*, October 20, 2004, 5.

5. "Briefing strategy in Iraq," *The Economist*, September 8, 2007, 28.

6. Anne Applebaum, "Why They Don't Like Us," *The Washington Post*, October 2, 2007, A19.

7. International Relations and Security Network Security Watch, "Brown Sets New Course for UK in Iraq," Zurich, September 25, 2007, 1–5.

8. "The Politics of Retreat," *The Economist*, October 13, 2007, 62.

9. Ronald Tiersky and Alex Tiersky, *Europe: A Year of Living Dangerously* (New York: The Foreign Policy Association, 2004), 19.

10. Paul Wolfowitz, "The Road Map for a Sovereign Iraq," *The Wall Street Journal*, June 9, 2004, 12.

11. Arthur M. Schlesinger Jr., *War and the American Presidency* (New York: W.W. Norton, 2004), 18.

12. George A. Lopez and David Cortright, "Containing Iraq: Sanctions Worked," *Foreign Affairs*, July–August 2004, 91.

13. "The UN's Revenge," *The Wall Street Journal*, October 29, 2004, 14.

14. James Traub, *The Best Intentions: Kofi Annan and the UN in the Era of American World Power* (New York: Farrar, Straus and Giroux, 2006), 299. On the UN role in Iraq, see also Stanley Meisler, *Kofi Annan: A Man of Peace in a World of War* (New York: John Wiley and Sons, 2007).

15. Colum Lynch, "Pressed by U.S., A Wary UN Now Plans a Larger Iraq Role," *The Washington Post*, August 8, 2007, A1.

16. Michael McFaul, "Turtle Bay Tango," *The Wall Street Journal*, October 14, 2003.

17. "Romey Backs 'Coalition of the Free' over UN," *Financial Times*, October 19, 2007, 5.

18. Rudolph Giuliani, "Toward a Realistic Peace," *Foreign Affairs*, September–October 2007, 14.

19. Hillary Clinton, "Security and Opportunity for the Twenty-First Century," *Foreign Affairs*, November–December 2007, 2 and 6.

20. Michael D. Huckabee, "America's Priorities in the War on Terror," *Foreign Affairs*, January/February 2008, online edition, 1.

21. Paul Collier and Anne Hoeffler, "The Challenge of Reducing the Global Incidence of Civil War," Center for the Study of African Economies, Department of Economics, Oxford University, March 26, 2004.

22. U.S. Government Accountability Office, "Peacekeeping Cost Comparison of Actual UN and Hypothetical U.S. Operations in Haiti," Report to the Subcommittee on Oversight and

Investigations, Committee on International Relations, House of Representatives, U.S. Government Accountability Office, 06-331, February 2006, 7.

23. Kofi Annan, "Our Mission Remains Vital," *The Wall Street Journal*, February 22, 2005, A14.

24. Jeffrey Laurenti, "The UN in Iraq—Handle with Care," The Century Foundation News and Commentary, www.tcf.org, July 27, 2007, 1.

25. James Traub, "The UN and Iraq: Moving Forward?" Policy Analysis Brief, The Stanley Foundation, October 2007, 1.

26. Joseph Nye, "America Needs to Use Soft Power," *Financial Times*, April 19, 2004.

27. Bill McInturff, Liz Harrington, and Geoff Garin, "The New International Consensus on International Cooperation: A Presentation of Key Findings from Focus Groups and a National Survey," Public Opinion Strategies and Hart Research study for the United Nations Foundation, New York, November 28, 2007.

28. Rosemary Foot, et al., "Conclusion: Instrumental Multilateralism in U.S. Foreign Policy," in Rosemary Foot, Neil MacFarlane, and Michael Mastanduno, eds., *U.S. Hegemony and International Organizations* (New York: Oxford University Press, 2003), 266 and 272.

29. G. John Ikenberry, *After Victory: Institutions, Strategic Restraint, and the Rebuilding of Order after Major Wars* (Princeton: Princeton University Press, 2000), 273.

30. Morton H. Halperin and Michael H. Fuchs, "The Pillar of the International System," Working Paper, The Stanley Foundation—After the Unipolar Moment Project, February 2007, 14–15.

Acknowledgments

I began writing this book soon after the invasion of Iraq by the United States and its allies, in early April 2003. At that time, I had left my position as minister secretary general of the government of Chile in the cabinet of President Ricardo Lagos. However, the book was interrupted when President Lagos requested that I accept the position of ambassador of Chile to the United Nations. As Chile was an elected member of the United Nations Security Council, it was an offer I could not refuse.

The hectic pace of the Security Council, focused on Iraq, impeded me from continuing with the book project. But in 2005, I decided to retake the effort, narrowing the focus to the circumstances surrounding the UN negotiations on Iraq in the run-up to the war and to the key developments that followed.

The book is based on episodes I personally experienced and on firsthand accounts by direct participants I interviewed. I made abundant use of primary sources such as UN documents, newspaper reports, governmental correspondence, and press releases. In a few instances, I consulted secondary sources such as books by journalists or key actors in relevant decision-making positions so as to confirm or reinforce my own data.

Here are personal views that do not necessarily reflect the views and positions of the Chilean government. This is a free scholarly exercise.

I am indebted to my literary agent, Scott Mendel, who stimulated me to persevere with this project, furnished valuable suggestions, and accompanied the long road from the writing up to the publication of this story. Elizabeth Zack helped me with the editing of a first draft of the manuscript.

I am very thankful to Sam Scinta and Robert Baron of Fulcrum Publishing for their interest in this book and for their professional guidance. Scinta offered me substantial comments that contributed to improving the text and gave me the kind of personal support and motivation that any author appreciates. Katie Wensuc, managing editor at Fulcrum, polished the text with very useful and precise editing suggestions.

I greatly appreciate the generous gesture by my friend Kofi Annan, former secretary general of the United Nations and Nobel Peace Prize laureate, in agreeing to write a foreword for this book. His unwavering commitment to multilateralism during the events narrated in this volume deserves my fullest respect.

My fellow diplomat Ambassador Munir Akram, permanent representative of Pakistan to the United Nations, took the time—in the midst of our busy diplomatic agendas—to go over the manuscript, and gave me valuable new information and intelligent reflections. Ambassador Ismail Gaspar Martins of Angola also collaborated with my research. Edward C. Luck, professor at Columbia University, and Tom Farer, dean of the Graduate School of International Studies at the University of Denver, read the manuscript and granted me sharp suggestions and generous comments. Paul Begala, former White House advisor, Abraham Lowenthal, professor at the University of Southern California, Paul Sigmund, emeritus professor at Princeton, and Patricio Navia of New York University read a first draft of the book and provided me with comments for which I am thankful. My friend and colleague Jorge Castañeda, former secretary of foreign affairs of Mexico, afforded me his acute insight into some of the episodes here narrated. Also, I recognize Claudia Aguilar, Isabel Seguel, and Claudia Hernández for having gathered some data for this book and for assisting me tirelessly in the correction of the draft chapters.

A special mention to former president Ricardo Lagos for taking the time, while he was president of Chile, to read a first draft of the manuscript, for providing me with encouragement and valuable unknown information regarding some key episodes narrated in this book, and for his enduring friendship.

I owe the most to my wife, Pamela, for her assistance, intelligent comments on an early draft, and for her patience and support when I worked until late hours of the night and on weekends to complete and revise the manuscript. The title of this book was her idea.

—Heraldo Muñoz
New York, January 2008

About the Author

Heraldo Muñoz is currently the ambassador–permanent representative of Chile to the United Nations. Formerly, he was president of the UN Security Council and chairman of the council's Al Qaida and Taliban Sanctions Committee. From 2006 to 2007, he served as vice president of the UN General Assembly's Sixty-First Session. In 2007, he was facilitator of the UN Security Council reform consultations.

Ambassador Muñoz has written or edited more than a dozen books on foreign relations and international political economy, as well as many essays for academic journals and national newspapers.

Prior to his present position, Ambassador Muñoz occupied the post of minister secretary general of government (from 2002 to 2003) in the cabinet of President Ricardo Lagos. Earlier, from 2000 to 2002, he was deputy foreign minister and was the chief negotiator of the free trade agreement between Chile and the European Union.

From 1994 to 1998, he was ambassador of Chile to Brazil, and from 1990 to 1994, he was ambassador of Chile to the Organization of American States (OAS), where he was responsible for conceiving and negotiating the Santiago Commitment to Democracy, which gave the OAS a new instrument to act collectively and peacefully to defend democracy in the Americas.

Muñoz was cofounder of the Party for Democracy (PPD) in 1987 and served as joint representative of the Socialist Party and the PPD in the executive committee of the NO Campaign for the plebiscite held in Chile in October 1988 that defeated General Augusto Pinochet.

He holds a PhD from the Graduate School of International Studies at the University of Denver, was a PhD guest fellow at the Brookings Institution, and has been a visiting professor or lecturer at Georgetown University, the University of Southern California, and the University of Miami.

Muñoz was born in Santiago, Chile. He and his wife, Pamela Quick, live in New York City.

More thought-provoking titles
in the Speaker's Corner series

Beyond Cowboy Politics
Colorado and the New West
Adam Schrager, Sam Scinta, and Shannon Hassan, editors

The Brave New World of Health Care
What Every American Needs to Know about the Impending Health Care Crisis
Richard D. Lamm

Condition Critical
A New Moral Vision for Health Care
Richard D. Lamm and Robert H. Blank

Daddy On Board
Parenting Roles for the 21st Century
Dottie Lamm

The Enduring Wilderness
Protecting Our Natural Heritage through the Wilderness Act
Doug Scott

Ethics for a Finite World
An Essay Concerning a Sustainable Future
Herschel Elliott

God and Caesar in America
An Essay on Religion and Politics
Gary Hart

No Higher Calling, No Greater Responsibility
A Prosecutor Makes His Case
John W. Suthers

On the Clean Road Again
Biodiesel and the Future of the Family Farm
Willie Nelson

One Nation Under Guns
An Essay on an American Epidemic
Arnold Grossman

Parting Shots from My Brittle Bow
Reflections on American Politics and Life
   Eugene J. McCarthy

Power of the People
America's New Electricity Choices
   Carol Sue Tombari

Social Security and the Golden Age
An Essay on the New American Demographic
   George McGovern

Stop Global Warming
The Solution Is You!
   Laurie David

TABOR and Direct Democracy
An Essay on the End of the Republic
   Bradley J. Young

Think for Yourself!
An Essay on Cutting through the Babble, the Bias, and the Hype
   Steve Hindes

Two Wands, One Nation
An Essay on Race and Community in America
   Richard D. Lamm

Under the Eagle's Wing
A National Security Strategy of the United States for 2009
   Gary Hart

A Vision for 2012
Planning for Extraordinary Change
   John L. Peterson

For more information, visit our website,
   www.fulcrumbooks.com